Taking Ethics Seriously

Taking Ethics Seriously

Why Ethics Is an Essential Tool
for the Modern Workplace

John Hooker

Carnegie Mellon University

CRC Press

Taylor & Francis Group

Boca Raton London New York

CRC Press is an imprint of the
Taylor & Francis Group, an **informa** business

A PRODUCTIVITY PRESS BOOK

CRC Press
Taylor & Francis Group
6000 Broken Sound Parkway NW, Suite 300
Boca Raton, FL 33487-2742

International Standard Book Number-13: 978-1-1382-9958-0 (Hardback)
International Standard Book Number-13: 978-1-3150-9796-1 (eBook)

Library of Congress Cataloging-in-Publication Data

Names: Hooker, John, 1949- author.
Title: Taking ethics seriously : why ethics is an essential tool for the
modern workplace / John Hooker.
Description: Boca Raton, FL : CRC Press, [2018] | Includes bibliographical
references and index.
Identifiers: LCCN 2017048093 | ISBN 9781138299580 (hardback : alk. paper) |
ISBN 9781315097961 (ebook)
Subjects: LCSH: Business ethics.
Classification: LCC HF5387 .H667 2018 | DDC 174/.4--dc23
LC record available at https://lccn.loc.gov/2017048093

**Visit the Taylor & Francis Website at
http://www.taylorandfrancis.com**

**and the CRC Press Website at
http://www.crcpress.com**

Contents

Preface

This book takes ethics seriously. It recognizes that ethics is an indispensable tool for the modern workplace, no less important to an organization than technology or finance. We need ethics not to decide who is good or bad, but to build social infrastructure that, like physical infrastructure, is vital to getting anything done. Simplistic platitudes cannot accomplish this. Only a sophisticated and subtle intellectual framework can guide us through the complexities of today's world. The book develops such a framework and equips you to use it.

The book develops the concepts and skills you need to analyze an ethical dilemma, come to a rational conclusion, and defend it convincingly. In so doing, it provides a basis for developing ethical policies for your organization. It analyzes a wide variety of situations that are taken raw, from real life. Many are based on the experiences of participants in business classes and professional workshops I have taught in several countries. The book begins with minor dilemmas that do not engage our egos and emotions, and works gradually toward larger issues that require more intellectual discipline.

Here are a few. What kind of content should a social networking site allow to be posted? Is it ethical to source smartphones from low-wage factories? Or to buy such a phone? Should one report a coworker who is padding his or her expense account? How frank must advertising be about the limitations of a product? Is it ethical to advertise pharmaceuticals to the general public? When should a defective product be recalled? When can we ethically say, "Let the buyer beware"? Is it always wrong to lie? Is it fair to use study drugs in school, or to share job interview questions with a friend? Is surge pricing ethical for companies like Uber and Lyft? When is it morally right to withhold treatment or surgery from a terminally ill patient? How should limited health care resources be allocated? Can robots have rights and duties? The book analyzes all of these issues and many more.

Author

John Hooker is a T. Jerome Holleran Professor of Business Ethics and Social Responsibility, and Professor of Operations Research, at Carnegie Mellon University, Pittsburgh, Pennsylvania. He has also held visiting posts at several universities, most recently the London School of Economics and the State University of Campinas, Brazil. He brings his extensive background in philosophy and logic to the rigorous analysis of ethical dilemmas, and his background in management science to making sure the dilemmas are realistic. He has published over 170 research articles, eight books, and five edited volumes on ethics, philosophy, operations research, and cross-cultural issues, including *Business Ethics as Rational Choice* and *Working across Cultures*. He is the founding editor-in-chief of the world's only academic journal dedicated to teaching business ethics, and he developed the ethics program in the Tepper School of Business at Carnegie Mellon.

1

The Central Role of Ethics

The departure area for my flight was noisy and crowded as passengers boarded by zones. My boarding pass was marked Zone 2, so I stepped back to allow the Zone 1 passengers to enter the gate. But they kept coming. A suspiciously large fraction of the crowd boarded before Zone 2 was even announced. I couldn't help noticing that most had bulky suitcases in tow.

I thought about how the airlines created a demand for more cabin luggage space when they began charging fees to check bags. The result is a scramble for overhead space every time passengers board a plane, not to mention the headaches for the flight attendants who must make sure the overhead doors shut. The advantage of boarding early is clear.

I managed to spot a couple of the boarding passes carried by Zone 1 passengers. They were not marked Zone 1. Apparently, the gate agent was lax about enforcing the zones. When I finally entered the plane, I noticed that the early boarders were sitting throughout the cabin, not in the back or along the windows as one might expect from an efficient boarding system. Perhaps the airline rewarded frequent fliers with early boarding, regardless of their seat location. But this many? I also noticed that the overhead space was nearly filled with large carry-ons.

Imagine that we debrief some of these passengers in a focus group. Those who dutifully boarded with their zone would doubtless defend their compliance, although they might regret the hassle that resulted. Those who boarded early would be equally vigorous in their defense. I can hear the arguments now: It's the airline's responsibility to enforce its rules. The airline created this situation, not me, by its ridiculous practice of charging for checked luggage. The airline gives me the option of a carry-on bag, and if I must board early to find space, that's the airline's problem. Besides, why shouldn't I have as much right to the space as anybody else? And on and on.

If this little matter doesn't generate enough heat, we could ask passengers in a cramped economy cabin whether it's okay to recline the seat all the way back, assaulting the knees and computer screen of the person behind it. Some would say that it is rude and selfish to make another person miserable for the slightly greater comfort of a reclined seat. Others will defiantly insist that their ticket gives them the right to use a certain seat, and that seat has a recline button. Everyone has the same right, and those who don't like this arrangement can take the train. I'm not making this up, as these are arguments I lifted from an online forum on the subject—minus the insults and hate speech that are always found in such places.

REACHING AGREEMENT

Perhaps airlines have a way of bringing out the worst in us, but I see these little disagreements as evidence of a larger phenomenon. If we can't agree on how we should board a plane, or even adjust a seat, can we agree on what to do about wealth inequality, immigration, or terrorism? More broadly, can we agree on how to manage the complex, interlocking systems that shape the world around us?

The complexity of modern life is no more evident than in the workplace. Whether we work in a business corporation, a healthcare facility, or a government agency, we find ourselves enmeshed in a vast web of social practices: commercial markets, legal regulatory frameworks, political discourse, media publicity, and the online world. We must not only somehow deal with these complex and conflicting forces, but we must rely on them to get anything done.

We all know that *physical* infrastructure is essential. Without energy supply, transportation, communication, and far-flung supply chains, we would quickly perish. It is no different with the *social* infrastructure that underlies everything we do. The physical systems themselves would collapse in an hour without the social cooperation on which they depend. We would not be able to turn on the light switch were it not for countless individuals who come together to finance, build, and maintain the power grid.

Making the parts of physical infrastructure interact properly requires a certain kind of know-how, which we call engineering. Maintaining social infrastructure likewise requires know-how, but there is a big difference: We are the parts that must work together. This means that we must all know what to do. Much of this knowledge is technical and domain specific. A banker must know how to assess a loan application, and a construction contractor must know how to write specifications for a supplier. But a broader type of knowledge is necessary. We must know how to agree on ground rules that make these social practices sustainable. We must agree on how much information should be shared in negotiation, what kind of competitive practices are allowed, what duties we owe our clients and customers, when employees can be fired, what we should post on the Internet, and what we can dump into the air and water. Fortunately, there is a field of study that provides guidance in this area. It is called ethics.

Some say that regulating conduct in the world of work is a task for lawyers and legislators, not ethicists. A legal framework is extremely useful, to be sure. But it is only part of the solution. To begin with, we must decide which laws are ethical and just, and this requires ethical judgments. Beyond this, after a moment's reflection, we realize that real life is far too intricate to be governed by the ponderous mechanisms of the law, particularly in the complex and rapidly changing world we inhabit today. A lawsuit or legal prosecution is an expensive undertaking that requires months of tedious evidence gathering and sometimes years for resolution. Only the most egregious transgressions can be regulated in this way, and the legal system is already overwhelmed with them. The day-to-day operation of our social systems requires that the vast majority of us voluntarily comply with norms of conduct that we agree are reasonable. Reaching this kind of rational consensus is precisely the task of ethics.

WHY WE ARE SOMETIMES UNETHICAL

Even those who acknowledge the importance of ethics often see the main problem as getting people to be ethical, rather than deciding what is ethical. This comes out in professional ethics workshops I lead. Many participants are impatient to get past normative analysis and move on to the issue of what to do about unethical coworkers and bosses. To be sure, there are plenty of unscrupulous people out there. More often than not, however, unethical behavior in organizations stems from an inability to identify and defend what is right, rather than from a failure to do what we know is right.

To illustrate this fact, look no further than one of the most famous case studies in the annals of professional ethics. In the early 1970s, the Ford Motor Company began to receive reports that its budget car, the Ford Pinto, occasionally burst into flame after a rear-end collision. Serious injury or death frequently resulted. Investigation revealed that even a low-speed collision could cause studs protruding from the rear axle housing to puncture the fuel tank, resulting in an explosion. Ford could have fixed the problem at a cost of $11 per car. But it decided against the fix, on the ground that the cost outweighed the benefit. As the problem became more widely known, Ford finally redesigned the gas tank in the 1977 model, but it did not recall earlier models until the National Highway Traffic Safety Administration declared them defective in 1978. Meanwhile, a spectacular 1978 crash that killed three teenage girls attracted media attention, and an Indiana grand jury indicted Ford on a criminal charge of reckless homicide. Ford escaped a conviction, but its executives were widely condemned for what was seen as a callous decision.

We have rare insight into this case because one of the Ford managers who supported the company's decision, Dennis Gioia, wrote an honest and self-critical article about the affair.[*] After leaving Ford, Gioia became a business school professor and summoned the courage to use the Pinto case study in his MBA classes. While at Ford, Gioia was convinced that he made the right decision, and he practiced what he preached by driving a Pinto himself. He remained convinced for several years while using the case study in his classes, even though some of his students were outraged by his conduct. He eventually changed his mind, but what is relevant here is that *his article gives no clear reasons for this change.* This suggests to me that there was no solid rational basis for Gioia's view either before or after he changed his mind.

Gioia neither was, nor is, a "bad person." Quite the opposite. His article tells us that he went into the auto industry with a strong desire to make a positive contribution to society, and one can presume that he entered academia with a similar motivation. What is needed here is not better character, but a better intellectual framework for deciding such issues.

---

[*] D. A. Gioia, Pinto fires and personal ethics: A script analysis of missed opportunities, *Journal of Business Ethics* 11 (1992): 379–389.

We will find in Chapter 12 that the Pinto dilemma is actually fairly straightforward to resolve, after the necessary conceptual equipment is at hand. Gioia's article goes to on analyze the organizational and psychological factors that influenced this thinking, which are important, of course. We ought to shape organizations and habits of mind that lead to ethical choices. However, we cannot do this until we know which choices are ethical. An essential part of shaping ethical institutions is building a capacity within them to identify and defend the right decision.

DOING ETHICS WITH OUR BRAINS

It's not obvious how to resolve ethical issues like Ford's, but it's not obvious how to drive a car, either, and yet we learn to do it. With training and practice, we can all learn to think about ethical issues in a rational and objective fashion, and work toward consensus. Then why don't we do it more often?

I think it's because we don't know it's possible. Popular culture tells us that ethics is a matter of gut feeling, simplistic platitudes, or personal values, with no objective way to resolve issues. Few of us have ever been exposed to rigorous ethical argumentation, and so we naturally have no idea what it is like. This is despite our centuries-old heritage of ethical reasoning, developed by some of the smartest human beings who ever walked the earth. We have forgotten this tradition. As the world becomes increasingly crowded and complicated, with an increasingly urgent need for rational consensus on how we are going to live together, we have cast aside the very tools our forebearers developed for this purpose. We have forgotten how to do ethics with our brains.

That's why I wrote this book. I attempt to lay a conceptual foundation for ethical analysis that I believe has the best chance of building rational consensus. It draws on insights from the past but goes beyond the classical theories by refining them and integrating them into a unified framework. This doesn't mean the framework allows us to turn a crank and get the right answer. Rather, it sets out requirements that any valid ethical argument must satisfy. To get results, we must take these as a starting point and work toward an ethical consensus.

One might think this is a job for professional philosophers and ethicists. The professionals preserve and develop our intellectual heritage, but unfortunately, they have largely failed to knit together ethical theory and practice. The theories provide insight but are typically too general to apply to messy, real-world cases. Even in the field of normative ethics, which focuses on the resolution of practical dilemmas, the dominant mode of reasoning is to seek a *reflective equilibrium* of moral intuitions and principles, an approach that cannot resolve fundamentally differing intuitions. This leaves us no alternative but to take on the ethical task ourselves. It has to be this way in any case, because ethics, unlike physics, biology, or mathematics, can't be left solely to the professionals. We must all be ethicists, because we are the parts of the system that must work together.

The heart of ethical reasoning lies in constructing arguments for why one choice is right rather than another. This requires more discipline than one might think. It is not enough for me to conjure up an argument that I think is convincing, because it probably won't sound convincing to someone with a different perspective. We humans are very talented at rationalizing our behavior, which means it is vital to distinguish mere rationalization from correct analysis. The only way to make progress is to agree on a few bedrock principles of ethical reasoning that everyone can accept before any specific issues are considered. Then we must stick with these principles when we analyze a dilemma, even when we don't like the outcome. We do this in other fields and we can do it in ethics.

WHAT IS IN THE BOOK

The book develops three conditions that an action must satisfy to be ethical: generalizability, utility maximization, and respect for autonomy. It then shows how to construct arguments by checking whether the act in question meets these conditions. No other kind of argument is allowed, even if it sounds convincing.

I didn't invent these conditions. They are based on ideas that have been discussed in the ethical literature for centuries. I think you will find them inherently reasonable, because they are grounded in the logical structure of action itself. The book refines and reinterprets the conditions so that they fit into a coherent framework and have the power and subtlety to deal with real-life dilemmas.

The book next illustrates ethical reasoning by applying it to a variety of ethical dilemmas taken from real life, especially in the world of work. Many of them were experienced by my students or professional workshop participants. I begin with small, everyday dilemmas that don't engage our emotions or egos, to provide practice. In later chapters I gradually move into more challenging issues that require greater intellectual discipline. Many of these deal with buying and selling, job hunting, issues on the job, and organizational policy. There are also chapters on educational ethics, medical ethics, and the ethics of artificial intelligence. At no point do I pretend to supply the final answer. My intention is to illustrate ethical reasoning and contribute to our collective effort to reach consensus.

I tried to keep the book short, because I know you are busy. I present the theory as concisely as I can without compromising its depth and subtlety. I analyze a representative sample of dilemmas, rather than aim for encyclopedic coverage. A more comprehensive collection of dilemmas can be found on my blog (ethicaldecisions.net), along with analysis. You can post dilemmas anonymously yourself, or help with those posted by others.

Despite its brevity, the book discusses a wide range of ethical concepts and controversies at one point or another, often in the context of specific dilemmas. These include responsible consumerism, self-interest versus altruism, career choice, "white" lies, study drugs, resumé padding, sexual harassment, fiduciary duty in business, sourcing from sweatshops, price gouging, manipulative advertising, obligations to future generations, behavior toward immigrants and religious minorities, killing to save lives, Internet privacy and content, refusing vaccines, end-of-life decisions, the rights and duties of autonomous machines, and many others.

I have also tried to make the book accessible to a broad audience by presenting the concepts as straightforwardly as I can. Yet I never dumb down the material. I use the degree of rigor and sophistication necessary to deal with the issues at hand, at times reaching a level that professional philosophers will find challenging. Life can get complicated, and when it does, ethics must be complicated enough to deal with it.

My focus is almost entirely on the Western ethical tradition. I would love to cover other ethical traditions, as this is a major part of my research. Having lived and worked in ten countries on six continents, I fully appreciate the importance of cross-cultural understanding in today's world. However, to supply the necessary cultural background for other ethical traditions, even in outline, I would have to write a far longer book, and so I leave this to another occasion.

We have achieved remarkable success at collective reasoning in fields such as physics, biology, and mathematics. We have not done so well in ethics, where it is particularly crucial. I believe this is due partly to a whole raft of popular misconceptions peculiar to ethics. The first order of business is to dispense with them.

2

Myths and Misconceptions

Popular culture has clogged our brains with layer upon layer of myths and misconceptions about ethics. These preconceived notions too often obscure the vital role of ethics in everyday life. They lead us to believe that there can be no rational analysis in ethics. It is imperative to clear out this sludge before we can make progress toward building a practical framework for resolving ethical issues.

WHY WE HAVE ETHICS

The first misconception is that ethics exists to judge our moral worth. It does not. Its task is not to decide whether we are good people or bad people. There may be a higher power that judges us, but the mistaken notion that ethics makes this judgment raises an unnecessary barrier to rational discourse. We go into an ethical discussion with an emotional investment in an outcome that vindicates our past actions or beliefs. We find ourselves fabricating arguments to support a preconceived position, which makes it practically impossible to come to consensus.

It's no surprise that we think this way, because people so often use ethics as a basis for judging us. When mom says to big sister, "It's wrong to hit your little brother. Bad girl!" she makes two very different statements, only the first of which is an ethical statement. Religions have made valuable contributions to ethical discourse, but they also may pass judgment on people who go astray, perhaps consigning them to eternal damnation or *samsara* (endless death and rebirth). This kind of judgment may or may not be a useful practice, but it doesn't come from ethics.

The purpose of ethics is not to judge us, but to help us agree on how we are going to live and work together. It is a negotiation tool. It provides a thought framework within which we can reach rational consensus on the ground rules.

We often fail to appreciate how important this is. We may think, for example, that we can just vote on the rules. But what if some people disagree with the outcome of the vote? We say that they should abide by the vote anyway. But this means we need prior agreement that we are going to honor the results of the vote. We can't arrive at this agreement by taking another vote, because people will ask why they should respect *that* vote, and so forth in an infinite regress. We have to agree, before any votes are taken, that we should respect the outcome of voting. Read that again: We *should* respect the outcome of voting. This is an ethical claim, and we have to agree on it. In fact, we must agree on a wide array of ethical principles if we are to live and work together.

It is tempting to believe that in the real world, law enforcement does the heavy lifting, not ethics. We behave decently because we get in trouble if we don't, not because of ethical scruples. Ethics helps now and then, but it's not central to the process. The truth is precisely the opposite. If you doubt this, imagine that tomorrow morning, every motorist in the city starts driving through red lights. What can the police do about it? There are thousands of intersections and not nearly enough police to watch them. The city might install video cameras at every intersection, but who is going to analyze the images, send out citations, and collect half a million fines every day? What if motorists simply refuse to pay the fines? Or suppose that tonight, people start burglarizing houses and apartments all over the city. There is no way the police can stop it. They can't be everywhere at once.

It is the same in the world of work. Law courts and regulatory agencies cannot enforce compliance. The legal system is clogged with a multi-year backlog of cases, even though only a fraction of disputes result in legal action, and most of these are settled out of court. Regulatory agencies have nowhere near the funding and staff necessary to police behavior. Even if they did, organizations can take advantage of legal loopholes or stay a step ahead of the rules.

Legal and ethical conduct will prevail only if most of us voluntarily comply with the rules (in both letter and spirit), leaving the regulators and police to take care of a few people on the fringes who don't cooperate. And most of us won't voluntarily comply unless we agree on how we should behave. We don't run red lights or break into houses because we agree that we shouldn't. On the other hand, we regularly violate the speed limit when we think it is too low. In fact, I am told that in some areas, traffic engineers first determine how fast people are driving and then set the speed limit so that most of them will be within it.

Agreement, not enforcement, is at the core of the process, and ethics is the way we reach agreement. In the Western tradition, ethics accomplishes this primarily through rational consensus. We adopt rules that seem reasonable. Law courts, for example, resolve disputes according to common law principles that were hammered out over the centuries so as to be acceptable to all parties. The loser, as well as the winner, must view the rules as fair. William Blackstone's eighteenth-century treatise, *Commentaries on the Laws of England*, was a major legal milestone because it provided a rationale for Anglo-Saxon common law. The book, which was written for ordinary people, made English law seem reasonable and even inevitable to them. The field of ethics must provide a similar service, but in a much larger context.

THE ROLE OF RELIGION

Why do we resist the idea that ethics can be a rational endeavor? One factor seems to be its historical association with religion. Popular culture today often views religion as a haven for stubborn belief in irrational doctrines, not to mention extremism and intolerance. I have two responses. First, we can carry out ethical reasoning perfectly well without reference to religious belief, and I do so in this book. Second, this is a one-sided view of religion that ignores its long and rich history of ethical analysis. I will focus on the Abrahamic religions (Judaism, Christianity, and Islam), which have had the largest role in developing our ethical sensibilities.

Despite the popular image of God handing down the Ten Commandments on stone tablets, these religions have viewed ethics as a matter of rational debate, not divine fiat, for at least twenty-eight centuries. It was in the eighth century BCE when the prophet Isaiah became concerned about corruption and moral decay. He saw God (Jahweh) as disapproving of this behavior but didn't portray God as laying down the law. The first chapter of the book of Isaiah quotes Jahweh as saying, "Come, let us reason together." Scholars tell us that the Hebrew words refer to the kind of argumentation that occurs in a court of law. Even in this ancient time, God is inviting the Jewish people to a debate about ethics, so they can resolve their differences in a rational manner. The juridical approach to ethics continued to develop in Jewish culture and eventually produced the great rabbi and pacifist Hillel, who helped to found the Talmudic tradition of scholarship. He is known for his enunciation of the Golden Rule and emphasis on civility and compassion for all human beings, both of which appear in the teachings of Jesus a few years later.

The Jewish respect for law and justice permeates Western civilization to the core and continues to shape our ethical outlook. To take just one example, the idea of public interest law (think about Ralph Nader) was introduced to the United States by legal activist Louis Brandeis, who later became a Supreme Court justice. Brandeis was deeply influenced by the Jewish perspective of his uncle Lewis Dembitz and even changed his middle name to Dembitz in his honor. His brilliant legal arguments were also largely responsible for establishing a legal right to privacy in the United States, a paramount concern in our age of electronic surveillance.*

The Christian faith has accumulated an equally impressive record of ethical thought. Perhaps best known is the natural law tradition associated with the Roman Catholic thinker Thomas Aquinas and ultimately grounded in Aristotelian philosophy. Natural law theory holds that ethical principles can be derived from a rational analysis of human nature. Its reliance on reason rather than divine edict was a strong attraction to such enlightenment figures as John Locke, Thomas Jefferson, and Francis Hutcheson. Hutcheson may not be a household name, but he was intellectual mentor to Adam Smith, whose statement about the "invisible hand" that governs a market economy is routinely quoted today.

Catholic thought is popularly viewed as fixated on abortion and contraception, but this overlooks centuries of social justice teachings that are as relevant today as ever. For example, Pope Francis released in 2013 an Apostolic Exhortation that addresses the pressing issue of economic inequality.† It contains analysis that might very well appear in a secular tract. Many readers will find the Pope's arguments unconvincing, but they are arguments nonetheless, not merely appeals to divine edict.

---

* See the seminal essay by S. Warren and L. D. Brandeis, The right to privacy, *Harvard Law Review* 4 (1890): 193–220.
† Pope Francis, *Apostolic Exhortation Evangelii Gaudium*, Vatican Press (2013): 47–48.

Islam has a long tradition of sophisticated ethical reasoning developed by the *ulema*, or community of Muslim scholars. A good example of Islamic teaching in today's world is Islamic finance. It is primarily known for its rejection of interest on loans (*riba al nasi'ah*), which is prohibited by the Qur'an and was for centuries regarded as usurious and exploitive. Modern finance dismisses this perspective as outmoded, but we are also beginning to recognize the tendency of modern finance to exacerbate income inequality, encourage excessive risk taking, and trigger capital flight. Excessive risk lay behind the global financial crisis of 2008, and capital flight magnified the Asian financial crisis of 1997 as short-term investors pulled their money out of the region. Recent Islamic thinking uses the old misgivings about *riba* as a springboard for a critique of modern finance.

Interest-bearing loans are seen as problematic because lending banks assume too little risk relative to the borrower, which over time results in excessive power for banks and their owners. It's an all-too-familiar issue in our era of banks that are "too big to fail." Socially responsible investment in stocks, by contrast, is encouraged because the investor assumes risk proportionate to gains. Derivatives, short selling, and speculative trading are frowned upon because they are too much like gambling. They incur unnecessary risk (*gharar*) and lead to instability and capital flight. At a deeper level, gambling is immoral because it exacerbates injustice. The world is unjust enough already, and gambling only makes it worse by transferring wealth on the basis of chance rather than who deserves or needs it.

One can debate the soundness or economic efficiency of Islamic finance, but there can be little doubt that the financial crisis of 2008 would have been unthinkable in an Islamic financial system. The highly leveraged trading, subprime loans, mortgage-backed securities, and credit default swaps that precipitated the crisis are all *haram* (forbidden). We are also seeing an intermingling of ideas from Islamic finance with secular thinking about sustainable development, particularly in the sustainable banking movement.[*]

---

[*] T. Spangler, Could principles of Islamic finance feed into a sustainable economic system? *The Guardian*, October 18, 2013; T. A. Myers and E. Hassanzadeh, The interconnections between Islamic finance and sustainable finance, IISD Report, International Institute for Sustainable Development, July 2013. The London-based publication *World Finance* lists the Arab National Bank of Saudi Arabia as one of the world's best sustainable banks; Best sustainable banks 2016, June 27, 2016.

Religion, then, has played a major role in the development of ethics, but not simply by laying down commandments. For centuries, religions have been working out a rational basis for moral precepts, much as Blackstone's Commentaries did for the laws of England. I don't claim that the ethical arguments in religious writings are adequate in today's world. But they remind us that Western civilization has long relied on rational discourse to build consensus around ethical norms, even in a religious context. We abandon this practice at our peril.

ETHICS AND SELF-INTEREST

Another barrier to ethical reasoning is the popular view that people and organizations are motivated solely by self-interest, not by ethical scruples. Philosophers call this view psychological egoism. Perhaps the most interesting thing about psychological egoism is how much people want to believe it. It is imperative to deal with this theory, because anyone who accepts it is likely to dismiss ethical reasoning as pointless. Why worry about ethics when you are going end up acting in your self-interest anyway?

Common sense tells us that psychological egoism can't be right. We all know of people who sacrifice self-interest to fight for their country or to care for children and elderly parents. We can't forget the 441 fire fighters and other emergency workers who gave their lives while responding to the 9/11 attack on the World Trade Center. There are countless not-for-profit (as well as for-profit) organizations that dedicate themselves to making the world better. None of this sounds like self-interest. Science also provides refuting evidence. Altruism appears to be in our genes, for example. There is a large literature on how biological evolution can favor altruistic behavior because it has survival value.[*] We are a stronger species when we support each other. Neurological research may have discovered a neurological basis for some of this behavior, in the form of mirror neurons in our brains that react to the experiences of others. These are neurons associated with pleasure or pain that fire when we observe pleasure or pain in others. They may help

---

[*] For a sampling of the literature, D. S. Wilson, *Does Altruism Exist? Culture, Genes, and the Welfare of Others*, New Heaven, CT, Yale University Press, 2015; D. W. Pfaff, *The Altruistic Brain: How We Are Naturally Good*, Oxford, Oxford University Press, 2015; M. Tomasello, A. P. Melis, C. Tennie, E. Wyman and E. Herrmann, Two key steps in the evolution of human cooperation: The interdependence hypothesis, *Current Anthropology* 53 (2012): 673–692.

give us the capacity for empathy, enabling us care about other people as well as ourselves (although their role now appears more complicated than originally thought).*

A remarkable volume by Matthieu Ricard, entitled *Altruism*, fills several hundred pages with research-based evidence for human altruism and empathy.† Yet such research has little effect on the determined psychological egoist, who always has a retort. What appears to be altruism is really perceived self-interest. People provide personal care to elderly parents to avoid the guilt feelings of putting them in an institution. People join the military for employment or to feel good about being patriotic, and they go into battle to avoid shame or court-martial. Organizations work for a better world because this helps people to feel satisfied with themselves, or at any rate provides them a paycheck. I'm not sure what egoists would say about the 9/11 responders, but I'm sure they can imagine some kind of self-interested motivation.

It is not hard to see what is going on here. No conceivable behavior is allowed to count as evidence against psychological egoism. No matter how utter the sacrifice, there must be some self-interested reason for it, or else one wouldn't do it. This strategy comes to the surface in an almost amusing way in the highly popular book *Freakonomics* by Steven Levitt and Stephen Dubner, which uses economic concepts to explain everyday phenomena.‡ Much of mainstream neoclassical economics rests on the assumption that incentives (i.e., perceived self-interest) motivate human behavior, at least in economic matters, and so it is no surprise that economists are partial to this view. In making a case for it, the book concedes that people sometimes appear to choose an action simply because it is right. But the authors say: Aha! In this case, people are motivated by *moral* incentives! Naturally, if any motivation (even a moral one) counts as an incentive, then it means nothing to say that behavior is motivated by incentives. As philosopher of science Karl Popper famously pointed out, a theory that has no conceivable refutation has no content.

---

* G. Rizzolatti and L. Craighero, The mirror-neuron system, *Annual Review of Neuroscience* 27 (2004): 169–192; S. Blakeslee, Cells that read minds, *New York Times* (January 10, 2006); C. Keysers, Mirror neurons, *Current Biology* 19 (2010): R971–R973; S. Acharya and S. Shukla, Mirror neurons: Enigma of the metaphysical modular brain, *Journal of Natural Science, Biology and Medicine* 3 (2012): 118–124; C. Jarrett, A calm look at the most hyped concept in neuroscience: Mirror neurons, *Wired* (December 13, 2013).
† M. Ricard, *Altruism: The Power of Compassion to Change Yourself and the World*, Boston, MA, Little, Brown and Company, 2013, English translation 2015.
‡ S. Levitt and S. J. Dubner, *Freakonomics*, New York, William Morrow, 2005.

Returning to common sense, beliefs about right and wrong motivate our behavior all the time, along with self-interest and other factors. We wait at the red light, even when there is no police officer in sight, because we believe it is wrong to drive through it. We make a right turn on red, under the same conditions, because we believe it is permissible to do so. We take care of our parents partly because we believe it is our obligation. We don't take care of the neighbor's parents partly because we don't believe it is our obligation. And similarly with a thousand other behaviors.

Why do so many of us want to deny this common-sense psychology? Adam Smith's "invisible hand," which I mentioned earlier, gives us a clue. Smith is the patron saint of our economic culture, because we credit him with showing us how self-interest lies at the foundation of the economy. We tirelessly quote his remark, "It is not from the benevolence of the butcher, the brewer, or the baker that we expect our dinner, but from their regard to their own self-interest."[*] By pursuing self-interest, one is "led by an invisible hand to promote an end which was no part of his intention," namely the "public interest."[†] We are presumably to infer from this that (a) people are motivated by self-interest, and (b) this is good, because at least in a market-based economy, it leads to the betterment of all.

This portrait of human beings as self-interested might be seen as justifying our economic system, and perhaps this is why we seize upon it. Yet it is a gross misrepresentation of Adam Smith's views. He entered the University of Glasgow at the tender age of 14, where he fell under the spell of Francis Hutcheson, a founding father of the Scottish Enlightenment. Hutcheson was an inspiring lecturer in moral philosophy who explicitly rejected psychological egoism, then and now associated with Thomas Hobbes. Hutcheson taught that many of our actions are motived by sympathy for others, a view that deeply influenced Smith. It is reflected in his book *Theory of Moral Sentiments*, which he wrote years later after returning to Glasgow as a professor.[‡] The very first sentence of the book states that human beings are often motivated by empathy, as well as self-interest, and the rest of the book elaborates on this proposition. I'm sure Smith would have felt vindicated by modern research on empathy.

The famous quotes about self-interest are lifted from Smith's second book, *An Inquiry into the Nature and Causes of the Wealth of Nations*,

---

[*] A. Smith, *The Nature and Causes of the Wealth of Nations* (1776) Book 1, chapter 2, paragraph 2.
[†] A. Smith, cited above, Book 4, chapter 2, paragraph 9.
[‡] A. Smith, *Theory of Moral Sentiments*, London: A. Millar (1759); 6th ed. (1790).

which receives far more attention today. Some think that Smith changed his mind and corrected his earlier, naïve views on the goodness of human nature. But there is no evidence for this. Smith always viewed *Theory of Moral Sentiments* as his best work. He revised both books several times, last revising the book on moral sentiments shortly before his death in 1790. There is no reason to doubt that it reflects his final views on the subject. In any case, he clearly recognized that markets cannot rely solely on self-interest. He called for government regulation and progressive taxation to tame the excesses of selfish interest and ensure equal opportunity for everyone. In fact, after writing *The Wealth of Nations*, he resigned his post at the University of Glasgow and became a government regulator.

Perhaps we cherry-pick certain Smithian quotes because they support the concept of *Homo economicus* (economic man), which many see as underlying the key regulatory mechanism in the West since feudalism gave way to a market-oriented society. Economic man is motivated by a desire to maximize personal utility, at least when making economic decisions and perhaps in life in general. Economists tend to be particularly enthusiastic about *Homo economicus*, and many fondly cite the invisible hand passage in support of general equilibrium theories that arose in the nineteenth century and still dominate mainstream neoclassical economics today. These theories, at least in their purest form, see a free market economy as consisting of atomistic, self-interested individuals that maximize personal utility subject to scarce resources, resulting in a supply/demand equilibrium that is optimal in some sense. Ironically, the idea of *Homo economicus* is almost invariably associated with Smith, even though his actual views of human nature are more balanced and consistent with common sense, as we have seen.

Smith and Hutcheson were scarcely the first moral philosophers to remark the human tendency to altruism. A notable example is Mencius, whom Chinese refer to as *Mèng Zǐ* (Master Mèng). He is probably the most important Confucian philosopher aside from the sage himself, and he may have studied with a grandson of Confucius. Mencius taught that human nature is innately good, and that bad character is the result of society's failure to cultivate this innate tendency through education and moral training. He was doubtless influenced by his mother, whom Chinese honor with the saying, *Mèng mǔ sān qiān* ("Mencius's mother, three moves"). It refers to the fact that his mother moved the family three times to find quality education for her son.

Mencius defended his perspective with a parable. Suppose you hear a scream and spot a young child who is clinging to the side of a deep well, about to fall in. How would you react? You would rush over and save the child. Anyone but a monster would do the same. But why would do you do it? Mencius says it is not because you would enjoy the gratitude of the child's family, or want to be recognized as a hero. You would rush to the rescue if the child were an orphan, or if no one ever learned about your heroism (and the child too young to remember). You would respond because it is part of your humanity. It is a manifestation of the altruistic impulse that lies in every human being, waiting to be cultivated.

I grant that we have selfish impulses as well as altruistic ones. The great truth in Mencian philosophy is the extent to which the resulting conduct depends on our training. We can learn almost any kind of behavior, from beastly to beatific. I will illustrate this with two stories of my own. One day while I was teaching in Zimbabwe, a student was scheduled to make a presentation in class. Malaria is endemic in parts of Africa, and it can become chronic in an individual, with the fever recurring after several weeks of dormancy. When I noticed that this student was not feeling well, I suggested that he take the day off. However, like all of my African students, he was very serious about education and insistent on attending every class. During his presentation, the fever became more intense, and he began to faint. Before I could move a muscle in response, fellow students rushed to his aid and helped him to a chair. While some hovered over him to offer comfort, others arranged to have him transported to the college clinic. I later learned that his classmates continued to be solicitous after class, checking on him regularly to make sure he was recovering. They told me that his relapse was brought on by news that his mother, who had been ill for some time, had died in a Sierra Leone hospital due to disruption caused by civil war. He managed to attend the next class (of course), during which his classmates watched him carefully for signs of trouble.

The second story takes place in my business school classroom in the United States. The room was packed with some seventy-five MBA students, nearly all of whom had several years' experience in the business world. During a team presentation, one of the presenters suddenly stopped speaking, became beet red, and literally collapsed into a chair. I was alarmed, as I had no idea what could cause this reaction in a young man. I rushed to the front of the room and asked his teammates if they knew anything about his condition. They shrugged. I was about to telephone medics when the stricken student recovered enough to tell me that someone in the hall was waiting to take care of him. He later explained that he had a problem with a slipped disk in his spine (as I understand it) that could suddenly cause unbearable pain. He had arranged for someone to be nearby in case of emergency. This was an occasion on which I had no problem beating his classmates to the rescue. I distinctly recall that during the entire episode, they chatted casually and checked their Facebook pages, with no apparent concern for a classmate in agony. A few, well aware of the value of their time, seemed annoyed at the delay in the proceedings.

My purpose is not to pass judgment on my African or American students. Neither I nor the field of ethics has any interest in judging character. My point is that the degree of altruism in our behavior is largely dependent on our social conditioning. The Shona and other ethnic groups represented in my African classroom are strongly collectivist cultures in which people are expected to take care of their neighbors. People will literally give the clothes off their back to those in need (I know of an actual incident of this). Competition is frowned upon, even in the classroom, where students who excel too much over their fellows are subject to reproach. It is better to spend time helping others to succeed rather than trying to outperform them. Some students make it to college in the first place because the people of their village pooled their meager assets to help pay the tuition fees.

My MBA students are the product of very different backgrounds. Many of them grew up in the world's most highly individualistic culture, that of the United States.* All have been shaped by a business environment that relies heavily on competition and individual incentives as organizing principles. They also preach what they practice. It's not only college sophomores who embrace psychological egoism, because MBA students are even more enthusiastic about it. If I suggest that altruism plays a role in the business world, they ridicule the thought. I personally know seasoned business people who want to make a positive contribution for its own sake and use business as a powerful instrument to accomplish this. Many of the twenty-somethings in my class bristle at this idea, viewing it as a fairy tale. One particularly outspoken student, who apparently learned about Thomas Hobbes in a philosophy course, kept insisting that a Hobbesian

---

* Geert Hofstede famously ranked national cultures with respect to individualism and other traits, based on survey data. The United States ranked first. See his book *Cultures and Organizations: Software of the Mind*, 3rd ed., New York, McGraw-Hill, 2010. For more extensive survey data of this kind, R. J. House et al., *Culture, Leadership and Organizations: The GLOBE Study of 62 Societies*, Thousand Oaks, CA, Sage Publications, 2004. I discuss the underlying concepts in my book, *Working Across Cultures*, Palo Alto, CA, Stanford University Press, 2003.

dog-eat-dog world is a far more accurate portrayal of human nature than my naïve faith in altruism. He instantly became a class hero.

The lesson in these stories is that our behavior is largely a product of our own self-conditioning and the ideology that goes with it totally so. Ethical analysis is, therefore, far from pointless. We can teach ourselves to reason together about ethics and, over time, condition ourselves to act in accordance with our conclusions. We can't afford to let specious theories like psychological egoism distract us from this vital task.

MORAL DEVELOPMENT

Still another source of resistance to ethical analysis is the notion that ethics is something we learn from Mom and Dad in early childhood. By the time we are old enough to think analytically, our values are already set. So again, ethical reasoning is pointless.

This flies in the face of decades of research in developmental psychology. Early childhood is important, but we can grow ethically throughout life, right up into old age. The well-known psychologist Lawrence Kohlberg identified six stages of moral development, characterized by increasingly sophisticated forms of moral reasoning. In his view, most people never reach the final stage, but if they do, it is likely to be late in life.[*] Robert Kegan, Carol Gilligan, Martin Hoffman, and John Gibbs provide alternative perspectives on moral development.[†] Kohlberg's work inspired a related literature on faith development, involving figures such as James Fowler and Sharon Parks.[‡]

---

[*] L. Kohlberg, *The Philosophy of Moral Development: Moral Stages and the Idea of Justice*, New York, Harper and Row, 1981.

[†] R. Kegan, *The Evolving Self: Meaning and Process in Human Development*, Cambridge, MA, Harvard University Press, 1981; C. Gilligan, *In a Different Voice: Psychological Theory and Women's Development*, Cambridge, MA, Harvard University Press, 1982; M. L. Hoffman, *Empathy and Moral Development: Implications for Caring and Justice*, Cambridge, UK, Cambridge University Press, 2000; J. C. Gibbs, *Moral Development and Reality: Beyond the Theories of Kohlberg and Hoffman*, Thousand Oaks, CA, Sage Publications, 2003. For earlier work, see W. G. Perry, *Intellectual and Ethical Development in the College Years*, New York, Holt, 1968.

[‡] J. W. Fowler, *Stages of Faith: The Psychology of Human Development and the Quest for Meaning*, New York, Harper and Row, 1982; S. D. Parks, Is it too late? Young adults and the formation of professional ethics, in T. R. Piper, M. C. Gentile and S. D. Parks (Eds.), *Can Ethics Be Taught? Perspectives, Challenges and Approaches at Harvard Business School*, Cambridge, MA, Harvard University Press, 1993.

The two main lessons from this literature, for our purposes, are that moral development is closely tied to cognitive and social development, and it can continue throughout life. The precise sequence of stages is less important, because there are alternative ways of usefully conceptualizing the developmental process. I find it helpful to recognize three broad phases that illuminate how the various facets of personal development relate to each other.

The first stage begins in childhood and may extend through adolescence or beyond. It is characterized by *heteronomy*, meaning that we take our beliefs and values from others. We don't reason critically or independently in any significant way but are dependent on family, friends, school, or some other authority for our views. Our interpersonal relations are similar, in that we rely on others for support or approval, whether it be family in the case of a child or peers in the case of an adolescent. Ethically, we live by norms handed down by others, which may reflect family discipline or school rules in younger years. If this stage persists into later years, we may uncritically accept company values in order to get ahead, or conventional legal constraints as defining right and wrong.

The second stage is one of *ideology*. It tends to begin in late teens, as we strive for independence. We learn how to think independently and criticize the ideas we passively accepted in earlier years. We may adopt an ideology that purports to explain everything, whether it be religious fundamentalism, Marxism, or laissez-faire capitalism as represented in the "objectivism" of Ayn Rand. Socially, we break away from the family and childhood environment as we consciously select a peer group that reflects our own values or point of view. Ethically, we choose our norms, but they must come in a neat package. They may flow from our religious or political ideology, or they may be based on some such maxim as, "Don't do anything you wouldn't want your mother to know about," or "Don't do anything you wouldn't want to go viral on the Web." Or like some college sophomores and MBA students, we may simply say, "Everybody is motivated by self-interest, so ethics doesn't matter."

The third stage brings *autonomy* in the sense that we work out our own views and values. If all goes well, it arrives in mature adulthood. We not only do our own thinking, but as a necessary part of this process, we learn to tolerate uncertainty and ambiguity. We accept that there is merit on both sides of an argument and that we will never reach a final answer. Nonetheless—and this is crucial—we persist in the quest for a reasonable solution. Socially, we learn to value others even when they have serious shortcomings. Our social circle expands from those of like mind to persons of widely different backgrounds and perspectives. Having established our independence, we are ready again to rely on others in a relationship of mutual support and community. Ethically, we recognize the complexity of issues and the multiplicity of legitimate viewpoints. Nonetheless, we continue working together toward rational consensus.

Notice how ethical reasoning develops in tandem with cognitive and social skills. We can't make our own ethical choices until we declare independence from those who dictate norms to us, and we can't declare independence until we find a basis for making ethical choices. Later on, we can't form community with people of different backgrounds until we develop an ethical perspective that considers their point of view, and we can't develop such a perspective until we have the intellectual capacity to arrive at rational consensus. Ethical reasoning is part of our development throughout life.

JUST A MATTER OF OPINION

We now arrive at the thorniest conceptual tangle of all. It takes various forms: Ethics is just a matter of opinion. Ethics is just about personal values. There is no objectivity in this field, unlike chemistry or biology. I have my view, and you have yours, and that's it.

I don't think anyone really believes any of this, but many claim to believe it—until their own rights are violated. A victim of mugging is not likely to say that the ethics of mugging is just a matter of opinion. My students who insist on moral relativism quickly become staunch absolutists if they think I graded their exams unfairly. There is no hesitation to "impose our values on others" in these cases.

This internal contradiction is particularly troublesome in the United States. Having taught classes and led professional workshops in several countries, I can report that the United States is one of the trickiest places in the world to discuss ethics. On the one hand, many Americans dismiss any possibility of objectivity in ethics, whereas on the other hand they are probably the most absolutist people on the planet. They take it for granted that everyone in the world should agree with their values of individual rights, free markets, and democracy. The last two U.S. presidents espoused very different political philosophies, but both told the world that American values are universal.*

We first must acknowledge how destructive it is to deny the objectivity of ethics, even if at some level nobody really means it. Ethics can't be about "personal values." It must be about *interpersonal values*, or else it can't perform its function. Remember that ethics exists precisely to bring us to rational consensus, to put us on the same page, as to how we are going to live and work together. If ethics is just a matter of opinion, it is pointless.

We can't deal with this kind of ethical nihilism until we understand why it exists. One explanation may lie the fact that we so often use ethical statements to admonish. When Mom says, "It's wrong to hit your little brother," she isn't just stating an ethical proposition. She is urging big sister not to hit. This is what philosophers of language, beginning with J. L. Austin, call a performative utterance.† When the minister says, "I now pronounce you husband and wife," she is not making a statement about what she is doing at the moment. She is marrying the couple. The utterance performs the act of marrying them. Or if I say, "I bet you a dollar," that very statement makes a bet. In similar fashion, Mom's statement, "It's wrong to hit," is a reproof as much as an assertion. So it's natural to think of ethical statements as admonitions rather than as claims that can be submitted to intellectual scrutiny. We may, therefore, be inclined to reject the possibility of objective ethical reasoning.

Yet ethical discourse has always had a performative function, and people nonetheless recognized its intellectual content for ages. Ethics is a sophisticated field of inquiry, at least as ancient as mathematics and medicine. As I mentioned earlier, some of the smartest human beings who ever walked the planet made it a central concern of their thought, including Confucius, Socrates, Aristotle, Adi Shankara, Siddhārta Gautama, Thomas Aquinas, and Immanuel Kant. The study of ethics became a key part of Western university education at least as early as the Italian Renaissance, with the establishment of the *studia humanitas* (humanities curriculum), and some universities today are trying to revive it. There must be other factors involved in our ethical anti-intellectualism.

---

* For example: G. W. Bush, at a press conference with European Union members, June 20, 2005, in Washington DC; Barack Obama, in a speech to UN General Assembly, September 25, 2012.
† J. L. Austin, *How to Do Things with Words*, J. O. Urmson and Marina Sbisá (Eds.), Cambridge, MA, Harvard University Press, 1962.

One possibility is warmed-over Freudianism in popular culture. The field of psychology has long since moved past this stage, but there is a lingering notion that human behavior is determined by irrational impulses emanating from the subconscious mind, and that any perception that we make rational choices is false consciousness. Sigmund Freud's brilliant and articulate nephew Edward Bernays popularized this interpretation of human nature as early as the 1920s. Bernays was the father of the public relations industry and the foremost propaganda expert of his day. He believed that citizens of a democracy are incapable of governing themselves rationally and must be manipulated from above, using a process he called the *engineering of consent*. Non-democratic states have also found this kind of engineering useful. According to Bernays himself, Joseph Goebbels relied on his book *Crystallizing Public Opinion* for his anti-Semitic propaganda campaign in Nazi Germany.*

Bernays' techniques have obvious relevance to the advertising industry, and he became a marketing consultant to a number of corporations. An early breakthrough was his successful campaign to induce women to smoke cigarettes. He played into the feminist movement of the 1920s, for which smoking already represented equality with men, presumably (in Bernays' view) due to the cigarette's subconscious role as a phallic symbol.

At about the same time, the behaviorist theory of psychologist John B. Watson began to influence advertising, partly due to his employment by a major New York City advertising agency, J. Walter Thompson. A favorite tool was (and is) affective conditioning. By juxtaposing a certain brand of toothpaste with a sexy model, an ad campaign might condition consumers to associate the toothpaste with sexiness. Celebrity endorsements were also a popular technique.

Vance Packard's bestselling 1957 exposé *The Hidden Persuaders* revealed psychological manipulation techniques to the public at large.† His most famous example was the technique of inserting images of popcorn into a movie. The images go by too fast to register with the conscious mind, but they presumably boost popcorn sales at the cinema. This kind of subliminal advertising turns out to be humbug, but Packard's general point was well taken, and his book further reinforced the popular conception of

---

* As reported in E. L. Bernays, *Biography of an Idea: Memoirs of Public Relations Counsel Edward L. Bernays*, New York, Simon and Schuster, 1965, p. 652. The book in question is E. L. Bernays, *Crystallizing Public Opinion*, New York, Boni and Liveright, 1923.
† V. Packard, *The Hidden Persuaders*, New York, David McKay, 1957.

human beings as directed by hidden impulses rather than rational choice. My conversations with marketing faculty suggest that advertising is still largely associated with "psychological" persuasion, which they see as far more effective than rational persuasion. Note, by the way, how we continue to use the word *psychological* as a synonym for nonrational.

Advertisers might point out that some of the same techniques Bernays used to induce women to smoke were later used, with considerable success, to induce people *not* to smoke. Nonrational persuasion can certainly be effective; however, this doesn't prove that human beings have no rational side. Even Bernays' pro-smoking campaign resorted to rational persuasion. It told young women that they could keep their slim figure by reaching for a cigarette rather than a snack, which is perfectly valid advice. It is well known that smokers often gain weight when they kick the habit, because eating replaces smoking.

Psychologists, in fact, gradually came to recognize our rational side, as developmental and cognitive psychology supplanted the Freudian and behavioral schools. Cognitive psychology, in particular, since the 1960s has acknowledged the importance of thought processes in determining behavior. The way we think influences the way we feel, just as feelings influence thoughts, and both influence action. Psychologists now recognize the value of cognitive therapy in treating depression, phobias, addiction, post-traumatic stress disorder, and even schizophrenia. Aaron T. Beck, who pioneered cognitive therapy, argued that thought patterns can help lead to a depressed state, as well as help pull us out of it.* For example, I might infer from a job loss, followed by breakup with a friend, that I am unworthy and incompetent, conclusions that reinforce the depressed feelings I already have. A more careful analysis might show, however, that my misfortune was caused by external factors that have little to do with my personal traits. Without denying the neural and genetic basis for depression, Beck maintained that repeated correction of illogical thought patterns can help tame negative feelings and restore functional behavior.

Cognitive therapy in fact has grounding in neurophysiology. The prefrontal cortex, where the brain carries out rational thought, interacts constantly with the limbic system of the brain, the seat of emotions. Neither completely dominates the other. The limbic system motivates thought and

---

* A. T. Beck, *Cognitive Therapy and the Emotional Disorders*. Madison, CT, International Universities Press, 1975; A. T. Beck, A. John Rush, B. F. Shaw, and G. Emery, *Cognitive Therapy of Depression*, New York, Guilford Press, 1979.

mediates long-term memory formation in the rational brain, while the prefrontal cortex tames emotions emanating from the limbic brain. It is, therefore, no surprise that disciplined thought can get our feelings under control and reform our behavior.

Recent neural research, therefore, confirms the common-sense view that humans are directed by reason as well as emotion. This is not only a common-sense view, but an ancient one. Aaron Beck himself traced the origins of cognitive therapy to such Stoic philosophers as Seneca, Epictetus, and Marcus Aurelius. Beck could have also pointed to Siddhārta Gautama (the Buddha), who was a cognitive therapist of the first order. His Eightfold Path is a regimen of mental training designed to get us through the ups and downs of life.

Dispensing with specious popular psychology, whether it be psychological egoism or warmed-over Freud, allows us to return to common sense and traditional wisdom. It also reopens the door to rationality-based ethics as a guide to conduct, as Stoicism and Buddhism themselves illustrate. It is no accident that the Stoics viewed ethics as based on what they called *universal reason*.

THE LIMITS OF REASON

Even those who recognize a rational component of human motivation may question our ability to live by reason. They may point out that Western civilization tried it once, in the Age of Enlightenment, and it led to Robespierre and the guillotine. Left to its own devices, reason is either too weak to direct our conduct, or it slips into ideology and extremism. The wide-eyed innocence of the Enlightenment, with its naive faith in reason, has no place in the real world.

I never said that we should live by reason alone. I'm only saying that we should use our brains as we decide how to live and work together. Reason is not something that came and went with the Enlightenment, but has been a survival tool for eons. Our prehistoric ancestors relied on encyclopedic knowledge of plant species, intimate familiarity with the habits of game animals, and clever strategies for hunting them. Nobody saw this knowledge as "just a matter of opinion." They had to get it right, because their existence was at stake. Agriculture and industry were not developed on the basis of "personal values." In today's crowded world, our environment consists primarily of other people, and we must apply the same intelligence to interpersonal relations. Ethics lies at the foundation of this effort. We have to get it right, because our existence is at stake.

This doesn't mean that ethics uses the same methods as science, engineering, or even sociology. It is not an empirical field, because it doesn't formulate theories whose consequences can be tested by observation or experiment. This itself erects a barrier, because in our age of laboratories and data collection, it may be hard to imagine how anything can be established except by empirical methods. On second thought, however, this shouldn't be so hard to imagine, because there is already an ancient and successful field that uses completely different methods. In fact, these methods are similar to the methods that are appropriate to ethics. I am talking about the field of mathematics.

Wait, don't panic! I am not saying that you have to be good at mathematics to do ethics, any more than you have to be good at nuclear physics to do botany. Ethics and mathematics resemble each other only in that their methods are analogous. This should be reassuring, not frightening, because it tells us that a nonempirical field can establish a wealth of useful results.

3

The Generalization Principle

The key to ethical reasoning is one central insight: To act ethically is to act rationally. However, by rationality I don't necessarily mean rational self-interest, even though we often think this way. We tend to identify rational action with enlightened self-interest, an identification that is almost axiomatic in much of economics. Still, ethical thinkers have for centuries conceived of rational action in a broader sense, and I am going to follow their lead. I am going to show how an ethical action is an action that has a coherent rationale. In particular, I will identify three characteristics that the action must have to be rational, and, therefore, ethical: It must be *generalizable*; it must *be consistent with one's goals*; and it must *respect autonomy*. This will provide a basis for making ethical decisions in a reasonably objective fashion.

These three characteristics obviously require explanation, which I will provide as we go along. Although, you may ask right away, "Why is an irrational choice necessarily wrong?" My answer may sound quite radical: You *can't* choose to act irrationally. Obviously you can choose to act against rational self-interest, but this is not what I mean by rational. What I mean is that none of us can choose to act without a coherent rationale, because an *action* with no coherent rationale is not an action. It is mere behavior, ethically equivalent to a twitch or the buzzing of an insect. Behavior must be freely chosen to be an action, and it is freely chosen only when it has a coherent rationale.*

---

* The connection between action and having reasons is deeply embedded in the philosophical tradition, having origins in the work of Immanuel Kant and perhaps ultimately in Aristotle. In recent decades, this connection has become part of what might be regarded as the textbook account of agency, as originally put forward by G. E. M. Anscombe in *Intention*, Oxford: Basil Blackwell (1957) and D. Davidson in "Actions, reasons, and causes," *Journal of Philosophy* 60 (1963): 685–700, and subsequently elaborated in the writings of several philosophers.

This means that it is impossible to *act* unethically. If we behave unethically, we are not acting at all. Morally, we are bugs without exoskeletons. It is only by being ethical that we are fully human. I told you that this might sound radical, but I hope that by the time I am finished, it will not only seem reasonable, but provide a foundation for making ethical decisions.

WHAT TO EXPECT

Before we get started, I want to be clear about what you should expect as we go along. First, I am not going to lay down a few simple rules for ethical conduct. Life is more complicated than that. It is interesting that we expect economics, physics, and medicine to be hard, but in ethics we want a cookbook with fast and simple answers. When we don't get it, we too often fall back into the attitude that ethics is just a matter of opinion.

At least, this is the reaction I have seen in hundreds of students and professional workshop participants. As soon as there is controversy over an issue, and the controversy is not resolved in a few minutes, everyone is thinking, "It's just as I suspected. There's no way to resolve these issues. This professor has had three full sessions to teach us ethics, and he still can't get us to agree." Suppose I were to pose a question in integral calculus, rather than ethics. How many *years* of mathematical training would it take to get the class to agree on the answer?

Ethical skills are very different than mathematical skills, but both require years of experience to develop, as developmental psychologists like Lawrence Kohlberg have been trying to tell us. There is controversy in ethics, but there is controversy in every field, even (or especially) among the experts. This doesn't mean there is no objectivity. It just means that the issues are hard. The remedy is to put our heads together and figure it out, as we do in other fields.

Although I will present three conditions for ethical decision-making, they are not rules to be used in cookbook fashion. They are types of analysis that one can apply to an action to test its rationality. The application itself may require a good deal of expertise and cleverness, especially in tricky cases. This means that merely reading my presentation of the three conditions will tell you very little about ethical decision-making. You have to learn to apply them, which takes practice, practice, practice.

Think about a geometry course in which you are presented Euclidean axioms. These axioms mean very little until you work through proofs and see what kind of role they play in the arguments. Or think about a physics course. You spend most of your time working the exercises, because this is the only way to understand what conservation of energy or momentum really means and why it is important to the field. It is the same with ethics, which is why most of this book consists of examples.

There is something else I should mention. If you were involved in an ethics course or training session at some point, it may lead you to expect something you will not find here. This is the idea that ethics is a collection of competing theories or frameworks, and to solve a given dilemma we must apply the framework that seems most relevant—or the one that delivers the outcome we want. The most popular frameworks taught in such courses are deontological, consequentialist, and Aristotelian. The deontological framework is associated with Immanuel Kant and focuses on the content of one's intentions. The best-known consequentialist framework is the utilitarian philosophy of Jeremy Bentham and John Stuart Mill. It states, roughly, that the right action is the one that results in the greatest good for the greatest number of people. The Aristotelian approach is often presented as *virtue ethics*. This pluralism of theories is completely unsatisfactory, because it abandons the project of achieving rational consensus.

Fortunately, it is possible to develop applied ethics in a unified way, and I do so in this book. While much of what I present resembles deontological and consequentialist theories, it is a reconstruction of these classical theories that integrates them into a coherent whole. I also discuss virtue ethics, which is historically important and often taught in ethics courses, but I find it to be less useful as a tool for rigorous analysis.

This brings me to another caveat about the content of ethics courses. Because the material I present here somewhat resembles Kantian and utilitarian ethics, you might naturally infer that I am exposing the same ethical theories you learned in an ethics or philosophy course at some point. I am not. Almost all courses present Kantian and utilitarian ethics in something resembling their historical forms, while the field has moved far beyond this. You will never take a physics course that presents the historical theories of Copernicus and Galileo. These thinkers had enormous influence, and we owe much to them intellectually, but physics has advanced beyond them. Likewise, we owe much to Kant and Aristotle, but the field has moved ahead. Although science courses contain too little historical consciousness, ethics courses contain too much. I suggest that you set aside whatever you may have heard in ethics or philosophy courses, and judge the ideas presented here on their own merits.

THE BASIC ARGUMENT

I begin with a premise: When we act, we act for a reason. It need not be a good reason, but there must be some reason that we take as justifying the action. If I choose to eat a sandwich, I have a reason in mind. Perhaps I am hungry, or I really enjoy tuna fish sandwiches. Just to clarify, by a *reason*, I don't mean a cause. If I hiccup, there is a reason for it somewhere in my gastric system, but there is not the kind of reason I am talking about. I don't choose to hiccup to accomplish some purpose.

I have already provided a glimpse at why I assume that we always act for a reason: This is precisely what distinguishes freely chosen actions from mere behavior. I will defend this premise in detail later, but for now it should seem reasonable enough to proceed. Maybe there is no particular reason for an action performed purely out of habit or impulse, such as biting one's nails or swearing. However, I want to focus for now on actions undertaken deliberately with some purpose in mind. I will come back to the matter of habit and impulse later.

The next step of the argument is this: If a certain reason justifies an action for me, then it justifies the action for anyone to whom the reason applies. Otherwise, it is not really a reason. Suppose, for example, that I walk into a department store and spot a display of watches. I would really love to have a new watch, and I notice that the display is not in a case or under glass. There are no sales clerks in the vicinity, and as far as I can determine, there are no security cameras in view or theft detectors at the door. So I discreetly pocket one of the watches and exit the store.

I stole the watch for two reasons: I want a new watch, and I can easily get away with stealing it. If these are really my reasons, and there are no other reasons, then I decided that they justify taking a watch. Any customer entering the store who wants a watch, and can get away with shoplifting one, should grab one. However, I also know perfectly well that if all customers who have these reasons were to act on them, the store management would enforce security. It would lock the watches in a case, install security cameras, or place a detector at the exit. It would no longer be possible for anyone to get away with the theft, including me. This means that I am *not* deciding that anyone who wants a watch and can get away with stealing it should take one. This would frustrate my own purposes.

There is a logical contradiction here: I am deciding that anyone who wants a new watch and can get away with stealing it should take one, and I am *not* deciding that anyone who wants a new watch and can get away with stealing it should take one. I want my reasons to justify the action for me, but not for others who have the same reasons. But either they are reasons or they aren't. If they are reasons for taking a watch, then they are reasons for taking a watch—whoever does the taking.

The precise inconsistency here is this: My reasons for taking the watch are inconsistent with the assumption that everyone who has these reasons acts in the same way. Or still more precisely: I cannot *rationally believe* that my reasons are consistent with the assumption that everyone who has these reasons acts in the same way (because I know that management would enforce security). The theft, therefore, violates the *Generalization Principle,* which can be stated as follows:

> *Generalization Principle.* My action is ethical only if I can rationally believe that my reasons for the action are consistent with the assumption that everyone who has the same reasons performs the action.*

I'm not saying that other people who want a new watch will in fact steal one when they walk into the department store. I am making no prediction about what people will do. I'm only saying that if they did steal watches, I wouldn't be able to get away with taking one myself. My theft is *ungeneralizable* (i.e., violates the Generalization Principle, or as I will sometimes say, fails the generalization test).

The core idea here is that if my action is ungeneralizable, there is no coherent rationale behind it, and it is not an action. It is mere behavior, like a twitch. It may have some "psychological" or neurological explanation, but it cannot be intelligibly explained as the outcome of deliberation. There is no way to reconstruct my thinking that makes sense. One part of

---

* This is inspired by Immanuel Kant's famous categorical imperative but scarcely identical with it. The categorical imperative in its various formulations is most directly stated in *Foundations of the Metaphysics of Morals (Grundlegung zur Metaphysik der Sitten)*, 1785. Kant's ethics is further elaborated in his *Critique of Practical Reason (Kritik der praktischen Vernunft)*, 1788, and to some extent in his *Critique of Judgment (Kritik der Urteilskraft)*, 1790. The interpretative literature is overwhelmingly vast, but a good place to start is O. O'Neill, *Acting on Principle: An Essay on Kantian Ethics*, 2nd ed., Cambridge, Cambridge University Press, 2014.

my brain says that wanting the watch and lax security are sufficient reasons for stealing it, whereas another part says that they are not sufficient reasons. This makes no sense and cannot be part of a coherent rationale.

It's important to understand exactly what the Generalization Principle requires. It's true that I don't *want* all those other people to steal watches, because if they did, it would frustrate my own purposes. But this is not the precise test. It doesn't ask whether I would want others with the same reasons to act the same way. The precise test is whether I can rationally believe that my reasons for the theft are *consistent* with others acting on the same reasons.

The Generalization Principle is not the same as the Golden Rule, which is much narrower. The Golden Rule says that I should do to others what I would want them to do to me. This is totally inadequate as an ethical guide, at least as it is popularly understood. To use Immanuel Kant's example, suppose I am a judge whose job it is to sentence a convicted criminal. If I were the criminal, I wouldn't want to go to jail. Nonetheless, as judge, it is my duty to pass sentence.

You may think that I am missing the point. Taking the watch is wrong because it is theft and theft is wrong, not because I wouldn't be able to get away with it if others did likewise. But this is not very helpful. How do we know that theft is wrong? Exactly why is it wrong? If we are going to judge what is right and wrong, we must have some principle that allows us to decide the matter. I have a suggestion: Theft is (almost always) wrong because it is (almost always) ungeneralizable, and it is ungeneralizable because it both presupposes and undermines the institution of property.

One reason I steal a watch is that I want it to be my property. Roughly speaking, property is something you get to keep, and I want to keep the watch I steal. But if people stole things whenever they wanted them, there would be no property. No one would bother to remember who owns what, because ownership would mean nothing. As soon as I take a watch, others would feel free to take it from me, along with anything else they want. So the reason for theft (I want this to be my property) is inconsistent with the assumption that everyone with the same reason acts the same way. Theft for this reason is unethical because it is ungeneralizable.

Another reason we can't simply appeal to a principle that theft is wrong is that it is not always wrong. Suppose Jean Valjean, the protagonist in Victor Hugo's *Les Miserables*, steals a loaf of bread to rescue his family from starvation. He has a special reason for theft that goes beyond merely wanting to possess the bread. Does this make it okay? We certainly don't want to say it is wrong simply because it is theft. We have think about it first, and one way to think about it is to apply the generalization test. The moral status of theft depends in complicated ways on the reasons and circumstances, and generalizability takes the reasons and circumstances into account. I will eventually deal with hard cases like this one, but we must develop ethical skills one step at a time. The next step is to look at some additional simple cases.

CHEATING AND FREE RIDING

I sometimes ask my students why it is wrong to cheat on an exam. Very few can give me a sensible answer. The simplest response is that cheating is wrong because the cheater might get into trouble. But this implies that cheating is ethical if there is no chance of getting caught, and few students want to insist on this—particularly if *other* people are cheating and getting the high grades. A more popular response is that cheaters don't know the material and therefore leave school unprepared for their jobs. But suppose that the exam is on a topic that is unrelated the cheater's future job. Does this make cheating okay? Again, most students would say no.

To me, it is revealing that practically none of my students can answer this simple question. The problem is not with the students, but with the broader culture they live in. Our level of ethical discourse is so primitive that few of us can articulate a reason even for a basic ethical precept we are taught from childhood.

This is actually an easy case. Cheating, at least in this type of situation, is ungeneralizable and therefore unethical. If I cheat on an exam, presumably I do so because it will improve my grade average and boost my chances of getting a good job. To simplify matters, let's suppose I cheat from an external source, such as a smartphone. If all students who want a good job (which certainly includes all the students I know) were to cheat, then every student would have an A+ grade average, and grades would be meaningless. Employers would have no interest in grades, and cheating would no longer increase my chances of getting a good job. So my reason for cheating is inconsistent with the assumption that everyone with the same reason cheats, or more precisely, I can't reasonably believe otherwise.

There may, of course, be other reasons for cheating, but if we run a similar test on them, cheating is likely to come out ungeneralizable. Broadly speaking, cheating both presupposes and undermines the practice of grading, much as theft both presupposes and undermines the institution of property.

Cheaters and thieves are like free riders, because they rely on a practice without paying the price of maintaining the practice. In some northern European cities like Copenhagen or Amsterdam, riders of public transit are supposed to buy a ticket or pass but are generally not asked to show it. The transit system assumes that riders are honest enough to pay the fare, although police occasionally make the rounds and check tickets. If I ride without a ticket, my behavior is ungeneralizable and unethical, at least if my reasons are the usual ones: I want a free ride, and there is only a small chance of getting caught. If everyone who has these reasons (i.e., practically all riders) were to ride the bus without paying, the transit system would start checking tickets all the time, which is inconsistent with my reasons. Not all violations of the Generalization Principle are cases of free riding, but many are.

IDENTIFYING THE REASONS

They key to applying the Generalization Principle is correctly identifying the reasons for an action. This can be subtle in practice, but with experience one can learn to do it. To illustrate, let's suppose Gertrude Grosvenor walks into a department store and sees the unguarded watches. She takes one, and does so for three reasons: (a) she wants a new watch, (b) she can easily get away with stealing it, and (c) her name is Gertrude Grosvenor. She insists that her theft is generalizable, because she happens to be the only Gertrude Grosvenor in the country. If everyone with these three reasons were to steal watches, then only one person would steal a watch, and this would have little or no effect on the level of security in department stores.

Gertrude is quite right. Given these reasons, her theft is generalizable. However, her choice to steal doesn't pass the generalization test, because (c) is not one of her reasons. In fact, there are two flaws in her rationale: Having the name Gertrude Grosvenor is not one of *her* reasons, and it is not even *a* reason. It is not one of *her* reasons because it has no role in her deliberation about whether to steal the watch. Suppose that just after entering the department store, her mom rings her on her mobile phone. "Gertrude, I was just rummaging around in the attic and came across your birth certificate. There was a transcription error, and it lists your name as Genevieve. You are really Genevieve Grosvenor!" Would hearing this news lead Gertrude (Genevieve) to conclude that stealing a watch is no longer justified? Of course not. She arrived at the decision to steal because she wants a watch and can easily get away with the theft, not because she has a certain name.

Even worse, having the name Gertrude Grosvenor is not even *a* reason to steal a watch, because it has nothing to do with the act. A reason need not be a good reason, but it must help explain why someone decides to steal a watch. The thief's name (normally) has nothing to do with the decision to steal and cannot help explain it.

The reasons for an act must be necessary and sufficient conditions for performing it. Gertrude's name is not a reason for theft because she would steal if her name were Genevieve. It is not a *necessary* condition for her act. Her desire for a watch and the lax security are *sufficient* conditions if they are enough to convince her to steal. They comprise the reasons for her act. In reality, they are probably not sufficient, because there are likely to be additional reasons. She is willing to steal because she believes she won't feel terribly guilty about it later, because it will have little effect on the department store's financial health, because she believes the loss will not come out of some salesperson's wages, and so forth. But once all of her reasons are acknowledged, they must be individually necessary and jointly sufficient for the act.

It is useful to introduce a technical term for this idea. The reasons for an act define the *scope* of the act, which is the set of necessary and sufficient conditions under which one decides to perform the act. The problem with Gertrude's generalizability argument is that she drew the scope much too narrowly. This is a common mistake that we must carefully avoid.

Satisfying the Generalization Principle is only one necessary condition for an ethical action. Another is satisfying the Utilitarian Principle, which is developed in the next chapter.

4

The Utilitarian Principle

An action is often a means to an end. There is some state of affairs we would like to bring about, and we take the necessary steps to bring it about. Because life often requires us to plan ahead, these steps often form long chains of means and ends that may extend over a period of years. I put fuel in the car so I can drive to Chicago. I drive to Chicago so I can interview for a job. I interview for a job so I have a chance of taking the job. I take the job so I can make a decent living. I make a decent living so I can raise a family… and on it goes.

People often ask whether "the end justifies the means." Of course, this is precisely what an end does. The end may not justify the means in the sense of showing it is ethical. The job interview does not justify stealing a car to drive to Chicago; nonetheless it justifies the means in the sense of explaining why it is undertaken. The explanation may be incomplete, because there may be alternative means to the same end. I could fly to Chicago or take the train; however, citing an end helps make my choice of end intelligible and serves as one of the reasons for the choice.

An explanation of this kind is intelligible only if the sequence of ends and means eventually terminates. There must be a goal at the end of the chain that is intrinsically worthwhile. Otherwise, one can always say, so what? The Chicago job will allow me to make a decent living, but so what? Why is this important? It may boil down to happiness. I want to make a decent living so I can live in a nice house, drive a nice car, support a family, and I want these because they are a ticket to happiness. Or I may have altruistic ends: I want my family to be happy, or I want my work to contribute to the welfare of society. Whatever the case, I must be willing to say that some state of affairs is valuable for its own sake. Otherwise, the whole sequence of means and ends has no purpose.

Frequently we find ourselves in just this situation. We focus on immediate ends and fail to reflect on what we are ultimately after. This kind of reflection is necessary if we are to be rational agents who make free choices. Without it, we are rats in a maze, oblivious to where we are going.

THE CONCEPT OF UTILITY

I will follow Jeremy Bentham, father of utilitarianism, and refer to an intrinsically valuable state of affairs as *utility*. Bentham himself recognized a single type of utility toward which all actions should be directed, which he identified as pleasure (and avoidance of pain). It is more likely, however, that my choice of means is explained by multiple ultimate ends. I may take the train to Chicago because it ultimately promotes my family's happiness, and because it contributes less to air pollution than driving. I may view an unspoiled natural environment as an intrinsic good and therefore a form of utility alongside happiness. At the other extreme, an action may also have no end beyond itself. I may play melancholy Chopin preludes, not because they make me happy, but for the sheer sake of playing Chopin. I may regard performing music of this caliber as a form of utility in its own right.

A means/ends justification is a particular way of providing a rationale for an action, and it leads to a particular condition for rational choice: the *Utilitarian Principle*. Because a means/end rationale commits us to regarding some state of affairs as intrinsically valuable, it requires us to treat this same state of affairs as valuable when making other decisions. Suppose I take the Chicago job for the sake of ultimate happiness. Then if regular exercise and medical checkups promote long-term happiness, I must regard happiness as an equally good reason for getting regular exercise and checkups.

This seems innocuous enough, until we realize that everyone's utility counts equally. If happiness is intrinsically good, then it is good, no matter who experiences it. When taking a job, I must consider not only my own happiness, and not only that of my family, but the happiness of everyone who is affected by my choice. It is at this point that many people balk. Why can't I regard only my happiness as intrinsically good (and maybe my family's) and simply not care about the happiness of others? I can certainly do this, but it isn't rational. It reduces my thinking to mush.

Conceivably I could escape irrationality by regarding my own happiness or pleasure as more valuable than that of others. John Stuart Mill, another influential utilitarian, suggested that pleasure comes in grades. If I find pleasure in listening to Brahms, and someone else finds pleasure in eating greasy french fries, then I can regard my pleasure as a higher order and give it precedence in my decision-making. At least I am consistent.

However, neither I nor most people I know regard our happiness as having an intrinsically different quality than that of others. This means that any distinction I make between my happiness and that of others is arbitrary. If it is arbitrary, there is no reason for it; that's what *arbitrary* means. And if there is no reason for it, it's irrational.

Many find this simple argument unconvincing, perhaps due to the strong emphasis our society places on self-interest. It may be helpful to apply it to disutility rather than utility. Suppose I enjoy watching late-night TV in my hotel room and turn the volume to a high level, disturbing the sleep of other guests. I have no hearing impairment or even a particular taste for loud TV, but I simple don't care about the other guests. Almost everyone finds something wrong with this behavior, but exactly why is it wrong? Perhaps it is against hotel rules. By checking into the hotel, I implicitly agreed to abide by its rules, and violating such agreements is not generalizable. But let's suppose the hotel has no such rule and doesn't care about noise. Several guests complain to the manager, who simply says, "We have no control over guest behavior." The loud TV is wrong nonetheless.

If one accepts the Utilitarian Principle, the explanation is clear. I regard lack of sleep and the resulting unhappiness as disutility. I am therefore committed to considering the unhappiness of other guests. Because loud TV has no benefit for me and reduces the utility of others, the only rational alternative is to reduce the volume. Those who reject the Utilitarian Principle must either find a substitute principle, or concede that it is all right to disturb the other guests—and engage in a million other behaviors that harm others. I have yet to hear of a substitute principle that is even remotely plausible.

MAXIMIZING UTILITY

If an action results in more utility for *everyone* than any other action, it is clearly the ethical choice from a utilitarian perspective. To use the language of economics, an ethical action must be *Pareto optimal*, meaning that no other action would increase utility for one person without reducing it for others.

Pareto optimality may not be enough, however. I may be able to benefit many people by disadvantaging only a few, and it seems that I should take this opportunity. Let's suppose I prefer loud TV at night because it takes my mind off my worries. Then I can grant the other guests a night's sleep only by reducing my own utility, which makes my obnoxious behavior Pareto optimal. Yet it seems clearly wrong, because I can boost the utility of others a great deal by absorbing a small cost to myself.

This suggests that an action should not only be Pareto optimal but should maximize total net utility in some sense. It should result in the optimal tradeoff between gains and losses across the population. Bentham's famous formula is that it should result in the greatest good for the greatest number, but this is slightly less precise than the idea of maximizing total net utility. The argument for this principle is far from airtight, and we have to refine the principle as we go along to make it more defensible. Yet the basic defense is similar to the argument for a Pareto choice. If I regard, say, happiness as intrinsically valuable, then to be consistent I should prefer more happiness to less happiness. Conversely, if I regard pain as intrinsically bad, I should judge more pain to be worse than less pain, other things being equal.

Utility maximization immediately raises the question as to how one can quantify utility. Can one measure happiness, for example? Utility theory proposes various methods for calibrating individual *utility functions*, but even after this is accomplished, we must assume a sufficient degree of interpersonal comparability of utility estimates to add them up across the population. This problem has been much studied in economics and social choice theory, with some interesting results,* but few of the dilemmas we will consider require so precise an analysis. When one option creates greater net utility than another, we can usually ascertain this by common sense. We don't need social choice theory to determine that a loud hotel TV at night causes more harm than good.

---

* An excellent exposition of these results can be found in W. Gaertner, *A Primer in Social Choice Theory*, Oxford, UK, Oxford University Press, 2009.

There are other questions, however, that deserve closer attention. One question is what to do when a choice has several possible outcomes, and it is hard to predict which one will occur. When the probabilities of the outcomes can be estimated, the classical solution is to maximize *expected utility*. The utility of each possible outcome is multiplied by its probability, and these products are summed to compute the expected utility of the action in question. Expected utility can be interpreted as the average utility that would result if the action were repeated many times.

However, in many practical situations, probabilities are hard to estimate. We can deal with such cases by recalling that the essence of ethical action is that it has a coherent rationale. We are, therefore, constrained only to make a choice that we can rationally believe maximizes total expected utility. An action that is consistent with this principle passes the *utilitarian test*. Or, more precisely:

> *Utilitarian Principle.* An action is ethical only if it is not irrational for the agent to believe that no other action results in greater expected utility.

If there is no rational way to identify which option creates the greatest expected utility, we are off the hook, as far as the Utilitarian Principle is concerned. All available actions satisfy the test, because any one of them can be selected as the most utilitarian without violating rationality. This does not, however, give us license to be lazy. We can't just throw up our hands and say that we can't predict the consequences and then do anything we want. This is equally irrational. It is like driving to a party in an unfamiliar part of town. I could simply hop into the car and start driving, in hope of coming across the right address by sheer luck. But no rational person would do this. A more reasonable approach is to research the matter, perhaps by consulting a map or GPS device. On the other hand, it is equally perverse to spend hours verifying the route, because I would miss the party. A *satisficing* approach is better, to use a term coined by my late colleague Herbert Simon. To satisfice is to find a reasonable tradeoff between research and action.

DEONTIC UTILITARIANISM

Some readers will detect a difference between the Utilitarian Principle presented here and the one normally taught in ethics and philosophy courses. Classical utilitarianism is a *consequentialist* theory, meaning that it judges an action by its effect in the real world rather than by what is in the mind of the agent. Varieties of consequentialism differ in part by how they assess the consequences, with utilitarianism assessing them by the amount of utility they create. The Utilitarian Principle described here, however, is a deontic as opposed to a consequentialist criterion. This means that it judges an action by whether the agent acts according to duty, rather than by the actual consequences. In this case, duty requires that I select an action I can rationally believe maximizes utility. If I am wrong and the action turns out to be a poor choice, it was nonetheless ethical because it was a rational choice.

Deontological ethics sometimes attracts ridicule from practical people. They accuse deontologists of valuing acts only when they are based on good intentions, regardless of how much benefit the acts create. If an entrepreneur markets a miraculous cancer cure for the sheer sake of making money, she allegedly doesn't get any moral credit for saving lives because her motivation is unworthy. Only philosophers with their heads in the clouds could think this way, we are told. It is much better to recognize, with Adam Smith, that self-interested acts create enormous benefit and should be valued for that reason.

Nothing I have said implies any of this. First of all, ethics as conceived here doesn't decide how much moral credit people should get. It judges actions, not people. Furthermore, deontic utilitarianism doesn't care about the motivation behind an action. The entrepreneur's effort gets full "credit" for saving lives so long as she can rationally believe that it maximizes total utility. She can build the business to get rich or to please her cocker spaniel; it makes no difference to the utilitarian test.

The generalization test, which is also deontic, does care about motivation in the sense that it examines the reasons behind the act; however, the reasons need have nothing to do with altruism or a good heart. They need only be generalizable. The life-saving entrepreneur passes the test so long as she could still achieve her purpose if other entrepreneurs with a desire for wealth pursued lucrative opportunities in a similar fashion.

JUSTIFYING THE MEANS

I remarked earlier that the end does not justify an unethical means. But what if maximizing utility requires an unethical means? Maximizing utility is an end that we have an *obligation* to pursue, and yet perhaps the only means to achieving it is unethical because it is not generalizable. There seems to be a conflict here. The Utilitarian Principle is asking us to violate the generalization principle.

This situation actually comes up all the time. For example, think about the case of stealing a watch I discussed in Chapter 3. The theft is not generalizable, but stealing the watch probably creates more utility than not stealing it. It brings a substantial benefit to the thief, who we may suppose cannot afford to buy a watch, and imposes only a minor inconvenience on the merchant, who doubtless carries theft insurance. The insurance company must pay the claim, but the effect on its employees and stockholders is imperceptible. The Utilitarian Principle, therefore, calls for theft, even while the generalization principle forbids it. We seem to have a conflict of principles. The end (maximizing utility) seems to justify an unethical means (theft).

Actually, there is no conflict. The Utilitarian Principle asks us to select the *action* that we can rationally believe maximizes utility. A choice that fails the generalization test is not, strictly speaking, an action at all, because it has no coherent rationale. It should not be considered in the utilitarian calculation. This leads to a clarification of the utilitarian test:

> *Utilitarian Principle* (*Clarified*). An action is ethical only if it is not irrational for the agent to believe that no alternative action satisfies the other conditions of rational choice and results in greater expected utility.

Utilitarianism asks us to create as much net utility as we can by ethical means, where ethical means are those that are generalizable and respect autonomy.

THE DEMANDS OF UTILITARIANISM

A much-discussed and serious complaint about the Utilitarian Principle is that it is too demanding. It seems to call for major personal sacrifice. For example, consider the fact that the marginal value of money decreases as one gets richer. An extra dollar is worth less to Bill Gates than to me, and less to me than people living on a subsistence wage. This means I could increase total net utility if I gave away most of my money to residents of a poor country. They would gain more utility than I would lose. Does this mean that I am required to take a vow of poverty?

As it happens, sacrificial giving merely for the sake of increasing total net utility is probably ungeneralizable. If too many people in rich counties gave sacrificially, the wealth transfer would be so great that their economies would collapse. There would be too few resources to build infrastructure and educate children for productive employment. Many people would lack motivation to study and work hard so as to make the most of their talents. Net utility would not be increased after all, because first-world economies would become third-world economies, and there would be little surplus wealth to give away.

The philosophers in the room will object to this response. They will point out that even if utilitarian demands are moderate, this outcome is contingent on the current state of affairs and does not address the matter of principle. In a different type of situation, utilitarianism could require a much greater sacrifice. So I have not defended the utilitarian *principle* from the objection that it can be too demanding.

This is correct, but my intent was not to defend utilitarianism as a principle. I was only arguing that utilitarianism does not ordinarily require sacrificial giving. If someone wants to attack utilitarianism as a principle on the grounds that it can demand a great deal, I have a simple response. The fact that an ethical theory is potentially demanding does not, in itself, show that the theory is false. In fact, we sometimes accept burdensome demands from morality.

Suppose I carry a deadly disease to which I am immune but that is easily communicated to everyone around me. Then I should quarantine myself, even if this makes severe demands on my lifestyle. Or suppose I am an organized crime boss who obtains my wealth from extortion and murder. I should reduce myself to poverty, if necessary, to avoid complicity in such crimes. Few of us would say that morality demands too much in such cases. Even when a moral theory seems too demanding, we may think better of it in the future. It was not so long ago that some people relied on slave labor for a comfortable lifestyle. A utilitarian imperative to forswear slavery could have seemed quite demanding at the time, but it was correct nonetheless. Ethical scruples were, in fact, an important factor in the eventual abolition of chattel slavery. A demanding ethical theory may not only be correct, but it can lift us out of entrenched thought patterns that rationalize an unjust society.*

---

* Similar arguments against the "demandingness objection" are echoed by some modern utilitarians. The best known is P. Singer, as in Famine, affluence, and morality, *Philosophy and Public Affairs* 1 (1972): 229–243. See also S. Kagan, *The Limits of Morality*, Oxford, UK, Clarendon Press,

Furthermore, a theory that does *not* require helping the disadvantaged is demanding in its own way.[*] It demands that the needy continue to suffer! Suppose, for example, that morality does not require those in prosperous regions of the world to assist refugees of the Syrian civil war. Such a morality makes merciless demands on the refugees by forcing them to endure miserable conditions.

Perhaps we don't recognize this as demanding because it doesn't require anyone to take affirmative action. We are more comfortable with a theory that tells us what *not* to do than with one that tells us what to do. It is okay if morality tells us not to infect others or not to extort money from them, even if this requires sacrifice, but it is not okay if morality tells us to take the positive step of rescuing others from misery. We prefer to regard altruism as admirable but beyond the call of duty, or to use the philosopher's term, as supererogatory.

All this suggests that the objection to utilitarianism is not so much that it is demanding, but that it demands acts that benefit others as well as forbidding acts that harm others. This is a deeply ingrained intuition that relies on a distinction of causing and allowing. It relies on an assumption that we can distinguish actions that cause harm from actions that allow harm, and that this distinction is morally relevant. So it is essential to examine the distinction carefully.

1989; P. K. Unger, *Living High and Letting Die*, New York, Oxford University Press, 1996; A. Norcross, Comparing harms: Headaches and human lives, *Philosophy and Public Affairs* 26 (1997): 135–167. The demandingness objection is reasserted in L. Murphy, *Moral Demands in Nonideal Theory*, New York, Oxford University Press, 2000; T. Mulgan, *The Demands of Consequentialism*, Oxford, Clarendon Press, 2001. Another line of argument is that the demandingness objection can be avoided by moving to "rule utilitarianism" (as opposed to "act utilitarian"), as advocated in B. Hooker, *Ideal Code, Real World: A Rule-consequentialist Theory of Morality*, Oxford, UK, Oxford University Press, 2000. Rule utilitarianism holds that a general rule of action, rather than an individual act, should be subjected to utilitarian scrutiny. There are serious weaknesses in this view, perhaps the most central being that there is no satisfactory way to define what scope the rule should have. In this book, scope (for purposes of the generalization test) is defined by the agent's rationale. One could conceivably adopt a similar definition of scope for utilitarian purposes, but this creates still more problems, and more relevant here, it sacrifices the argument for deontic utilitarianism. One is not rationally constrained to reject an action plan that would create less utility than another if generally adopted, unless one is rationally constrained to believe that adopting it would cause it to be generally adopted, which is rarely the case. It is true that if *part of the rationale* for such an action plan is that it would increase utility, then it must be rejected, because there is an internal inconsistency. Action plans of this kind were considered earlier in the chapter, for example when analyzing the obligation to give sacrificially. In such cases, the generalization principle already rejects the action plan, and there is no need for a rule utilitarian principle.

[*] D. Sobel points this out in The impotence of the demandingness objection, *Philosophers' Imprint* 7 (2007): 1–17.

CAUSING VERSUS ALLOWING

One problem with the distinction of causing from allowing is that it is fiendishly difficult to define. We can easily think of some clear cases, as for example throwing a bomb into a crowd, versus watching someone throw a bomb into a crowd. Our seemingly clear intuition about this breaks down, however, when we try to capture it in words. Every definition seems to either misclassify or to be too vague to be useful. Specific examples can be unclear as well. If I leave a manhole uncovered while working under the street, do I cause injury when someone falls in, or do I only allow it to happen? There are several attempts in the philosophical literature to draw the distinction, all of which are problematic and end up being unsuitable for the purposes of ethics anyway.* Legal theorists have invested even more effort trying to understand causation, because it is related to criminal culpability, and yet the field seems to remain as controversial as ever.

The Utilitarian Principle, as developed here, avoids these difficulties by making no distinction between causing and allowing. All results of a decision become part of the utilitarian calculation. By *results*, I mean simply the state of affairs that would exist if the decision were made, whether there is causation in some particular sense or not. So if there are two options, I compare the utility in the state of affairs A that would result from selecting one option with the utility in the state of affairs B that would result from selecting the other option. Most of the world is the same in A and B, but parts of the world are different, and these determine the outcome of the utilitarian test.

The argument for this basically is the same as for the Utilitarian Principle in general. Utility is, by definition, the state or quality I value intrinsically. If I have an opportunity to select a state of affairs A with greater total utility than state of affairs B, then rationality constrains me to select A, because otherwise I don't intrinsically value utility after all. The total utility in A and B is therefore relevant to the utilitarian test, not some portion of that utility that I caused in some sense.

---

* One strategy for defining causation, as opposed to allowing, is based on counterfactual conditionals: If I had not done A, then B would not have occurred, or some more complicated variation of this idea. J. Mackie, *The Cement of the Universe*, Oxford, UK, Oxford University Press; 1974; A. Donagan, *The Theory of Morality*, Chicago, IL, The University of Chicago Press, 1977; D. Lewis Causation, in *Philosophical Papers* (vol. 2), New York, Oxford University Press, 1986; S. Kagan, *The Limits of Morality*, Oxford, UK, Oxford University Press, 1989. But then one must explain why allowing cannot be expressed as a counterfactual conditional.

Think about Mencius' parable of the child about to fall in the well, which I brought up in Chapter 2. The child is clinging to the side of the well and will fall in unless I rush to the rescue. Many view rescuing the child as supererogatory, while tossing the child into the well is immoral, because it causes the injury rather than allowing it to happen. The Utilitarian Principle treats the two cases equally. It requires a rescue just as strongly as it prohibits an assault. We may be uncomfortable with this because it would be poor *public policy* to require a rescue, whereas it is good public policy to prohibit an assault. If there is an injury, it would be impractical to identify which bystanders could have intervened to prevent it, apprehend them, and punish them accordingly.* On the other hand, it is relatively easy to identify a perpetrator of injury, and our primal urge for retribution is satisfied by punishing the person who "caused" the harm. Legal theorists agonize over theories of causation, but behavior that we don't want to prohibit by law may be unethical nonetheless. For example, it would be impractical to outlaw double-crossing a friend or lying to your spouse.

The failure to distinguish causing and allowing has a serious implication, however, that deserves careful examination. It allows us to use a futility argument: "If I don't do it, someone else will." A prison guard who is ordered by a commanding officer to torture prisoners can point out that if he were to refuse, someone else would comply with the orders, and the utilitarian effect would be the same. In fact, it could be worse, because he could be disciplined for insubordination. U.S. personnel involved in torture at Abu Ghraib prison in Iraq claimed that abuse of prisoners was already standard practice.† They could have told themselves that if they didn't participate, someone else would take up the slack, and the result would be the same. It doesn't matter who directly causes the torture.

---

* In a recent notorious case, bystanders who had an opportunity to help *could* be identified. A group of teenage boys used their smartphone to record a man drowning as they stood by and laughed at the spectacle. When they posted the video on social media, there was a public outcry for their prosecution even though they broke no law, which indicates a widespread belief that they had an ethical duty to intervene. At this writing, the local police chief has relented by suggesting that the boys might be arraigned on a charge of failing to report a death to a medical examiner, which is a misdemeanor. T. Turner, Teens film, laugh as Florida man drowns, *Washington Post*, July 21, 2017; R. Ellis, N. Valencia, and D. Sayers, Chief to recommend charges against Florida teens who recorded drowning, CNN, July 22, 2017. Interestingly, a ship captain is required to rescue persons in distress at sea, under U.S. and international maritime law.
† S. M. Hersh, Torture at Abu Ghraib, *The New Yorker*, May 10, 2004. Referring to the 372nd Military Police Company stationed at the prison, the article states, The 372nd's abuse of prisoners seemed almost routine.

This kind of argument strikes us as grotesque, and yet it seems to have a certain validity. How can we resolve this paradox?

The resolution is straightforward. If it is really true that "If I don't do it, someone else will," this fact may well establish that a piece of behavior passes the utilitarian test. Yet passing this one test does not show than the behavior is ethical, because the behavior must respect generalizability and autonomy as well. Torture, for example, is a grievous violation of autonomy. As we will see in Chapter 6, the logic of autonomy is different than the logic of utility, and torturing someone is wrong regardless of whether others would be willing to do it. Passing the utilitarian test does not suggest that there is anything right about torture. It only recognizes that one individual's decision won't have an effect on the amount of torture that occurs.

"If I don't do it, someone else will" can also be used as a reverse futility argument. It may convince one *not* to take action, on the grounds that someone else would step in anyway. An infamous case of inaction occurred in 1964, when Kitty Genovese was brutally murdered in the streets of Queens, New York. Thirty-eight nearby residents allegedly failed to call the police as she screamed for help over a period of half an hour, during which she was attacked three times by the same assailant.* The incident became a standard example of the *bystander effect* in social psychology textbooks. The popular account of events has since been questioned,† but supposing something like it is true, these bystanders might have reasonably surmised that if they didn't call the police, someone else would. Failing to respond could therefore pass the utilitarian test.

Again, however, an ethical decision must pass the other tests as well, and this time there are problems with generalizability. Some of the bystanders, at least, described their rationale for not picking up the phone as a reluctance to get involved, as well as an assumption that someone else would respond. These reasons do not generalize. If everyone with the same rationale failed to call, no one would call, and in fact no one did. This is inconsistent with the assumption that someone else would respond. If some bystanders were not convenient to a phone or had some other impediment, and they failed to call for this reason, then they are off the hook, because this argument against generalizability does not apply. But for those who

---

* M. Gansberg, Thirty-eight who saw murder didn't call the police, *New York Times*, March 27, 1964.
† For example, R. Manning, M. Levine, and A. Collins, The Kitty Genovese murder and the social psychology of helping: The parable of the 38 witnesses, *American Psychologist* 62 (2007): 555–562.

were sitting next to their phones, a failure to call was not generalizable. The verdict of the utilitarian test is again appropriate. Passing the test does not say that inaction is right, but only helps direct attention toward the true source of the ethical problem.

UTILITARIANISM AND FAIRNESS

Even those who can accept the demanding and comprehensive nature of the Utilitarian Principle may see its demands as unfair. One reason the principle asks us to render so much assistance is that most people fail to live up to this obligation. If everyone pitched in, less would be required of everyone. If every person of means contributed to developing economies, those economies would be more developed, and there would be less need to contribute. Perhaps it is unfair to ask a few ethical individuals to carry the weight that others should bear. Liam Murphy, for example, proposes that we are obligated only to render the level of service that would be necessary if all others were to pull their own weight from now on.[*]

One problem with this kind of objection is that people have many different ideas about what is "fair," and these ideas change from one occasion to another. But aside from this, it is unclear why the unfairness of the situation relieves one of the obligation. Suppose I come across an injured hiker on the trail who cannot survive without assistance. It would be much easier to give assistance if other hikers helped out, but let's suppose they pretend to ignore the problem and walk on past. It is "unfair" for me to be the only Good Samaritan, and Murphy's principle lets me off the hook. Yet it is my obligation to help, because doing so would result in greater utility.

Murphy deals with this case by distinguishing a "loss" from a *gain*, relative to the status quo. On his view, the main Utilitarian Principle applies to actions that cause others to gain, but a secondary principle requires that my action not result in a *loss* greater than what would occur if others helped out. This means I must not let the injured hiker perish, because he would not perish if others rescued him. But then we must judge allowing a hiker to perish as resulting in a *loss* relative to the status quo, even though his demise *is* the status quo. Perhaps puzzles like this can be addressed, but

---

[*] L. Murphy, *Moral Demands in Nonideal Theory*, New York, Oxford University Press, 2000.

it is hard to see what would be the principle for distinguishing loss from gain in a satisfactory sense. More generally, it is unclear how to defend Murphy's principles except to say that they result in a less demanding utilitarian theory that we are more comfortable with in particular cases.

Before moving ahead, I should be perfectly clear about something. I am not claiming there is an obligation to help the injured hiker because this seems reasonable to you or me. There is an obligation because it is required by the utilitarian test, which I have defended as a general principle on general grounds. I say this because it relates to a fundamental issue of epistemology that will arise later. Ethics must rest on general argumentative strategies that can be defended on their own merits, like the generalization and utilitarian tests, not on common-sense intuitions in particular cases.

UTILITARIANISM AND LIFESTYLE

Utilitarianism can in principle require onerous sacrifice for the sake of others, but we can take comfort in the fact that its demands are usually moderate. In fact, we can normally maximize utility by focusing on self-interest much of the time, because we have the greatest control over our own welfare. I am in the best position to determine my state of mind and body. No one else can get me up in the morning, study my lessons, make me go to work, and keep me in good physical shape. Furthermore, I can make a greater contribution to others if I take care of myself. This is particularly true of young people, who should invest in themselves so they can contribute more in the future. As we get older and take on responsibilities—family, children, clients—we have greater influence on the well-being of others and assume utilitarian obligations accordingly. Fortunately, we mature ethically with age and acquire the ability to meet these obligations.

If I am like most people, I can also maximize utility by investing most of my time and effort in everyday concerns like my job and family. I am uniquely positioned to take care of my family, not only because I have legal authority to look after their interests, but because of the intimate relationship we share. Even if my occupation is not the world's most productive one, I can ethically give it much of my time and energy, because I am trained for it. It is simply a matter of efficiency. Heart surgery may create more utility per hour than writing ethics books, but this does not oblige me to attempt heart surgery, as the results would be deadly.

The amount of time I should spend on charitable causes depends on the marginal productivity of my job and the needs of my family. If an extra hour with the family or at work would create less benefit than an hour of pro bono activity, then I should think about getting into volunteer work. A heart surgeon might well maximize benefit by working long hours, short of becoming too fatigued, whereas a department store clerk may feel called to community service outside normal working hours. Both should also find a reasonable tradeoff between work and recreational activities that recharge their batteries.

I said earlier that the Utilitarian Principle does not require taking a vow of poverty, but I certainly don't want to imply that self-imposed penury is necessarily wrong. Sacrificial giving for the sole purpose of increasing total utility is ungeneralizable, but self-denial for more complex reasons may be ethical. One may enter a monastery, for example, not simply out of concern for the poor, but because one feels called by God to do so, or judges oneself to be particularly suited to a monastic life. If these reasons apply to a minority of the population, the choice is generalizable, and it may be utilitarian as well because it conserves resources. Living simply, without committing oneself to poverty, is equally defensible, even for a majority of us. It conserves resources while retaining enough capital to maintain a productive economy. Sam Walton, founder of Walmart and one of the world's wealthiest men of his day, drove an old pickup truck and reportedly never paid more than $5 for a haircut. His prize possession was not a 130-foot yacht, but his hunting dog Ol' Roy.

An extravagant lifestyle, on the other hand, is more difficult to justify from a utilitarian viewpoint. It not only consumes resources that may be more productively allocated elsewhere, but it often fails to provide lasting benefits even to the privileged. A safe, stable, and reasonably comfortable environment is easily justified, because it is conducive to better education for the kids, greater productivity at work, and better health for everyone. But a middle-class lifestyle can provide these. There are cases in which one's work may require high-end living, perhaps to associate with or impress well-to-do clients. The promise of opulence may be necessary to motivate some talented individuals, such as business entrepreneurs, to operate at a high performance level at which they generate extraordinary utility. Aside from such cases, however, extravagance seems nonutilitarian and therefore unethical.

UTILITARIANISM AND CAREERS

The Utilitarian Principle doesn't require me to try my hand at heart surgery, because I would make a mess of it. Yet it may seem to require a young person to train for a career that maximizes utility, whether it be medicine, disaster relief work, or whatever. Actually, it doesn't, due to a generalizability issue. If I become a surgeon or relief worker to increase my utility production, then I am committed to saying everyone who can create greater utility this way should do the same. This obviously would not work, because too few people would be left to stock the grocery shelves and pick up the garbage. These and many other occupations may create less utility per hour, but they are essential to a functioning society. Becoming a heart surgeon or relief worker solely to maximize utility is, therefore, ungeneralizable, which means there is no utilitarian obligation to do so.

However, if I have more complex reasons for going into surgery or relief work, then these choices are likely to be generalizable as well as utilitarian. If I become a heart surgeon because I have a keen intelligence, coolness under pressure, good hand-eye coordination, and an interest in surgery, then a career in the field is clearly generalizable. Even if everyone with my reasons were to act on them, there would probably be no surplus of surgeons.

In practice, the job market tends to enforce this particular generalization test, albeit very crudely. If too many people like me want to be surgeons or relief workers, it will hard for me to find a job in these fields. A generalizable decision often boils down to selecting a career that attracts me and in which a person with my talents and motivation is likely to find a job. Within these parameters, the Utilitarian Principle asks us to choose a career with the greatest potential for positive impact. If I have a keen intelligence, coolness under pressure, good hand-eye coordination, and interests in both surgery and playing pool, it is better to become a surgeon than a pool shark.

If an extravagant lifestyle is problematic, how about a career with an extravagant salary? There is certainly no ethical problem with making a lot of money. The issue is whether you make a contribution in your work and what you do with the money you earn. Both overpaid CEOs and underpaid school crossing guards can create a great deal of positive utility. As for disposing of the money, you can always live simply, as I mentioned earlier, and put the large income to productive use. However, entering a lucrative career simply for the money, without investigating the kind of contribution it makes to society, is ethically problematic.

Ethics does not tell us exactly which career to pursue. In fact, it leaves most life choices largely up to us. It only asks that we have reasons for these choices, and that these reasons meet certain general criteria for coherence. These criteria can, however, provide useful guidance in a society that offers some people a range of choices but no clear set of values for making them.

RESPONSIBILITY FOR THE CHOICES OF OTHERS

There is a persistent notion in popular culture that we are not responsible for the choices others make, at least if they are competent adults. We are only responsible for our own choices. I'm not sure what *responsible* means here, but it is often taken to mean that if I give others an opportunity to make good or bad choices, and they make bad ones, that's not my fault. I need not consider their potential mistakes when judging my own actions. The Utilitarian Principle rejects this idea. It says that I must take into account all the consequences of my actions, including those that result from the free choices of others. I will try to explain this through a series of examples. These examples don't prove that utilitarianism is right, but they clarify its implications and may show that it is closer to popular beliefs than one might think.

Suppose I operate a chain of fast-food restaurants and introduce a new menu item, the Superburger. It proves to be a runaway success, and some customers eat several Superburgers a week. The only problem is that Superburgers are high in saturated fat, high-fructose corn syrup, and LDL cholesterol. A hospital study finds that Superburger enthusiasts incur a significantly increased risk of diabetes and heart disease. Demand continues to soar, despite a Superburger box label that clearly discloses the ingredients, and despite the fact that kids never eat Superburgers because of the lettuce on them.

Should I take this product off the market? Many would say there is no obligation to do so, despite the health effects, because I am only satisfying consumer demand. My customers are adults who freely and knowingly choose to eat Superburgers, and kids are unaffected. Nonetheless, I should take the disutility of disease into account when applying the Utilitarian Principle. The health effects are, in fact, consequences of my marketing decision, in the sense that they would not have occurred otherwise. Since rationality requires me to maximize utility, it requires me to make a choice that, in fact, results in the greatest utility.

If this is not convincing, consider another example. I run a health food company, and one of my nutritionists discovers a concoction that provides a fantastic high. I decide to sell it in my health food stores under the name Crack II. Word gets around, and sales go through the roof. Unfortunately, Crack II is addictive, and thousands of customers are losing their jobs and families because they have become addicted. Due to political gridlock, there is little chance the government will outlaw the product in the near future.

Should I take Crack II off the shelf? Remarkably, a significant number of people continue to insist that I need not consider its health effects, because I am not responsible for the free choices of others. (I know this to be true, because I have used this example in classes and professional workshops.) Again, I'm not sure what it means to be "responsible" for the choices of others, but in any case, those choices are a consequence of my decision and should be factored into the utilitarian analysis.

I conclude with an example in which even Crack II defenders may find utilitarianism to be reasonable. Suppose I run a pharmaceutical company and have two product proposals on my desk, with equal potential to generate revenue for the company. Due to limited development funds, I must choose between them. One proposal is for a miracle cancer cure that will save millions from a miserable death. The other is a remarkably effective anti-wrinkle cream. The salutary effects of the cancer drug rely on the free choices of physicians to prescribe it and patients to take it, yet nearly everyone urges me to market the cancer drug rather than the anti-wrinkle cream. They rightly say that I should take into account all the consequences of my decision. Then I should do the same in general.

THE POPULATION PUZZLE

The Utilitarian Principle, at least when conceived in a consequentialist fashion, seems to generate a paradox. Maximizing utility can be interpreted as maximizing total utility or average utility, and both can lead to strange conclusions. Suppose we have the option to promote a high birth rate that would lead to an overpopulated world. People would be worse off in this world than they are now, but the total utility would be higher due to the sheer number of people. Maximizing utility requires us to overpopulate even though it reduces everyone's welfare. This seems strange. It is called the *repugnant conclusion* in the philosophical literature.*

So perhaps we should maximize *average* utility over the population rather than the total. Yet this can lead to even more grotesque outcomes. We could raise the average utility level by murdering everyone who suffers from a chronic disease. Of course, murder violates autonomy and is wrong for that reason, no matter what the utilitarian consequences. But the same problem surfaces in cases where there is no violation of autonomy. Suppose we have the option of developing drugs that prolong the life of chronically ill patients. Despite their illness, these patients derive enjoyment from life and would gain utility from a longer lifespan. Nonetheless, prolonging their lives would result in a lower average utility, because a larger fraction of the population would be ill. Maximizing average utility would require us to deny them longer life, even if we could develop the necessary drugs for free. This seems bizarre.

The population paradox is much debated in the ethical literature, with no resolution in sight.† The paradox loses much of its urgency, however, when the Utilitarian Principle is deontic, as it is in this book, rather than

---

* D. Parfit, *Reasons and Persons*, Oxford, UK, Oxford University Press, 1986. A slightly different formulation of the problem is discussed in L. Temkin, Intransitivity and the mere addition paradox, *Philosophy and Public Affairs* 16 (1987): 138–187.

† Problems with averaging utility are discussed in R. I. Sikora, Utilitarianism: The classical principle and the average principle, *Canadian Journal of Philosophy* 5 (195): 409–419; B. Anglin, The repugnant conclusion, *Canadian Journal of Philosophy* 7 (1977): 745–754. An alternative approach is to suppose that total utility is a nonseparable function of individual utilities. That is, the utility change that results from adding another person to the population depends on the number and/or utilities of those already in the population. T. Hurka, Value and population size, *Ethics* 93 (1983): 496–507; Y.-K. Ng, What should we do about future generations? Impossibility of Parfit's Theory X, *Economics and Philosophy* 5 (1989): 135–253; T. R. Sider, Might Theory X be a theory of diminishing marginal value?, *Analysis* 51 (1991): 265–271. Functions for which the utility change is zero if the added person's welfare is below a critical utility level are discussed in G. S. Kavka, The paradox of future individuals, *Philosophy and Public Affairs* 11 (1982): 93–112; C. Blackorby, W. Bossert and D. Donaldson, Critical level utilitarianism and the population-ethics dilemma, *Economics and Philosophy* 13 (1997): 197–230. Other functions are discussed in R. B. Edwards, *Pleasures and Pains: A Theory of Qualitative Hedonism*, New York, Cornell University Press, 1979; J. Griffin, *Well-Being: Its Meaning, Measurement, and Moral Importance*, Oxford, UK, Clarendon Press, 1986; N. M. Lemos, Higher goods and the myth of Tithonus, *Journal of Philosophy* 90 (1993): 482–496; S. Rachels, A set of solutions to Parfit's problems, *Noûs* 35 (2001): 214–238. There are many other perspectives in the literature. For a collection of articles with reference lists, see the T. Tännsjö and J. Ryberg (Eds.), *The Repugnant Conclusion: Essays on Population Ethics*, Dordrecht, the Netherlands, Springer, 2004.

consequentialist. A deontic principle requires us only to acknowledge our rational commitments. Sometimes rationality requires us to maximize average utility, sometimes total utility, and often it imposes no clear commitment.

Suppose, for example, I regard happiness as intrinsically good. It is clearly rational for me to take an action that creates greater happiness for everyone who is now alive and makes no future persons less happy than they would be otherwise. This raises both average and total happiness. However, if overpopulation increases aggregate happiness while reducing the average, it is hard to say that I would be irrational in avoiding overpopulation, simply on the grounds that I value happiness. It is still harder to say that I would be irrational in prolonging the lives of the chronically ill, if they gain in happiness and others don't lose, simply because this reduces average happiness.

Since the aim of ethics is to develop rational consensus, we should recognize only those rational commitments that are clear and uncontroversial. Such a rule might be formulated by taking into account *lifelong utility*, and by requiring action only when it clearly benefits more lives than it harms.

Clearly Beneficial Lifelong Utility Tradeoff. If an act results in greater lifelong utility for many in the present and future, at the cost of less lifelong utility for a few (or slightly less lifelong utility for many), then it is preferred by the Utilitarian Principle.

It's unclear what is meant by *many*, *slightly less*, and *few*, but the idea is to apply the Utilitarian Principle only in clear cases, not in borderline or controversial cases. The classical Benthamite criterion of maximizing total utility, which I have relied on up to now, can be regarded as a rough approximation of this rule that should not be forced when the tradeoff is less decisive.

This rule can be applied to actions that affect the total population. Suppose that reducing fertility would create a better life for many people, present, and future, and would reduce lifelong utility only for a few people. Then people should have fewer babies, even if the total utility is less. Suppose that prolonging the lives of the chronically ill would substantially raise their lifelong utility and only slightly reduce the lifelong utility of others. Then their lives should be prolonged, even if it reduces the average.

A deontic Utilitarian Principle places a heavy burden on identifying rational commitments. Yet the same problem arises in the sciences and other fields of endeavor, and we forge ahead just the same.

PRESENT VERSUS FUTURE UTILITY

Another puzzle for utilitarianism deals with the present versus the future. How much should we discount future benefit before weighing it against present sacrifice? Should I study hard today to avoid unemployment in the future, or just live one day at a time? As a society, should we invest in solar panels or drive electric cars to reduce global warming in the future, or let future generations take care of themselves?

The first thought that comes to mind is the Utilitarian Principle's noble egalitarianism. Everyone's utility counts equally in the calculation, regardless of race, background, or social station. The same kind of equality would seem to apply across the generations. Why should people living in 2120 count less than people living in 2020? If the calendar date makes no difference, then my own future should count equally with the present.

To understand why one might want to discount future benefits, let's have a brief look at the practice of discounting in business and finance. It is standard procedure to compute the *net present value* of an investment by discounting future costs and returns. The time value of money is also reflected in interest rates, which imply the discounting of future loan payments. There are at least three distinct justifications for this kind of discounting: uncertainty, impatience, and opportunity cost.

Suppose I lend you $100. I want my expected payback to be at least as great as the amount of the loan. If there is only a 90 percent chance you will repay the loan, I must charge a risk premium of $11.11 interest to compensate for the uncertainty. This makes my expected payback 90 percent of $111.11, which is $100, as desired.

Even if there is no risk, I may prefer to have $100 now rather than later. Being human, I am impatient and don't like to defer gratification. So I charge a *risk-free interest rate* to make it worth my while to part with my money a few years.

On top of this, there are other ways to invest my $100. Even if there is no risk in lending to you, and even if I don't care about the time value of money, lending $100 to you deprives me of the opportunity to invest it elsewhere. I therefore charge you an interest rate that matches what another type of investment would pay.

Now let's see if any of these justifications are relevant to the Utilitarian Principle. Risk is certainly relevant, but it is already factored into utilitarian calculations. The Utilitarian Principle asks me to maximize *expected* utility, which takes account of the probability my actions will have the intended effect. There is nothing inherently temporal about this. What matters is the degree of risk, not whether the risk is due to uncertainty of predicting the future. So I must give equal weight to present and future generations, while taking in account the uncertainties involved in either case.

The Utilitarian Principle also considers opportunity cost. It examines all options that pass the other ethical tests and judges which one yields the greatest expected return. It takes into account the opportunity cost of investing in the future by comparing it with investing in the here-and-now. Again, there is no need to discount benefits to future generations.

That leaves the matter of deferred gratification. If I am willing to discount my own future benefits, it hardly seems inconsistent to give less weight to future generations. The problem with this argument is that discounting my own future is already irrational, except when it is based on uncertainty. There may be some rationality in saying, while a young person, that I may as well eat sweet desserts and enjoy myself, because nobody can predict the consequences of any particular diet, and we all die one way or another. But suppose I know with absolute certainly that eating desserts while young will cause me to be diagnosed with a serious case of type II diabetes on my fiftieth birthday, and I will otherwise enjoy good health into old age. It would be idiotic to afflict myself with this wretched disease.

It's hard for me to avoid the conclusion that the Utilitarian Principle cares as much about the future as the present, without any discounting beyond that already implicit in the calculation of expected utility. I therefore return to the principle's core insight: Everyone deserves equal consideration, whether they dwell in the present or the future.

5

Everyday Dilemmas

Everyone loves to talk about the hot-button issues, which in the United States at the moment include immigration, wealth inequality, gun rights, police brutality, terrorism, and healthcare reform. Sounding off on these questions may seem like fun at first, but in the end it is frustrating and demoralizing, because we just talk past each other and resolve nothing. It is much more useful to start with everyday dilemmas and build our ethical reasoning skills gradually. Going straight to the big issues is like going straight from $2 + 2 = 4$ to integral calculus. Besides, the everyday issues are the ones we deal with every day.

I am going to take us through some seemingly humdrum dilemmas that will help hone our ethical skills. I think you will find them interesting, and they will give us the satisfaction of being able to resolve something on the basis of sound reasoning rather than mere opinion or gut feeling. In addition, some of these little issues are subtler than you might expect.

BOARDING THE PLANE

Let's start with the question that opened the book. Is it okay for me to board the plane before my zone is announced, so I can find space for my carry-on bag?[*]

This certainly doesn't seem like a generalizable strategy, because if everyone used it, it wouldn't work. The whole point of boarding too early is to have some assurance of getting ahead of most people. If everyone boards

---

[*] Based on an exercise in my book, *Business Ethics as Rational Choice*, Boston, MA, Prentice Hall, 2011: 14.

early, there is no such assurance. Everyone mobs the gate, and whether I find space for my bag depends on how hard I shove to get to the front. To put it differently, any advantage of boarding with the Zone 1 passengers presupposes a system of boarding by zones, just as the advantage of cheating on exams presupposes a grading system. If everyone boards with Zone 1, or if everyone cheats, the system breaks down.

This is the right idea, but it is instructive to apply the Generalization Principle more precisely, because precision will become important as the issues become harder. I will make three attempts to apply it, and only the third will be correct. To get started, I have to identify my reasons for boarding early. Presumably there are two: It will allow me to find space for my carry-on, and I won't be caught.

> *Attempt Number 1.* I might think that boarding early is ungeneraliz-able because I wouldn't *want* everyone who had these same reasons to board early. There are so many people in this category that, if they acted accordingly, I probably wouldn't find space for my bag. True, but this is not the correct analysis. What I want is not part of the test.
>
> *Attempt Number 2.* I might also think that boarding early is ungener-alizable because if everyone did so, it would defeat the purpose of the boarding system. People would still crawl over each other as they try to access rear rows and window seats in the cramped econ-omy cabin, and the boarding process would be as inefficient as ever. Yes, it would defeat the purpose of the system, but this again is not the precise test.
>
> *Attempt Number 3.* The correct test is whether *my* reasons for boarding early are consistent with the assumption that everyone with these reasons acts on them. They are not. If everyone with these reasons boarded early, then either there would be no advantage in boarding out of turn, or else gate attendants would start checking the zone number on boarding passes. So at least one of my two reasons would no longer apply, and the generalization test fails.

Lack of generalizability is enough to show that early boarding is unethical, but for the record, it fails the utilitarian test as well. If I board early, then I will impede the boarding process at least slightly, because at least one person will have to crawl over me to reach his or her assigned set. It is true that I will be more likely to find space for my carry-on, but this only means that someone else will be denied space. Everyone's utility counts the same, and the space issue is therefore a wash. Because total net expected utility is slightly less if I board early, it violates the Utilitarian Principle.

THE AMBULANCE

I am an emergency paramedic who drives an ambulance. It happens that I have an appointment with my boss in half an hour, and due to heavy traffic, I am not going to make it on time. This would be unfortunate, because we are going to discuss the possibility of a promotion. So I decide to use the siren and lights, justifiably confident that no one will report me. Is this ethical?

Your reaction is probably that this is obviously unethical, and we shouldn't waste time with such elementary issues. However, the reasoning process is not so obvious and provides a useful lesson. To begin with, abusing the siren is almost certainly illegal. Violating the law merely for personal convenience is normally unethical because it is normally ungeneralizable. In most cases, breaking the law incurs an advantage only because most people obey the law. For example, if everyone parked illegally for greater convenience, streets would be so clogged with parked cars that any thought of convenience would be forgotten (perhaps Rome is approaching this condition). More generally, if everyone were a scofflaw for the sake of convenience, we would live in such a state of anarchy that it would be well-nigh impossible to accomplish anything, conveniently or otherwise.

To make the case more interesting, however, let's suppose that ambulance drivers in my city are so ethical that it has never been necessary to pass a law governing emergency vehicles. Given this, why is abusing the siren unethical? It seems ungeneralizable on the face of it, because if ambulance drivers made a habit of abusing the siren, no one would pay attention to it, and I would be late even with the siren.

However, I claim that when my reasons are properly taken into account, my action is perfectly generalizable. I am using the siren and lights for three reasons: The traffic is heavy, the siren will allow me to meet my boss on time, and it is very unlikely anyone will catch me. This is generalizable because such a convergence of circumstances is unlikely to occur in a given city more than two or three times a year. The resulting abuse of the siren will have no effect on my ability to achieve my purpose.

These reasons are, in fact, generalizable. The problem is that they are not my reasons, much as Gertrude Grosvenor's name was not one of her reasons for stealing a watch. Their scope is too narrow, because there are many occasions on which siren and lights would be equally useful to ambulance drivers in a hurry. Suppose that rather than meet my boss, I am supposed to pick up my kids at day care before closing time. Or suppose I am running late, not because of heavy traffic, but because I misplaced my car keys. And so on with a thousand other possibilities. Why wouldn't I use the siren and lights in these cases? There is no evident reason I would not. My real rationale for using the siren is simply that I really want to get somewhere in a hurry, and my misconduct probably won't be caught. If all ambulance drivers were to abuse their position on all such occasions, the public would become suspicious, the abuse would be exposed, and the city would crack down. It would no longer be possible to get away with such behavior.

I can, of course, insist that I wouldn't abuse the siren under any other circumstances. I am only going to break the rules this one time. This sounds suspiciously like the dieter who insists she is going to eat dessert just this one time, but psychology is not the issue here. I need not psychoanalyze myself to determine if I would abuse the siren on other occasions. The relevant criterion is whether, as part of my decision-making process, I adduced a rationale to distinguish this particular situation from the thousand other occasions on which I might abuse the siren to save time. I might conjure up such a rationale after the fact, but it is not part of my deliberation. It is only an excuse. I am abusing the siren simply because I really want to get somewhere fast, which is not generalizable.

What is to prevent me from *claiming* that my excuse is truly part of my rationale? Who can prove otherwise? Nothing, and nobody. Ethics doesn't force me to be ethical, or to analyze issues correctly. It doesn't prevent me from kidding myself about my true reasons. Ethics, at best, only tells me what is ethical and how to analyze the issues. It is my choice where to go from there. Nutritional science doesn't force me to eat properly, or prevent me from kidding myself about the calories in my diet. We don't reject the science on that basis.

Another problem with abusing the siren is that it is deceptive. I am deliberately misleading motorists into believing that I am responding to an emergency and should be given the right of way. Deception for mere convenience is ungeneralizable, because if it became universal, people would no longer be gullible enough to fall for it. In particular, motorists would no longer take ambulance sirens seriously, because they would know that drivers abuse the siren whenever they find it convenient to do so. I might maintain that I am being deceptive for a very particular purpose, not just for convenience, but again I must explain why I would not deceive on other occasions when it is convenient, and this explanation must be a factor in my decision to abuse the siren. It is not a factor, and so my deception is not generalizable.

Abusing the siren also fails the utilitarian test, but we must be careful about why it fails. If ambulance drivers made a habit of abusing the siren and lights, then motorists would ignore them, and it would take much longer to deliver patients to the emergency room. This would result in a great deal of negative utility, due to serious medical complications and death. This is all true, but the consequences of general behavior are irrelevant to the utilitarian test. What matters are the consequences of my individual action.

My abuse of the siren nonetheless fails the utilitarian test, because screaming through traffic with siren and lights increases the risk of an accident. It creates less *expected* utility than not using the siren. The probability of an accident is small but must be multiplied by its *very* negative utility, and this more than offsets the expected utility of arriving on time. So the net expected utility of using the siren is less than that of not using it.

This argument doesn't apply if I am responding to a real emergency call, because screaming through traffic for a real emergency is worth the risk. But using the siren for my own purposes is both nonutilitarian and ungeneralizable.

TAKING A SHORT CUT

Let's suppose that while commuting home from work, I take a detour through a residential area to avoid a congested main artery. Because only a few drivers take the detour, it removes several minutes from my commuting time due to the light traffic. This seems a little sneaky, but is it wrong?

To make the issue harder, let's also suppose that driving through a neighborhood will not risk an accident any more than driving on the main artery. At this time of day, there are no kids on residential streets, and few other people. If my shortcut increased the accident risk, then I should avoid it on utilitarian grounds, but it doesn't.

The Generalization Principle is easy to apply. If all motorists wanting to avoid congestion took the alternative route, there would no longer be an advantage in doing so. It is, therefore, ungeneralizable. This does not imply that it is unethical in general to take the fastest route. Generally, motorists already choose the route that is best for them, given the choices of other drivers. They tend to reach an equilibrium in which no driver has an incentive to reroute. This behavior is perfectly generalizable because it is already generalized. In fact, traffic engineers typically model traffic patterns on the assumption that drivers will find an equilibrium. However, if motorists are avoiding my residential route even though they know it is faster, then they are *not* seeking an equilibrium, and my shortcut is not generalizable.

Suppose, however, that few motorists are clever enough to find my shortcut, and this is one of my reasons for taking it. The shortcut would continue to benefit me even if everyone who knew about the residential route took it (perhaps they are doing so already). So this makes it okay, right? It is okay if general ignorance of the shortcut is part of my rationale for taking it. That is, I would stop using the shortcut if others learned about it and deliberately avoided it. However, if I have no reason to believe I am cleverer than other drivers, then their ignorance of the shortcut can't be part of my rationale, and my behavior is ungeneralizable.

THE DAMAGED CAR

This is one of many dilemmas that my students have experienced and submitted for discussion in class. I want to trade in my old car for a new one. I negotiate a price for the new car with a certain dealer, as well as a price for the trade-in. However, the salesman sees that I am hesitant to close the deal and offers me a free lunch voucher for a nearby restaurant. "Why don't you have a nice lunch, think it over, and let me know your decision." I see no harm in accepting a free lunch, and I drive to the restaurant. On the way back I have a little accident. The damage to my car is scarcely visible from a distance, but close examination reveals that the bumper must be replaced. Familiar with the high cost of body work, I estimate the bill at $1000.

When I return to the dealer, I park the car at the far edge of the lot, at some distance from the showroom entrance. When the salesman doesn't notice any damage to my car, I decide not to mention it. This is only fair, because I checked the book value of my old car on my smartphone while eating lunch. The dealer's offer was about $1000 below book value!

From a utilitarian point of view, my decision is probably acceptable. The marginal cost to the dealer of fixing the damage is doubtless well under $1000, because body work estimates reflect overhead, as well as perhaps some padding for the insurance claim. The cost to me of revealing the damage, however, could well be a full $1000, because the salesman will reduce his offer to offset the damage. Furthermore, $1000 is worth more to me than to the dealer, due to the decreasing marginal utility of money. A high-volume dealership like this one would scarcely notice a $1000 expense, whereas it is a tidy sum to me. So concealing the damage probably results in greater net utility than revealing it.

There is a problem with generalizability, however. If I accept the dealer's offer, then I enter into an agreement to exchange a certain car for a certain price. The damaged car is not the car I agreed to exchange. Violating a sales agreement, merely for personal gain, is not generalizable. The possibility of making agreements in the first place presupposes that people don't break them whenever it is convenient. After all, the point of having agreements is that we are supposed to honor them when we would rather not. If we keep our agreements only when we would perform the same action anyway, there is no point in having agreements.

I might question whether I truly violated the sales agreement. After all, no one expects me to deliver the car in a completely unaltered condition. Driving the car to lunch will result in some additional wear on the tires, some bug splats on the windshield, and perhaps even some misalignment of the wheels after hitting a pothole. No one would call these a violation of the sales agreement. How does one draw the line between what violates the contract and what does not? The answer, of course, is that wear and tear the salesman expects is not a violation. Because he suggested the excursion to lunch, any such deterioration is part of the sales agreement; however, the salesman did not anticipate a traffic accident over lunch, and any resulting damage is not part of the agreement.

Even if I grant that I violated the agreement, I can argue that my reason for doing so is not simply that it benefits me. Part of my reason is that I can easily get away with it, which seems a plausible interpretation of the scope. Yet it does not salvage generalizability. If it were universal practice to break sales agreements whenever one can easily escape detection, the parties to an agreement would make sure it is not easy to escape detection. The salesman would check my car to make sure I did not remove the CD player or change the tires during the lunch hour. The fact that I parked it at the far edge of the lot would arouse his suspicions still more.

I might maintain that I am breaking the sales agreement because it is unfair, due to the salesman's lowball offer. The problem here is that it is hard to assess what is "unfair." People have all sorts of ideas about what is unfair, normally one that favors their side of the argument. One advantage of the generalization and utilitarian tests is that it is reasonably clear how to apply them, but a fairness test does not share this advantage. I may view the salesman's offer as unfair, but he may view my dishonesty as equally unfair, and nothing is resolved.

As a final exculpatory gambit, I might use the fairness argument in a different way. Rather than claiming that concealing the damage is ethical because the offer was unfair, I claim that my belief that it was unfair is an additional *reason* for breaking the sales agreement, and this narrows the scope enough to make my action generalizable. First of all, the business about fairness seems more of a justification after the fact than an element of my decision-making. Would I have really fessed up about the damage if I had not seen the book value? Aside from this, my action fails the generalization test even with this reduced scope. Suppose people always violated sales agreements when they could easily get away with it and viewed the agreement as unfair. If they came to see the agreement as unfair only in retrospect, perhaps commerce could tolerate a practice of breaking such agreements, although it would be very different from business as we know it. In my case, however, I see the transaction as unfair before I even conclude the deal. After all, I can still decline the salesman's offer if I don't like it. If people universally broke agreements they saw as unfair from the start, then they could negotiate bad deals with the intention of breaking them later. Business would be well-nigh impossible in such a world, or else merchants would be extremely wary of customers like me, and the salesman would take no chances with my trade-in car.

My only ethical recourse is to show the salesman the damage, then show him the book value, and go from there.

THE CASHIER'S ERROR

This may seem like a trifling issue, but it has come up repeatedly in my ethics classes and workshops. Suppose I select several expensive items in a store and take them through the checkout. On arriving home, I notice that the cashier forgot to ring up a $300 computer. What should I do about this?

It seems straightforward enough. By taking the computer through the checkout, I entered into a sales agreement with the store. I agreed to pay the sticker price of $300 in exchange for taking possession of the computer. As we discussed in the previous case, breaking sales agreements merely for personal gain is not generalizable. I should therefore return to the store and pay for the computer. I might argue that the store *gave* me the computer, and there is nothing unethical about accepting a gift. However, a gift must be intentional, and nobody at the store intended to give me a computer.

So far, so good, but suppose that rather than a $300 computer, the cashier forgot to ring up a 25-cent pack of chewing gum. Does this mean that I have to jump into my gas-guzzling SUV and drive across town to settle up with the store? This seems ridiculous, but an agreement is an agreement. The amount due should make no difference to the ethical principle, right?

Actually, a slight deviation from the terms of an agreement may be generalizable, but there is another escape. Modifying an agreement by mutual consent is clearly generalizable. The practice of making agreements would not be undermined if the parties were to modify or even discard them when they both agree to the change. They already do so routinely. Furthermore, mutual consent can be understood as a counterfactual conditional, to use a philosopher's term. There is mutual consent if I am certain the other party *would* be okay with a change in the agreement if asked about it afterwards. This applies to my 25 cents. If I were to telephone the store manager to report that I underpaid by 25 cents and don't plan to make it up, the manager would undoubtedly be okay with this. We therefore have mutual consent, and I am in the clear.

It is important, however, that the other party be okay with the change if asked *after* the modified agreement is fully executed. It is not enough that the other party would have been willing to go along with the change when the agreement was made. Let's suppose I bought a computer for $300, but the store manager would have been willing to let me have it for $250 if I had asked. I can't assume on this basis that there is mutual consent for me to get a $50 refund the next day.

There may also be an obligation to inform the other party about a change in terms, even when there is mutual consent, to avoid deception. Suppose I agree to paint the interior walls of your summer cottage green during the winter, but I paint them blue instead. I happen to know that you are indifferent between blue and green, and you would be totally satisfied if I told you about the color change. So there is mutual consent. However, I should inform you about the change, because you may buy matching furniture for the cabin before returning to it for the summer. There is no issue of deception in the case of the chewing gum, however, and it is okay just to forget about the 25 cents.

FINDING MONEY

I am often asked if it's ethical to keep money found in a public place. This, too, is not an issue of cosmic importance, but people seem to enjoy debating it. Actually, it isn't hard to resolve. Let's suppose I spot a $20 bill in a New York City subway car. Is it okay to keep it? The basic principle is that violating property rights, merely for personal gain, is not generalizable. This is because my purpose in taking someone's property is to make it *my* property, and if everyone disrespected property, there would be no property or concept of ownership in the first place. People would just take whatever they want, including "my" money.

Does keeping the $20 violate property rights? Taking property means depriving the owner of it, without permission. So the question is whether picking up the cash deprives the owner of it. If the owner would never find it anyway, then the owner is already deprived. Someone who drops $20 somewhere in the New York City subway system will never find it, even if no one picks it up. So I can keep it.

On the other hand, someone who drops an envelope containing $10,000 cash in a parking lot is going to search every place he has been since losing the money and will find it if nobody picks it up. If the lot is deserted, and no one else will find the money, then I deprive the owner of it by taking it myself. If there are other people around, I can take the money and place a conspicuous note at the spot where I found it. I can also leave my business card with the lot attendant. The owner can then telephone me and describe the lost article. However, if it becomes evident that the owner is deprived of the money no matter what I do, I can ethically keep it, subject to legal restrictions I will discuss in a moment. One might argue that I actually have an *obligation* to take the money if the lot is full of people, because the next finder is not likely to be so honorable. This is another issue, which I leave as an exercise for the reader.

The law actually helps to define the basic ethical principle in this case, because it is through property law that the social practice of property and ownership has evolved. Anglo-Saxon common law allows me to keep lost property until and unless the owner claims it. Common law also distinguishes lost property, which is unintentionally left in some location, from *mislaid* property, which is intentionally left but forgotten. If a hotel guest sets his wallet on the check-in counter and forgets it, the wallet belongs to the hotel (until claimed by the guest) even if I find it. Several U.S. states strengthen common law with lost property statutes. They typically say that if I find something worth more than a certain amount, I must turn it over to the police for a certain period, after which I can keep it if unclaimed.

SURPRISE BIRTHDAY PARTY

Mary and her friends have arranged a surprise birthday party for Joan. Mary must somehow convince Joan to show up at her apartment after work Friday, without spoiling the surprise. As it happens, Joan has been talking about buying a smart electric range that she can control from her phone. So Mary tells Joan that she just bought such a range and would be happy to show it to her after work Friday. This is a fib, but it lures Mary to the party, which is great fun. Yet lying is unethical, right?

Some people think that ethics guys like me take all the joy out of life. Surprise birthday parties require a little dishonesty, but shouldn't we be allowed to enjoy them anyway?

Actually, we ethics guys love to have a good time. It's utilitarian, too! What about the dishonesty? I'm not going to say it's a "white lie" and therefore okay. *White* presumably means that the lie is harmless. But telling white lies is as ungeneralizable as telling any kind of lie, if the lie must be believed to serve its purpose. If everyone told white lies when convenient, the lies would no longer work. An occasional surprise birthday fib is okay because we are misleading our friends only for this socially recognized purpose. It is generalizable because one of our reasons for doing it is that it is socially sanctioned and regulated, which makes it different from other lies. It works because it is used only for birthday parties, and infrequently at that.

It is a little like flattery, which is also socially sanctioned and regulated. Flattery relies not on outright deception but on a certain amount of ambiguity as to whether the flatterer really means it—and on the fact that we like to pretend it's true anyway. We can tell when flattery becomes dishonest and manipulative rather than kind. At this point it begins to violate social norms and is no longer generalizable. This is not to say, by the way, that any violation of social norms is unethical. It only says that if an action's generalizability depends on the fact that its social acceptability is one of the reasons, then it becomes ungeneralizable and therefore unethical when it violates social norms.

THE BOSS'S TRAVEL EXPENSES

This is another dilemma experienced by one of my students, and a typical one. A perennial question is whether one should blow the whistle when colleagues at work behave unethically. This particular case is of minor consequence, but whistleblowing cases can take on major importance, pose vexing ethical questions, and call for extraordinary moral courage. As always, it is best to start small.

In this scenario, my boss asks me to accompany him on a business trip to San Francisco. Eager to visit an interesting city, I drop by the company travel agent's office to pick up the flight schedule. While looking over the travel requisition, she remarks that a third party will accompany us and shows me the name. It is my boss's wife, who uses a different surname than he. The travel agent sees nothing amiss, but I realize immediately what is going on. The boss is taking his wife along for a little holiday, at company expense. Should I report this to someone, or mind my own business?

This is a small case of internal whistleblowing. There are two issues in such cases: (a) is the activity in question really unethical, and if it is, (b) what should I do about it? In the present instance, issue (a) is easy. The boss is deceiving the company for his personal benefit, which is not generalizable. He is also violating his employment contract with the company, which at least implicitly obliges him observe company policy. This isn't generalizable, either. So he is batting zero.

Issue (b) is usually the sticky one, because it is notoriously hard to foresee the utilitarian consequences of blowing the whistle. This is true in my case, because I can't predict the consequences for either myself or the company. Raising the issue could invite retaliation from my boss, or at the opposite extreme, make me a company hero for exposing widespread abuse.

The company has an ethics hotline, but I am worried that it won't protect my anonymity. If someone confronted the boss about travel expenses, he could put two and two together. He could write an unfavorable annual performance review, resulting in my being laid off at the next reduction in force. The positive consequences for the company, if any, are equally hard to foresee. I don't know whether the boss makes a habit of this, or whether it is a widespread practice in the company. Even if it is, the compliance people may ignore my tip or make only a token effort to address it.

Given the uncertainty, keeping quiet passes the utilitarian test by default. It is not irrational to believe that silence would create at least as much net utility as speaking up.

In some situations, failure to report malfeasance is clearly ungeneralizable. If it were part of my job to monitor expense accounts, then I would have an obligation to report irregularities, because I would otherwise violate my employment agreement with the company. However, this is not part of my job. We can also apply the generalization test directly: Would I be able to accomplish my purpose if all employees in my situation failed to report small-scale misconduct like padding travel expenses? My purpose is presumably to keep my job and stay out of trouble. If universal failure to report such things would cause companies to collapse under the weight of employee fraud, then I would not achieve my purpose, because I wouldn't have the job anyway. But this seems very unlikely, because most companies have controls in place to prevent such abuse from getting out of hand, without relying on employees to finger their bosses and colleagues. So silence is generalizable. I conclude that I can forget about my boss's misbehavior and enjoy the trip to San Francisco without ethical misgivings.

The ethical landscape can be different in other scenarios, particularly when there is large-scale misconduct involved. If I stumble across evidence that the company controller is cooking the books in a way that could endanger the firm, and there is no reliable mechanism to uncover fraud at this level, the Utilitarian Principle can be merciless. It can demand that I risk my career, or possibly more, to save the careers of many.

Whistleblowing situations pose some of the most excruciating moral dilemmas. The consequences of speaking up are notoriously hard to predict and can be personally devastating. The whistleblower frequently endures the loss of career, friends, mental and physical health—and freedom, in cases of political dissidence.

One of the most famous whistleblowers of recent times is the late Roger Boisjoly, who warned in 1986 that O-rings may fail during the launch of the Space Shuttle *Challenger*. His warnings were to no avail. The craft disintegrated before a stunned worldwide television audience 73 seconds after launch, killing the seven crew members. Boisjoly also told his story in a Congressional hearing after the disaster. Even though his warnings were on the mark, his colleagues reacted angrily. He was shunned by company managers and neighbors, blacklisted by employers, and eventually obliged to collect disability benefits due to posttraumatic stress disorder. As he put it, the experience "destroyed my career, my life, everything else," although he was later recognized with awards for his courage.* In the right circumstances, high-profile whistleblowing can trigger reform on a significant and even global scale, but it is not for the faint of heart.

BLOCKED TRAFFIC LANE

This dilemma was posed by a participant in one of my ethics workshops. Police have closed one lane of a highway due to construction and have posted a sign, "Left lane closed," some distance ahead of the closure. A long queue of traffic has formed in the lane that remains open, because drivers slow down while driving past the construction site. However, a few drivers bypass the queue by driving in the left lane up to the point of closure and then rely on polite drivers to let them merge at the front of the queue. Is this behavior ethical, assuming it is legal?

"Cutting line" probably passes the utilitarian test in this case. The line breaker saves a great deal of time, and many other drivers are slightly delayed. I will assume this is a wash, or at least that we are not irrational in believing as much. There is a problem with generalizability, however. Presumably the reason for cutting line is to save time. If everyone who could save time by cutting line did so, it would no longer save time. So cutting line is ungeneralizable and unethical.

The same behavior may be generalizable under another rationale. I might drive to the merge point because the police posted signs urging motorists to use both lanes up to the merge point. It is just that most drivers are ignoring the signs. I would obey the signs regardless of any

---

* As reported in multiple sources, including Man who warned of Challenger disaster dies at 73, *The Guardian*, February 9, 2012.

time saved or lost. In this case, the behavior is generalizable, because drivers would be able to use both lanes to the merge point if all others did.

Suppose, however, that there is no sign asking motorists to use both lanes, and a few unethical drivers are cutting line. Is it ethical for a driver at the front of the queue to allow one of them to merge? Doesn't this encourage unethical behavior?

Actually, this kind of courtesy is generalizable if the policy is properly formulated. Let's suppose the polite driver's policy is to yield to at most one driver, because this is polite and causes very little delay for herself and those in the queue behind her. Then even if a general practice of courtesy encouraged many drivers to use the other lane, we would have a situation in which drivers use both lanes to the merge point (a policy that traffic engineers tend to recommend anyway). In this situation, a driver who yielded to one other could still be polite while creating minimal delay for herself and those behind her.

This is not to say that cutting line is ethical when no one else is doing so; it is not. Whether one should cut line, and whether one should cooperate with someone who has already cut line, are two different questions. It may seem wrong to *condone* unethical behavior this way, but this depends on the situation.

LAST WILL AND TESTAMENT

Another workshop participant posed a dilemma similar to this one. Millicent, who was widowed some years ago, is now in failing health and is belatedly getting around to writing a will. She is conflicted about how to divide her sizeable estate among her five children. The oldest, Alice, is an accountant and mother of three grown children. She visits Millicent regularly, helps out around the house, and takes care of Millicent's health insurance paperwork. Betty is a wealthy investment banker who never visits or even telephones. Charles is a ne'er-do-well who can't hold down a job, has lived with various women, owes child support for two kids, and is always asking for money. David earned mediocre grades in school but has a big, happy family. He works hard at a low-paying job but can't afford to send his kids to college. Edward is a wounded veteran of the Iraq war who lives alone on disability benefits. His fiancée dumped him while he was in Iraq, and he can't find a job due to his medical problems.

Millicent wants to do what is "fair" and reward the children who are most "deserving." The problem is that people have all sorts of ideas on what is fair and who is deserving (especially when they have a stake in the game), and there is no reliable way to resolve these differences. Ethics, at least as developed here, avoids this quagmire altogether by focusing on logical consistency criteria that can be applied more or less objectively.

The most obvious criterion for Millicent's decision is utilitarian. She should apportion the estate in a way that she can rationally believe will do the most good. A purely utilitarian decision, however, would probably have her disinherit her children altogether and direct her money to an agency that, say, aids starving children or war refugees. They would probably benefit more from her largesse than any of her children (I assume that Millicent knows the agency makes good use of the donation). Disinheriting her family is nonutilitarian in some respects, because it could create ill will between them and herself, and it could even plant seeds of bitterness and self-pity that would grow for years in some of her children. Nonetheless, a sufficiently worthy cause could outweigh even these liabilities.

A purely utilitarian solution may fail the generalization test, however, because it may violate an implied promise to Millicent's children. They might reasonably expect to be included in the will, as this is standard practice and the legal default, and she has never suggested anything to the contrary. Her silence on the matter over the years has in effect led them to rely on an implied promise that they will inherit something, and they may have made financial plans accordingly. Millicent is bound by that promise. While she clearly has no legal obligation to provide for them, she arguably has an ethical obligation.

However, any implied promise is quite vague as to the amount of their inheritance, which means that the Utilitarian Principle can still require her to turn over a significant portion to a relief agency or some other worthy cause. The rest goes to her kids. The disposition of their money is likewise governed by the Utilitarian Principle. Millicent may feel that she *owes* more to Alice than the other children, because of Alice's devotion to her, and Alice may agree. But there is no basis for such an obligation. It would be different if Millicent signaled to Alice that she would get more than the others, or if Alice signaled that she expected more and Millicent continued to accept her services. But absent this, there is no implicit agreement that Millicent will *reward* Alice for her services, and the Utilitarian Principle governs.

A straightforward utilitarian allocation would exclude Betty, who already has more money than she can spend, and perhaps Charles, who would waste it. However, it could include trust funds for his two kids, depending on their mother's financial situation, and certainly educational funds for David's children. It would also set up an annuity that would allow Edward to live comfortably. It is difficult to predict the utilitarian outcome of any more specific allocation, and so Millicent is ethically at liberty to define it any way she wants.

The children, however, may have strong views about what is a "fair" allocation. Inheritance situations often bring out the worst in people, rekindling old resentments and sibling rivalries. It is not uncommon for squabbles of this sort to create permanent rifts in the family. These consequences could outweigh any benefit of allocating a larger share to Edward and the minor grandchildren. Millicent may decide that it is better on balance to allocate everyone an equal share, which her children may be more likely accept as "fair." Ethics doesn't require her to predict their reaction, but only to make a decision that, so far as she can reasonably judge, has no worse prospects than any other decision.

RECLINING THE AIRLINE SEAT

Are we ready to take on the emotional issue of reclining airline seats? If you think I am overstating the emotional component, consider that just days before I write this, an altercation broke out over this very matter during a flight.* The trouble started when a man using a computer attached a "knee defender" to his tray table, which prevents the seat ahead from being reclined. When the woman in that seat was unable to recline, she summoned a flight attendant, who instructed the man to remove the device. He complied, at which point the woman slammed her seat back and sent the computer flying. The man shoved the seat forward and re-installed the knee defender, whereupon the woman doused him and his computer with a cup of soda. The flight was diverted to Chicago's O'Hare Airport so that the belligerent parties could be escorted off the plane.

---

* M. Hunter and M. Ahlers, Legroom fight diverts flight, CNN Travel, August 26, 2014. The story was updated by S. Mayerowitz, Knee defender passenger speaks out about in-flight dispute, Associated Press, September 3, 2014.

One might think that is an isolated incident, but apparently not. Within the next seven days, two additional U.S. flights were diverted due to squabbles over reclining seats.*

Reporters covering the first story conducted some on-the-street interviews about this, during which the debate continued to rage. Long-legged interviewees insisted that people should have the decency not to assault the knees of those behind for a slight increase in comfort. Short-legged interviewees dismissed this view as ridiculous, with one woman asserting that it is her "God-given right" to recline an airline seat (yes, that is a direct quote). I step into this debate with some trepidation, but it will give us an opportunity to think about the concept of courtesy.

Courtesy in the Western tradition was originally *courtly* behavior, or conduct that marked one as a member of the royal court or upper class. It became particularly important with the rise of a wealthy commercial class in Europe, who sought access to the old aristocratic circles by imitating their social manners. Courtesy today has great significance in some cultures, such as Japan, where the rules of etiquette can be exacting. It is a fundamental concept in Confucian philosophy, where rituals of courtesy are seen as acknowledging the divine element in another human being.

In the West, however, courtesy has evolved to refer to thoughtful behavior that is not required by the rules in effect at the moment. Due to the central importance of rules in Western cultures, this gives the impression that courtesy is nice but optional. It is not surprising that someone would say that she has a "right" to recline the airline seat, presumably because airline rules allow it (I can't speak to God's rules). From her perspective, keeping the seat upright may be nice but is entirely optional.

From the perspective of ethics, however, conduct that we view as courtesy is usually obligatory, on utilitarian grounds. I am obviously not talking about mere *manners*, such as using the correct fork at the dinner table. I am talking about everyday conduct that affects the welfare of others. Ethics requires me to hold the door for someone who is carrying a load, because a trifling inconvenience for me avoids a greater inconvenience for the other. I am required to relinquish my bus seat to someone who has difficulty standing, because the seat is of greater value to that person than to me. I may prefer to think of myself as acting out of kindness or thoughtfulness rather than bending to the demands of duty, but neither

---

* K. Hetter, Airline seat reclining sparks another skirmish, CNN Travel, August 29, 2014; Associated Press, It's no longer safe to recline your airline seat, *DallasNews Business*, September 2, 2014.

excludes the other. Ethics only tells us which actions are ethical, not how they are motivated. Ethical actions can arise psychologically from kindness and concern as well as from a plodding devotion to duty.

Thoughtfulness is often an element of ethical action, because one cannot apply the Utilitarian Principle without thinking about how others are affected. When courtesy is lacking, it is often because people don't take a moment to consider the effect of their actions on those around them. An airline passenger of smaller stature may not have noticed that taller passengers must sit with their knees pressed against the seat ahead of them, even before it is reclined. She may not have considered that working stiffs may have to use flight time for computer work that requires a keyboard, and their employers won't fly them business class. One has to be a contortionist to type on even a small computer in the economy cabin, and it becomes impossible when the seat ahead is reclined.

So how can we resolve the issue of reclining seats without fighting like kids in a sandbox? It's not so hard, really. Reclining a seat for greater comfort is generalizable, and so it comes down to the utilitarian test, as in most issues of courtesy. I should recline only if my added comfort will offset the pain inflicted on the person behind me. If that person is tall or a computer user, I should sit upright. Naturally, it makes no sense for me to leave the seat reclined while I lean forward to eat or play a game on my tablet. On the other hand, if it is a long-haul flight and I sleep better while reclined, then I can certainly recline during the lights-out portion of the flight. Sleep is important and increases utility. But I should recline slowly, to give the passenger behind me time to move knees and computer out of danger.

How about passengers with long legs or work to do? What are their obligations? Using a device to prevent reclining is unethical, unless it becomes generally accepted practice at some point. It may violate airline rules, and even if it doesn't, it is nonutilitarian because it may antagonize another passenger and get both thrown off the plane. Worse, it may force 120 other economy-class passengers to endure additional hours of cramped confinement while the fight is diverted. A better solution is to book a seat with extra leg room, if it is available for a reasonable price (business class and "premium economy" are far from reasonable). At this writing, unfortunately, only one airline offers such seats on a dependable basis. Personally, I take the train whenever possible and avoid the stress of air travel altogether. I wrote a large fraction of this book while on the train.

6

Moral Agency and Autonomy

While I lie sleeping on a warm night, a mosquito wanders through my open window and bites me. I don't judge the mosquito's behavior as ethical or unethical, although I might be tempted to do so if it gave me dengue fever. The mosquito's bite has no moral significance because it is just a matter of chemistry and biology. Chemical receptors on the mosquito's antennae detected carbon dioxide from my breath and lactic acid from my skin, which initiated a series of chemical and neurological mechanisms that led to the bite. There's nothing more to say.

Later that night, an experienced burglar notices my open window, discreetly peers inside, and spots my wallet on the nightstand. He quietly slips through the window and snatches the wallet, and I am none the wiser until morning. I don't hesitate to judge the burglar's behavior: It is illegal and unethical. Yet it is no less the result of chemical and biological causes than the mosquito's, even if it is mediated by a more complex mechanism. Give this, how can I consistently attach a moral judgment to the burglar's conduct?

One answer is that the burglar is a creature whose behavior, at least potentially, admits *a second type of explanation*. Namely, it is the result of ratiocination. It can be explained as resulting from a process of deliberation in which he adduces reasons for the actions. The burglar stole the wallet because he needed cash, wallets often contain cash, and he could probably snatch my wallet without being caught. The ability to act on reasons this way makes the burglar a *moral agent*. In this particular case, the reasons turn out to be incoherent and, therefore, not a comprehensible explanation for his behavior, because they are not generalizable. So he is not exercising moral agency when he steals the wallet. Nonetheless, the burglar is *capable* of behavior that can be reasonably explained as resulting from a consistent rationale. This makes him a moral agent and makes his behavior ethical or unethical, in this case unethical.*

MORAL AGENCY

The concept of moral agency is the linchpin of Western ethics, because only moral agents are capable of morally significant conduct. Only they are bound by obligation. In addition, the duty to respect the autonomy of other moral agents is a bedrock principle that lies behind much of what we believe about the value of life and freedom and the immorality of coercion and oppression.

Most importantly, moral agency is the Archimedean point from which we can develop ethical norms. I began with the premise that when we act, we act for a reason, and from this I derived the generalization and utilitarian tests for ethical choice. I defended this premise on the ground that action is not action unless it is based on reasons. The proper analysis of moral agency is therefore the foundation of ethical theory as developed here.

Some will continue to object that even if the burglar's behavior is based on reasons, the behavior and the reasoning behind it are nonetheless the result of chemical and biological causes and thus not freely chosen. So we can hold him no more responsible for his behavior than the mosquito. This is the old conundrum of free will versus determinism. The puzzle goes back at least to the ancient Greek philosopher Epicurus, who (like his

---

* This idea has roots in Kant, who saw human beings as part of a natural order of cause and effect *and* as part of "noumenal" world of thought. An autonomous action can be explained as the necessary result of natural causes *and* explained as based on intellectual activity in the noumenal realm. This sounds excessively metaphysical to modern ears, but Kant himself suggested that the metaphysical baggage might be removed when he said, "the concept of a world of understanding [the noumenal world] is therefore only a *standpoint* that reason sees itself constrained to take outside of appearances *in order to think of itself as practical.*" In other words, to see oneself as taking action (in Kantian language, to think of oneself as "practical"), one must interpret oneself as existing outside the natural realm of cause and effect. Or to use more modern language, one must be able give one's behavior a second kind of explanation, based on reasons the agent adduced for it. This idea eventually evolved into the "dual standpoint" theories of recent decades, which have some similarities with the dual-explanation theory advanced here. T. Nagel, *The View from Nowhere*, Oxford, Oxford University Press, 1986; C. M. Korsgaard, *The Sources of Normativity*, Cambridge, Cambridge University Press, 1996; D. K. Nelkin Two standpoints and the belief in freedom, *Journal of Philosophy* 97 (2000): 564–576; A. Bilgrami, *Self-Knowledge and Resentment*, Cambridge, MA, Harvard University Press, 2006.

predecessor Democritus) held the curiously modern view that everything, including the human body, is made of tiny atoms. Because these atoms are governed by physical law, our every thought and action is determined by a complicated chain of causes and effects. Epicurus was uncomfortable with this implication and tried to sidestep it by suggesting that some atoms make random motions that are not predetermined, and these atoms are responsible for our free choices. It is scarcely comforting, however, for our choices to be the result of chance rather than physical law.

Recent skeptics about the possibility of free will point to neurological research showing that we often make choices before we are aware of them. By measuring brain activity with an MRI machine, researchers can sometimes predict a subject's action (such as moving a finger) a few seconds before the subject is conscious of deciding to perform the action. This supposedly shows that when we seem to be deliberating about whether to act, our brain has already made the decision for us. The experience of "consciously deciding" is just an after-effect. In some sense this is true, but the key point is that there is absolutely nothing new about this puzzle. Determinists have told us for 2300 years that our experience of conscious deliberation is predetermined by prior causes. It is just that we are now beginning to detect some of those prior causes. This could present an interesting challenge to someone who is equipped with this kind of neural feedback. It may be impossible to deliberate in any meaningful sense if one knows the outcome of deliberation before it occurs. But this shows at most that moral agency cannot occur in the presence of neural feedback. We can still explain much of our behavior as the result of deliberation, even if the deliberation is itself chemically determined by prior causes. This is the behavior we classify as moral agency.

Granted, this may not resolve the free-will-versus-determinism debate. It has an exceedingly long and complex history, with almost every conceivable position having been adopted at some point along the way. Epicurus' own solution has had very few takers, with the notable exception of the American philosopher William James, but other opinions range from despair (there is no free will) to dismissal (this is no problem here). I won't try to resolve this question of the ages, because we have before us a reasonably intelligible and practical distinction between moral agency and mere behavior. This is all we really need for ethics.

The distinction is practical because we apply it all the time. It is one of life's basic skills to be able to understand why people do what they do, and so we get a great deal of practice attributing reasons to people. We can then check if these reasons (if any) are coherent or self-contradictory. On the other hand, we don't attribute reasons to mosquitos and roaches and therefore don't treat their behavior as morally significant. There are certainly hard borderline cases, as when a profoundly schizophrenic person acts on the basis of inner voices or paranoid delusions. Yet these cases are hard because of the vexing nature of schizophrenia, not because there is a problem with the concept of moral agency.

Another practical advantage of moral agency as conceived here is that it is adaptable to new technology. Some households already have robots that do housework and babysit the kids. This raises the question of whether you should be nice to your robot. The answer is yes, if you reasonably regard your robot's choices as based on reasons. The robot's behavior can always be explained as the result of an algorithm that is written into its computer code, much as human behavior results from chemistry and biology. But as robot behavior reaches a certain level of complexity, we might equally well give it a high-level explanation based on the robot's rationale, particularly if the robot can explain why it neglected to do the dishes or clean the toilet. I will explore the implications of this in the final chapter of the book.

DISPENSING WITH BLAME

The account of moral agency I have advanced has the seemingly strange consequence that one cannot choose to be evil. An unethical piece of behavior is one that has no coherent rationale and is therefore not deliberately chosen; thus, one cannot deliberately perform an unethical action. This means that it makes no sense to blame anyone for being unethical, which may strike us as a disturbing consequence. The whole edifice of morality seems to be built on possibility of holding people responsible for their conduct, rewarding good behavior, and punishing bad behavior.

Yet if the purpose of ethics is to arrive at consensus on what kind of behavior is ethical, ethics has no need for blame. It need only decide what kind of behavior has a coherent rationale. We can still reward and punish behavior, but not due to some metaphysical judgment that the agent is "responsible" for the behavior. We all know how hard it is to make this judgment anyway. For example, many crimes are committed by people with disadvantaged backgrounds that include poverty, stressful family situations, and violent neighborhoods. Are they fully "responsible" for their crimes? There is no need to decide the issue. Rather, we can follow the advice of Jeremy Bentham, father of utilitarianism, and adopt social policies that tend to result in ethical behavior. It may be useful to reward certain kinds of behavior and punish others. It may be equally useful to rehabilitate offenders and change the environment in which they live. We decide on the basis of what is effective. In so doing, we acknowledge that physical and psychological causes determine behavior—and take advantage of this fact. The goal is to produce behavior that can *also* be explained as the result of rational deliberation and is therefore ethical.

This addresses an old objection to rationalistic ethics, one that goes back at least to Adam Smith's contemporary, David Hume. Namely, it makes no sense to blame people for having an incoherent rationale, because this is a logical mistake, not a moral transgression. If we get rid of the concept of blame altogether, this objection evaporates. The goal of ethics is to define what kind of behavior is ethical, not to decide who is blameworthy.

Dispensing with blame may seem to disrupt much of ordinary life. If Suzie hits her little brother and leaves a bruise, we want to scold or punish Suzie. But if Suzie trips over a toy and injures her brother, we neither scold nor punish because it is not "her fault." Yet these responses are consistent with rationalistic ethics. Scolding Suzie for tripping over toys is likely to have little effect on aggressive behavior toward her brother. We can even use the language of blame when it is helpful. Telling Suzie that her brother's bruise is "her fault" may encourage Suzie to think about the consequences of her behavior, eventually resulting in conduct that has a coherent rationale. What is the role of ethics in all this, if it doesn't, strictly speaking, assign blame? Ethics tells us what kind of behavior we should encourage. How we encourage it is a matter of psychology and sociology.

HABIT AND EMOTION

An ethical theory based on rational agency may seem to misunderstand human nature. Human beings are not primarily rational beings. We are multidimensional creatures who run on habit, sentiment, prejudice, and impulse as well as reason. An ethical theory that asks us to make rational choices all the time seems unrealistic. However, ethics doesn't require this. It can guide our behavior even when we are governed by habit and sentiment most of the time.

Take the case of habit. It is essential to human survival, because the conscious mind lacks the computational power to direct the many complex activities we undertake. So we turn over much of our behavior to habits, which are preprogrammed sequences of behavior we can perform unthinkingly. Some habits are good for us, such as morning exercise, and some are bad, such as lighting up a cigarette. Others are simply necessary for daily existence, such as driving a car. Psychologist George A. Miller observed decades ago that we store memories by *chunking* them, or grouping them into sequences, as one might remember the telephone number 432-1212 by noting a descending sequence and then a repeating pattern.[*] We then recall information by retrieving chunks, each of which plays itself out automatically. We use a similar mechanism to learn habits and the skills they support. Herbert Simon and Kevin Gilmartin suggested that we build expertise in any given domain by efficiently chunking our knowledge, which typically requires at least a decade of experience and a store of some 50,000 chunks.[†] Jazz musicians, for example, improvise by drawing from a large internal library of licks and riffs, which are note sequences or chord progressions they can perform unconsciously. By necessity, we are all jazz musicians. We spend much of our time unconsciously performing habits based on chunked behavior patterns.

We can nonetheless exercise moral agency. To begin with, we can form habits by repeating deliberate actions. This is how we learn to drive a car or play a D-flat major scale. We can consciously decide whether to enable habitual behavior, as when we decide whether to own a car or keep cigarettes in the house. We can also decide whether to turn ourselves over to a habitual pattern at any given time. We can park the car or toss the unlit cigarette into the trash. Some habits may be compelling addictions, but in these cases we can decide to take steps toward addressing the addiction. The upshot is that people who engage in habitual behavior most of the time may nonetheless continuously exercise moral agency, provided they are making rational choices to cultivate, initiate, and tolerate these behavior patterns. Aristotle taught that being ethical is largely a matter of learning good habits.

---

[*] G. A. Miller, The magical number seven, plus or minus two: Some limits on our capacity for processing information, *Psychological Review* 6 (1956): 81–97.

[†] Based on my conversations with Simon and the article, H. A. Simon and K. J. Gilmartin, A simulation of memory for chess positions, *Cognitive Psychology* 5 (1973): 29–46.

Behavior based on impulse or emotion, without self-reflection at the time, can likewise result from moral agency. If I consciously decide to give myself over to emotion, the situation is similar to that of habit. I deliberately set in motion a behavior pattern that plays itself out without conscious control. I might allow anger to take over if I see someone threating my children, or allow sympathy to take over if I come across victims of an accident. Then I can examine my reasons for allowing emotion to rule.

Naturally, a tendency to reflect on our actions, rather than simply to act spontaneously, itself has neurological causes. This is actually fortunate, because it means we can train or condition ourselves to act deliberately. For example, we can reward children when they can rationally justify their behavior, and we can explain why bad behavior is wrong. We can design school curricula that develop our thinking power. We can even read ethics books. It is fine to teach and encourage particular behaviors in particular contexts, but teaching ourselves the art of ethical reasoning is more efficient. It allows us encourage ethical behavior in a million different contexts by teaching one skill and encouraging its exercise.

RESPECTING AUTONOMY

Some of our most deeply felt moral imperatives tell us not to murder, maim, or enslave people without the most compelling of reasons. What is the basis, if any, for these imperatives? Probably not the Generalization Principle, because crimes like these may well be generalizable under certain rationales, even when the rationale is far from compelling. They are not only generalizable but were generalized at various times in history. Some societies routinely murdered, maimed, and enslaved oppressed classes of people for centuries, and they more or less achieved their purposes by doing so. It takes a little ingenuity to think of cases in which murder would clearly pass the utilitarian test, if we take into account the disutility of extinguishing a life. Yet even if we can't imagine such a case, I don't think we want to say that murder is wrong because of its utilitarian cost. We want a more fundamental reason.

This reason is supplied by the concept of moral agency. This concept not only undergirds the development of ethical obligation, but it leads to some special obligations to moral agents. The obligations are based on the inherent inconsistency in any rationale for violating the autonomy of an agent. Similar arguments are used to show that coercion, injury, imprisonment, and enslavement may be wrong not only because of their disutility, but in certain cases because they violate autonomy. When this is so, we can never justify them solely on utilitarian grounds, because the Utilitarian Principle requires us only to consider actions that are otherwise ethical.

Autonomy is a central concept in Western civilization, due to our historical concern with individual freedom, and much has been written about it. Yet it is hard to find consensus in this literature, even on what autonomy is. The Greek roots of the word (*self-law*) connote self-determination in some sense, but there is little agreement on what sense. This may seem to make a concise treatment of the subject a hopeless task. However, much of the literature is concerned about when the state can legitimately compromise autonomy with police action, legal penalties, paternalistic laws, and so forth. To keep things manageable, I will set aside the issue of state authority in the discussion that follows. Given this, I believe we can achieve a great deal by defining autonomy simply as the exercise of moral agency.

DESTRUCTION OF AGENCY

The most basic moral implication of agency is that it is wrong to kill a moral agent. Killing implies permanent destruction of agency, as opposed to temporary destruction, as when someone is knocked unconscious for a short time. This is unethical because any rationale for it is inconsistent.

The basic argument is pretty simple. If I have a rationale for destroying another moral agent, then that same rationale calls for destroying me if our roles are reversed, and they could conceivably be reversed. But my own destruction is inconsistent with *any* purposes I might have at the time of my destruction. So my rationale for killing another, no matter what it is, implies inconsistency and is therefore incoherent. This means, in particular, that no utilitarian argument can justify killing. I will have to refine this argument when I introduce the concept of joint autonomy, but it contains the basic idea.

I am sure you are thinking, "But what about killing in self-defense?" I will get to this, but first there are more basic matters to clear up. One is the seemingly questionable premise that my victim necessarily has purposes at the time of death. This is true if the victim is exercising agency at that moment, but what if not? What if I kill people in their sleep? Actually, people have rationales and purposes even when not exercising agency. It is correct to say of someone asleep that he or she intends to cut the grass tomorrow, or intends to retire at age 65. There may be situations in which a person literally has given up on life and has no purposes any more, and suicide or euthanasia *may* be defensible in such cases, but I would like to postpone discussion of these extreme cases to the chapter on medical ethics.

COERCION

Another issue is whether and when less extreme forms of coercion than killing are ethical. It seems that they are sometimes permissible and sometimes not. If I see someone about to step inadvertently into moving traffic, it is acceptable to pull her to safety against her will. If I see a mugger about to hit someone from behind, it is acceptable to grab his arm. In cases like this, coercion is ethical even though it seems to compromise autonomy. Yet in most cases, we want to say that coercion is unacceptable. One popular formula is that we should have the freedom to do whatever we want, as long as we don't violate anybody else's rights. Yet this begs the question of what "rights" others have.

Can the logic of rational agency help us here? I think it can. We can establish one principle right away, which we might call the Interference Principle:

> *Interference Principle.* Using coercion to prevent unethical behavior does not compromise autonomy, because unethical behavior is not an exercise of agency in the first place. However, the coercion must be *minimal*, meaning that it prevents nothing more than the unethical behavior.

Unfortunately, this principle is hard to apply in practice, because one can rarely apply minimal coercion. There are a few neat cases. If the mugger is about to slug someone, I can grab the mugger's arm. If a thief is about to steal a bicycle, I can stand between him and the bicycle. But if my neighbor is cheating on his income taxes, I can't break into his house and handcuff him to stop him from filling out a false tax form.

This prevents him from taking hundreds of perfectly ethical actions. Using deadly force to prevent a crime is an extreme case of what one might call *overkill*, since it prevents the perpetrator from doing anything ever again.

The Interference Principle may seem too permissive because it allows prior restraint. A staunch libertarian might say that I have no "right" to prevent my neighbor from breaking the tax law if he so pleases, although the government has a "right" to prosecute him when he does. However, the language about rights only restates the claim rather than providing an argument. If the objection is that I have no legal right, then perhaps this is true, but I am not claiming that I have a legal right, only that I would not compromise his autonomy. Suppose, for example, that I can wave a magic wand that causes any false numbers on his tax form to disappear as he writes them. This would perhaps be the minimum coercion necessary to thwart unethical behavior. One might claim that even this violates autonomy, but we need an argument. Meanwhile, I have an argument that it does not: My neighbor is not exercising agency in the first place (if falsifying the form is in fact unethical). However, I concede that in practice, we can't wave magic wands and must often use coercive overkill. So far, I have no justification for doing so.

To deal with the problem of overkill, we have to explore the logic of moral agency more deeply. This will provide us the resources to deal with several ethical dilemmas that arise in later chapters, particularly in product liability, medical ethics, and machine ethics. It will also lead to some conclusions that may surprise you, particularly concerning self-defense.

PATERNALISM

It's helpful to begin by considering another case in which violating autonomy sometimes seems acceptable: paternalism. One case is pulling someone out of the path of a car. A classic case can be found in Homer's Odyssey, which tells us that Odysseus had his crew to tie him to the mast of his ship so that he wouldn't yield to the irresistible song of the Sirens. He ordered them not to release him from his bonds even if he demanded it, until they had passed the rocky coast where the Sirens lived.

Coercion seems to be acceptable when people are forced to do what they "really want" to do, so that there is no denial of autonomy. One way to analyze this is to distinguish first-order desires from second-order desires or objectives, a move that is associated with philosophers Harry Frankfurt and Gerald Dworkin.* On this view, coercion is acceptable if it is consistent with second-order desires, which represent what one really wants in some sense. Odysseus' determination not to yield to the Sirens was presumably a second-order desire. This *hierarchical* theory has its problems, not the least of which are how to identify second-order desires, and how to justify giving them priority. In any event, we have undertaken the project of analyzing ethical behavior based on the logical structure of one's rationale, not the psychological structure of one's desires. Let's try to explain cases of acceptable paternalism without making psychological assumptions.

This can be accomplished by recognizing that decisions actually have a conditional character, because they are based on reasons. Suppose, for example, that I decide to cross the street because there is a bus stop on the other side, I want to catch a bus, and there are no cars approaching. This can be interpreted as making a conditional decision, "If you want to catch a bus, and there is a bus stop across the street, and there are no cars approaching, then cross the street." A decision is really what might be called an *action plan*,† because it calls for a certain action in a certain set of circumstances. If someone pulls me back out of the path of an approaching car, that person has not contravened my action plan and has not compromised my autonomy. As for Odysseus, his action plan is to resist the Siren song at all costs, and so being bound to the mast is no violation of autonomy.

---

* H. Frankfurt, *The Importance of What We Care About*, Cambridge, Cambridge University Press, 1988; G. Dworkin, *The Theory and Practice of Autonomy*, Cambridge, Cambridge University Press, 1988. Recent discussion of this approach can be found in A. R. Mele, *Autonomous Agents: From Self-Control to Autonomy*, New York, Oxford University Press, 2001; L. Ekstrom, A coherence theory of autonomy, *Philosophy and Phenomenological Research* 53 (1993): 599–616; M. Bratman, *Structures of Agency*, Oxford, Oxford University Press, 2007; J. Christman, Autonomy and personal history, *Canadian Journal of Philosophy* 21 (1991): 1–24; D. T. Meyers, Decentralizing autonomy: Five faces of selfhood, in J. Christman and J. Anderson (Eds.), *Autonomy and the Challenges to Liberalism*, Cambridge, UK, Cambridge University Press, (2005): 27–55.

† The Kantian term is "maxim" (German *Maxime*), but it has the wrong connotation in English, and I want to avoid importing the Kantian baggage associated with this term. One might use the term "policy" rather than "action plan," but in popular usage, a policy is an action plan for an organization or government.

IMPOSING VALUES ON OTHERS

A potential problem with the Interference Principle is that it may permit us to impose controversial values on others. If I think that purchasing and eating meat is immoral, I can block your access to the meat counter without violating your autonomy. I don't see you as exercising agency at this point, and the coercion is minimal, because there is no reason you would approach the meat counter other than to buy meat. Or if I believe abortion is immoral, I can block your entrance to an abortion clinic without violating your autonomy. The problem here is that you may believe that eating meat or aborting a pregnancy is perfectly ethical. How do we deal with differences of opinion on what is ethical? What is to stop me from interfering with anyone who happens to think differently than I do?

First of all, the Interference Principle doesn't say that it is *permissible* for me to block your access to the meat counter or the abortion clinic. It only says that it does not violate your autonomy. In fact, blocking your access is unethical, if only because it is illegal. Even if it is legal, interfering with controversial behavior almost certainly fails the generalization test. If people universally felt free to interfere with any controversial action they view as unethical, then strident steak lovers would prevent *me* from blocking meat counters, thus defeating my purpose. We already see this kind of tug of war in front of some abortion clinics. More generally, the kind of society I want to achieve by discouraging unethical action would be impossible if people regularly "took the law unto their own hands" by imposing controversial values on others. On the other hand, this only applies to controversial values. Grabbing the arm of a mugger is generalizable, because there is little disagreement and about the evil of mugging. If everyone stopped behavior they see as uncontroversially evil, no one would stop my rescue attempt. The problem of disagreement would re-emerge at a higher level if we disagreed over what is controversial, but we don't. There is relatively little controversy over what is controversial.

It may seem that I am skirting the basic issue, however. Imposing controversial values happens to be unethical, but the fact remains that it does not violate autonomy (when the interference is minimal). This seems to reduce violations of autonomy to my personal opinion about whether your behavior is unethical. But it does not. Your behavior must, in fact, be unethical. It must fail one of the rationality tests for ethical action. Mere opinion doesn't matter.

I grant that we can disagree over whether an action plan satisfies the rationality tests, yet this is a risk we inevitably take when relying on rationality to generate consensus. We don't mind taking this risk in other endeavors, such as science and mathematics. Scientists disagree over whether certain fossil finds are evidence for a new hominid species, or whether the experimentally determined mass of the Higgs boson is evidence of a stable universe. Even mathematicians have disagreed over whether proofs that use infinitesimals or nonconstructive methods are valid. These are disagreements over what is rational. We nonetheless forge ahead under the working hypothesis that these disagreements won't undermine the overall project of reaching rational consensus, and we can do the same in ethics.

It helps to make this a collaborative project, of course. Scientists work out their theories as a community and must defend their views convincingly to critical peers or lose prestige. In like fashion, working out what is ethical must be a collective endeavor in which we call upon each other to explain and justify our views.

JOINT AUTONOMY

We have yet to find a principle that explains why compulsion is a violation of autonomy, beyond the extreme case of killing someone. We have two principles that *allow* limited compulsion—the Interference Principle and paternalism—but we have found nothing inherently wrong with compulsion in general. We can derive such a principle, however, by drawing out one more implication of the concept of agency.

The idea is this. If I regard any one person as exercising agency, I must attribute to that person a coherent action plan; that is, I must explain that person's behavior coherently as the result of reasons. Now if I regard *several* persons as exercising agency, I must be rational in attributing to them a set of action plans. The action plans must be consistent with each other, or else my attribution is irrational. In other words, these persons must have *joint autonomy*. This has ethical force when one of those persons is myself. Suppose my action plan violates joint autonomy with respect to the other action plans, but the other plans are consistent with each other. Then I can escape self-contradiction only by changing my action plan. This is another way of saying it is unethical.

Some examples will help explain this. Suppose that I block your path as you enter a restaurant for lunch. I grant that there is nothing unethical about eating lunch at a restaurant, and I therefore regard your behavior as an exercise of agency. This means there is a contradiction between my action plan and yours. I am rationally constrained to believe that my action plan of blocking your path is incompatible with your action plan of having lunch. So the action plans I attribute to you and myself are incoherent when considered together. This means I cannot consistently regard us both as exercising agency. Blocking your path is a violation of joint autonomy. If I am to be ethical (i.e., do something that I can rationally regard as an exercise of agency), I must adopt some other action plan.

Now suppose I am the restaurant owner and tell you that no tables will be available for an hour. This frustrates your intention to have lunch in my establishment. It does not, however, violate your autonomy, because it is consistent with your action plan. Only actions that you choose can go into your action plan. You can choose to walk into my restaurant and request a table; however, you cannot choose that a table be made available or that your lunch be prepared. I did nothing to block the actions you in fact choose.

Finally, suppose I close the eatery just as you arrive, perhaps due to a power failure. This is not a violation of autonomy even though it physically prevents your chosen action of entering the restaurant. The Autonomy Principle does not require me to give you whatever you want. Your action plan to enter my restaurant, if it is to be ethical and therefore genuinely an action plan, must be conditional on the restaurant's being open for business. An action plan of entering my restaurant, no matter what, is unethical, because forcing your way in is illegal. My closing the restaurant is perfectly consistent with an ethical action plan of entering restaurant if it is open, and it is no violation of your autonomy.

To take another example, suppose I select a theater seat that you prefer, because I arrive first and prefer that seat myself. Although I prevent you from taking the seat you want, this is normally not a violation of joint autonomy. I can reasonably attribute to you the action plan, "Select the best seat that is available at the time I arrive." I have the same action plan myself, and because we both successfully execute this action plan (at different times), there is no conflict.

Now suppose the seats are reserved, and your action plan is, "Take the seat whose number is printed on my ticket." Since I grant that your action plan is ethical, there is a conflict between our action plans. Taking your reserved seat is a violation of joint autonomy and therefore unethical. We can sum up the situation in the following principle.

> *Joint Autonomy Principle.* Violation of joint autonomy is unethical. That is, it is unethical for me to select an action plan that is jointly inconsistent with ethical action plans that I attribute to any given set of other agents, where the actions plans of the other agents are themselves jointly consistent.

Killing is an extreme violation of joint autonomy, because it wipes out all of the victim's ethical action plans. Slavery is a violation for a similar reason. If I enslave you, I almost certainly thwart ethical action plans that you cannot carry out as a slave.

Bodily injury can also violate joint autonomy, aside from the obvious negative utility it creates. An injury can interfere with many ethical activities, and when it does, an action plan that causes injury violates autonomy. This raises the thorny issue of when my action *causes* injury. If I slug someone, then there is no question that my action causes the injury. But suppose I am working under a crowded street and decide to leave the manhole uncovered to allow in fresh air. I know that anyone falling into the manhole will be seriously injured. Furthermore, a rational assessment of the situation requires me to believe that at least one pedestrian will walk into the manhole while texting on a smartphone. Nonetheless I erect no barrier or warning to pedestrians. My behavior is obviously unethical, even if no one falls in, because it is grossly nonutilitarian; I could have placed barriers around the manhole. But this is because the Utilitarian Principle considers all consequences, including those that result from the free choices of others. If someone freely chooses to walk across the path of the manhole and accidently falls in, did I *cause* the resulting injury? Is my behavior unethical because it violated autonomy?

Legal scholars have developed complicated doctrines of proximate causes, causes-in-fact, intervening causes, independent sufficient causes, concurrent actual causes, and so forth. But for our purposes we need only the concept of consistency between action plans. For example, we can check whether leaving the manhole open is consistent with action plans I rationally attribute to others. It is not. I am rationally constrained to believe that my negligence is incompatible with ethical action plans of at least one pedestrian. I essentially set a booby trap. So my action plan violates joint autonomy. Here, however, the inconsistency doesn't arise between two persons (myself and the injured party) as in previous examples, because rationality doesn't constrain me to believe that any particular person will fall in. Rather, the inconsistency arises only when everyone on the street is considered. Rationality constrains me to believe that it is impossible that the action plans of myself and everyone on the street be jointly carried out. So there is a violation of the joint autonomy of this group of agents. Since my action is the source of the inconsistency, I am obligated to change it.

The Joint Autonomy Principle takes into account fewer consequences than the Utilitarian Principle. It cares only about autonomy violations that I am rationally constrained to believe will occur, and not those that could possibly occur or would probably occur. Suppose, for example, that my manhole is on a suburban street where pedestrians seldom walk. Rationality does not constrain me to believe that someone will fall into the hole, and so I am not constrained to believe that my action plan is incompatible with anyone else's ethical action plan. So there is no violation of joint autonomy, even if someone by chance falls in. The Utilitarian Principle, by contrast, must consider all possible consequences. I must take into account the negative utility of a possible accident by factoring it into my calculation of expected utility. My negligence may therefore fail the utilitarian test even though it does not violate joint autonomy.

This distinction rules out the kind of futility argument that utilitarianism allows. I can't satisfy the Autonomy Principle by saying "If I don't do it, someone else will." I earlier used the example of the prison guard who is ordered to torture prisoners. He could conceivably claim that someone else would follow these orders if he refused, and if so, his torture passes the utilitarian test. To apply the Joint Autonomy Principle, we note that there are three agents involved: the prisoner, the commanding officer, and the subordinate ordered to torture the prisoner. The commanding offer need not be considered, because his action plan is unethical due to a necessary violation of the prisoner's autonomy. Even if the subordinate refuses to torture, the commander will order someone else to do it.

We therefore consider the subordinate and the prisoner. Torture is violation of their joint autonomy, and refusing to torture is not a violation of joint autonomy for any group of agents. If he tortured the prisoner, then his action plan would be inconsistent with many ethical action plans of the prisoner, and he would violate joint autonomy. If he refused to inflict torture, and another guard took on the task, then his action plan would at worst be inconsistent with the action plan of the commanding officer.

But the officer's action plan is unethical because it violates joint autonomy with respect to the prisoner. The dissenting guard does not violate autonomy, due to the Interference Principle.

INFORMED CONSENT

The next step is to investigate the concept of informed consent, which is often viewed as a major factor in judging whether autonomy is violated. Consent will also play a major role in addressing the problem of overkill. The basic idea behind informed consent is that exposing you to a risk of harm doesn't violate your autonomy if you consent to be exposed. The concept is perhaps best known in medicine, where patients are routinely asked for consent before they undergo treatment or surgery, or before they participate in a clinical study. Informed consent presumably implies that patients *assume the risk* inherent in the treatment, although not the risk of an improperly administered treatment.

Does the logic of autonomy provide a theoretical basis for any of this? It does, to a certain extent. One can argue that creating a risk of injury doesn't violate joint autonomy when everyone's action plan deliberately factors in the risk. Suppose, for example, that I introduce automobiles in a country that is now blissfully free of them. I know that some people will suffer injury and death from road accidents after they start driving. If everyone else knows this, I might say they assume the risk of driving when they get behind the wheel. More precisely, their action plans include (a) driving a car if the risk is such-and-such, as well as (b) carrying out any number of other actions *if* they are not injured or killed in a road accident. Part (b) is necessary, because if people take on the risk of driving a car, they must recognize that their other activities are contingent on surviving this risk. Then accidents that occur as a result of assumed risk are not contrary to the action plans of the drivers. This means that I can sell the cars without violating joint autonomy, and the ethics of my decision depends on generalizability and utilitarian factors.

On the other hand, suppose I know that the automobiles I sell contain a steering defect that will cause a certain number of accidents, over and above those that can be expected from the normal hazards of driving. When drivers "assume the risk" of driving my cars, they don't assume that defective steering is part of the risk. An accident that results from this unassumed risk is not consistent with their action plans. This means that selling the defective cars is a violation of joint autonomy. I can't ethically sell them, no matter what benefits they may bring.

These ideas lead to the following principle.

> *Principle of Informed Consent.* I can expose an agent to risk without violating joint autonomy if that agent gives informed consent, meaning that the agent (a) adopts an action plan that implies accepting the risk, (b) the agent is aware of the risk, and (c) I can rationally attribute to the agent a coherent rationale for assuming the risk.

Suppose, for example, that a physician performs orthopedic surgery on you that carries some risk. The physician is not violating joint autonomy if you adopt an action plan of undergoing the surgery, you are aware of the risk, and she can attribute to you a coherent rationale for accepting the risk, perhaps after talking with you about it. You might explain that after looking at the statistics, you concluded that the probability of a serious complication from surgery is on the same order of magnitude as the probability of being injured in an auto accident in 20 years of driving. Because you were willing to take this risk for the convenience of driving a car, you are certainly willing to take a similar risk for the convenience of walking without impairment. The physician need not agree with your reasoning, but only understand it; however, if your rationale is confused or self-contradictory, the physician has not obtained informed consent, and serious complications would imply a violation of joint autonomy.

OVERKILL

We are now ready to return to the problem of overkill. This is the problem that arises when interfering with unethical behavior often requires inference with ethical actions, which means it is not sanctioned by the Interference Principle. To make this concrete, suppose a burglar breaks into my home and is determined to attack me and my family unless forcibly restrained. I am lucky enough to be able to knock him to the floor and tie him up until the police arrive. This prevents him from performing actions that are perfectly ethical, and it therefore exceeds minimal interference. Yet if I release him, he will give me the same treatment or worse.

Ideally, I would install a force field around the criminal that activates only when he is about to attack someone. Tying him up appears to be a violation of joint autonomy and therefore unethical, as is releasing him.

I can observe, however, that the burglar almost certainty has an action plan to defend himself from attack under similar circumstances. To be consistent, he must choose the same action plan when I am under attack. That action plan calls for restraining the assailant, by tying him up if this is what it takes. That assailant happens to be himself. His action plans, including his ethical action plans, must contain an if-clause: He will carry them out if he is not restrained by victims of any burglaries he attempts. In effect, he has given consent to being restrained. Tying him up is consistent with his action plan and does not violate joint autonomy. On the other hand, I can't handcuff my neighbor to prevent him from cheating on his income taxes, without violating autonomy, because it would never occur to him to do the same to me.

This does not mean that I can do another whatever that person would do to me (a kind of counterfeit Golden Rule). It says only that I can restrict another's conduct *without violating joint autonomy* if the other person has an action plan that would restrict my conduct in the same circumstances. Restricting conduct may be unethical for other reasons, as is locking the burglar in my basement overnight, which is unethical even assuming he would do the same to me in the same circumstances.

This analysis opens the door to the use of a certain amount of overkill to stop an unethical action, without violating joint autonomy. We can sum up the situation as follows.

> *Principle of Implied Consent.* I can interfere with the action plan of an agent without violating joint autonomy, if (a) the agent implicitly consents to the interference, and (b) giving this consent is itself a coherent action plan. The agent consents to the interference if rationality constrains me to imputing to that agent an intention to interfere with the same action plan in the same circumstances.
>
> *Principle of Overkill.* I can ethically apply coercion that stops another person's unethical behavior, even if it interferes with other actions that are ethical, if my intervention satisfies the Principle of Implied Consent as well as the generalization and utilitarian tests.

Proviso (b) in the Principle of Implied Consent is necessary, because giving consent to interference may itself be inherently irrational and therefore not a coherent action plan. The burglar cannot implicitly consent to being killed, for example, because as noted earlier, death is incompatible with every conceivable action plan. This leads us, finally, to the matter of killing to save a life.

KILLING IN DEFENSE OF SELF OR OTHERS

We can now deal with the question everyone is waiting for: Is it ethical to kill in self-defense? Or to kill someone who is about to kill another? No, it is not ethical. Since killing is incompatible with every ethical action plan the killer might have in the future, the killer cannot implicitly consent to being killed (except perhaps when he or she is suicidal and has no action plans). The killer's victim, likewise, cannot consent to being killed. This means that one cannot ethically kill the killer, and one cannot ethically fail to kill the killer, because either results in a violation of autonomy. No ethical action is possible.

This conclusion will strike many as horribly unsatisfactory; however, the problem is not with ethics, but with the circumstances. There are many situations in which no action, and therefore no ethical action, is possible. A person rendered mentally incompetent by late-stage Alzheimer's disease can take no actions. This is the fault of cruel nature, not ethics. Human beings can likewise create conditions in which agency is impossible, as when one must kill or be killed. In such an environment we can only fight for survival, as do animals in a state of nature. It was only through a remarkable process of evolution, after all, that nature gave rise to the capacity for rational action. Our planet could have easily been a place where there is only animal behavior and no deliberation. Even in the actual state of affairs, the necessary conditions for deliberate action often do not exist.

Fortunately, we have some control over how often agency is possible. On occasions when we can exercise agency, we can take decisions that create other such occasions. We can plan carefully to avoid scenarios in which we must kill or be killed. In fact, we have an ethical obligation to do so, not only for utilitarian reasons, but because an action plan that we know will eventually result in death violates autonomy. However, after conditions deteriorate to the point where we must kill to survive, we cannot act. We are reduced to our animal nature and can only behave according to instinct or prior conditioning. We should, therefore, do our utmost to avoid such desperate situations.

TROLLEY CAR DILEMMAS

This is as good a point as any to deal with the famous trolley car dilemmas, introduced by philosopher Philippa Foot.* In the original dilemma, a runaway trolley is barreling toward five men who are working on the track. I can save their lives by pulling a level that will divert the trolley to another track, but in this case it will kill a single man working on that track. Should I allow five men to be killed, or save them by taking an action that kills one man? This dilemma is usually presented to tease our intuitions about the difference between allowing deaths and causing deaths.

Judith Thompson proposed a variation of the dilemma in which there is only one track with the five men, but I can derail the trolley by pushing a fat man off a bridge into its path.† Reportedly, more people balk at pushing the fat man off the bridge than pulling the lever, even though the results would be the same.

These dilemmas are much discussed in the media as well as introductory philosophy and psychology courses. They engage the audience and generate debate, but in my view they are an unfortunate way to introduce people to ethical reasoning. People puzzle over them endlessly, because they are aware of no conceptual framework that allows for their resolution. Even a proper analysis results in an uncomfortable and counterintuitive conclusion. This can create the impression that ethics is a field of unfathomable conundrums and therefore ends up being a matter of personal opinion.

The Joint Autonomy Principle applies immediately to these dilemmas. First, neither diverting the trolley car, nor failing to divert it, is a violation of the Joint Autonomy Principle when all the agents are considered. This is because the track workers themselves already have inconsistent action plans, no matter what I do. They can't all survive. However, we recall that the Joint Autonomy Principle must be satisfied when applied to any set of agents. There is a violation of joint autonomy when we apply it to the set of agents consisting of myself and the five on one track, or to the set consisting of myself and the one on the other track. In the one case, diverting the

---

* P. Foot, The problem of abortion and the doctrine of double effect, *Oxford Review* 5 (1967): 5–15.

† J. J. Thompson, Killing, letting die, and the trolley problem, *The Monist* 59 (1976): 204–217. A survey of views on the problem can be found in J. M. Fischer and M. Ravizza (Eds.), *Ethics Problems and Principles*, Fort Worth, TX, Harcourt Brace Jovanovich, 1992. Thompson reassesses her analysis in Turning the trolley, *Philosophy and Public Affairs* 36 (2008): 359–374.

car is inconsistent with the other action plans, and in the other case, failing to divert the car is inconsistent with the other action plans.

So no ethical choice is possible, and I am reduced to acting out of impulse or instinct. The only ethical action we can take is to build trolley systems that don't impose such choices. This outcome may be more palatable if we recall that it is not as though I am "being unethical." Rather, I have no choice in the matter. I cannot act.

The trolley examples are, of course, highly contrived, but other kinds of impossible choices can arise in extreme situations, such as on the battlefield, in police work, or in disaster situations that overwhelm medical personnel. The only way we can preserve the possibility of ethical action is to avoid war and other situations that force the violation of autonomy.

7

Virtue Ethics

Virtue ethics is rooted in the philosophy of Aristotle and remains a major force in ethical thought. As reinterpreted for Christianity by Thomas Aquinas, it is widely taught in Roman Catholic schools, where you might know it as *natural law theory*. Virtue ethics turns up in nonsectarian classrooms as well, and it has been quite fashionable at times.

Despite all this, virtue ethics is not part of the ethical framework developed in this book. Natural law theorists may find this exasperating and throw the book in the trash. So let me try to explain briefly what virtue ethics is all about and why I exclude it. This will also give me an opportunity to say something about the philosophical underpinning of the methodology I use in the book.

Although I don't find virtue ethics useful as an analytical tool, I hasten to acknowledge its positive contribution historically. Natural law theory has been a major civilizing force in the West, both by providing an intellectual framework for Christian sensibilities and by allowing enlightenment-era intellectuals to think about ethics *without* making religious assumptions.

OBLIGATION VERSUS EXCELLENCE

Aristotelian theory is inadequate for our ethical needs, because it has no concept of obligation—even if we may anachronistically and incorrectly believe otherwise. It is ironic that this philosophy would be grafted onto Christian ethical thought, where obligations to those less fortunate take center stage. Aristotle was interested in excellence, not obligation. The good life for him is one that fully realizes human potential, not a life of service and sacrifice.

The good life is something entirely different. One might imagine a successful nuclear physicist who has broad intellectual interests, stays fit and trim, lives in an architecturally well-appointed house with a view of the Rocky Mountains, is a connoisseur of good wine and food, plays late Beethoven string quartets on weekends, and is loyal to family and a circle of equally sophisticated friends. This notion of the good life resonates with many people. Universities and other organizations often describe their mission as achieving excellence, rather than as serving others. Aristotle would be pleased.

What, exactly, is excellence? Aristotle derives the answer from his idea of teleological explanation. Explanation is how we make sense of the world, and he recognized four ways to do this. The one we primarily use today is "billiard ball" explanation, or what Aristotelians call efficient causation. A billiard ball moves because it is hit by another, and in general, an event occurs because it is the result of a prior cause. Science takes this mode of explanation very seriously, tracing a chain of causation back to the Big Bang, albeit with some randomness thrown in at the quantum level.

Aristotle realized that other types of explanation can be equally enlightening, and teleological explanation is one of those, along with the so-called material cause and final cause. One way to understand the human body, for example, is to assign a purpose or *telos* to the various organs. The heart pumps the blood, the kidneys cleanse it, and so forth. One could, in principle, explain bodily function as the result of a complex chain of causes: The Krebs cycle creates adenosine triphosphate, which transforms to adenosine diphosphate during metabolism, and so forth. This is perfectly valid, but confusing. Everything is so much clearer when we view the body as composed of organs that have specific functions in a system. It is not necessarily to claim that a creator assigned a purpose to the organs, but only that things make more sense when *we* do so. This style of explanation has regained some currency in recent decades, as we speak of ecosystems in which various species have a role to play.

Aristotle carried this idea quite far, because he made sense of the world largely by seeing it as made up of entities (or *substances*, to use the medieval term) with a purpose embedded in their essential nature. As is often remarked, he was inspired by biology. Every living organism has an essence that is gradually realized as the organism develops, or to use Aristotelian language, as its potential is actualized. Today we speak of DNA rather than essence, but the idea is remarkably similar. The *purpose* of an organ or organism is to actualize its potential, much as an embryonic heart or kidney eventually realizes the potential encoded in differentiated stem cells. A similar analysis can sometimes be applied to nonliving things. The purpose of a paring knife is to peel fruits and vegetables, and its potential is actualized when it is sharpened and ready to slice.

Excellence is achieved when potential is fully actualized. An excellent paring knife is one whose sharp blade and ergonomic design maximize its cutting efficiency. An excellent human being is one who fully actualizes his or her potential. It's not so obvious what that potential is, but Aristotle offered a suggestion. Much as the heart brings to the body a unique pumping capability, he saw humans as bringing to the world certain splendid characteristics that no other being possesses. Aristotelians call these the virtues, whence the name virtue ethics. They include intelligence, honor, courage, loyalty, a sense of beauty, and *sophrosyne*, which is the ability to find the right balance among these. Lions and tigers are brave, but only humans have courage, because only they consciously overcome fear. Wolves stick together, but only humans are consciously loyal to friends and family. Aristotle can't prove that our purpose is to exhibit virtues we uniquely possess, just as no one can prove that the heart's purpose lies in its unique pumping ability. But if we allow him to draw this conclusion, life makes some kind of sense. Otherwise, he doesn't know why we are here.

I have only begun to tap into the resources of this rich and satisfying theory, and it's no wonder that it captivated the Western intellectual world for centuries. But it does not provide grounding for obligation as we understand it. It may seem otherwise, due, for example, to its emphasis on showing loyalty to friends and family. This sounds like obligation to our modern ears, but it is not. It is a reminder that loyalty is part of the good life. Without a sense of loyalty, we do not fully experience the splendor of human existence.

LOYALTY AS OBLIGATION

If Aristotelian loyalty is not an obligation in the modern sense, then I must explain why we often feel loyalty obligations and why these so often seem to conflict with other obligations. To cite a textbook example, suppose you are riding in your friend's automobile when she is involved in an accident. There is a dispute about who is responsible for the accident, and you are called to testify in traffic court. The judge asks whether your friend was exceeding the speed limit, because if she was, she would be legally liable. You are torn about how to answer, because you know that she was in fact driving too fast, but she has already asked you not to say anything about this in court. This dilemma is often discussed in connection with cross-cultural ethics, because in many cultures, the choice would be clear: Protect your friend, whereas in other cultures, including northern European cultures, there is a strong sense of duty to tell the truth to authorities. My students face a similar dilemma when their friends ask them to help write an essay or cheat on an exam. They think I don't know this is going on, but I know. There seems to be a conflict of obligations in these examples.

The Generalization and Utilitarian Principles impose loyalty obligations of their own and can explain the sense of conflict. For example, friendship and marital relationships imply mutual commitment, or a kind of mutual promise to take care of each other. Violating this commitment is not likely to be generalizable, depending on the reason for the violation. Duties to one's children are not based on an agreement of this sort, but they are solidly grounded in utilitarian obligation. Parents (or other designated caregivers) are in a unique position to take care of their children, because no one else has the close relationship, intimate knowledge of their needs, and legal authority that are necessary to carry out this responsibility. Neglect of children is ungeneralizable as well, because no society could survive such neglect if generalized, and no purposes of any kind would be realizable. None of this is meant to suggest that friendship, marriage, and family are reducible to generalization and utility obligations. There is much more to life than ethics, and part of life is developing our capacity for loyalty.

The traffic court dilemma can also be resolved within a deontic framework. Perjuring oneself in court is illegal, and breaking the law is ungeneralizable under most rationales. It is not hard to see why. If people broke the law whenever they thought they had a good reason, we would all be scofflaws and descend into anarchy. It would be difficult or impossible to achieve any purpose we might have. To be ethical in lying to the court, you would have to find a rationale for breaking the law in this case but not in a thousand other cases where you might think you have a good reason, and this rationale would have to be generalizable. Perjury is probably nonutilitarian as well, if only because your testimony could be refuted by other witnesses or surveillance videos, and you could end up in worse trouble than your friend.

Beyond this, it's unclear that friendship necessarily implies a mutual obligation to protect the other party by illegal means. Having a friend implies being a friend, and perhaps a true friend would not ask another to break the law on her behalf, unless there is a compelling reason. Avoiding a penalty for a traffic violation that one deliberately committed is not a compelling reason. In some cultures, friendship may imply a much stronger promise, and honoring this promise may be generalizable because society is designed to tolerate and even rely on such behavior.

NATURALISTIC ETHICS

I have argued that Aristotelian ethics is inadequate for our needs because it offers no concept of obligation in the modern sense. But there is a more fundamental weakness. It is a form of naturalistic ethics, which means it isn't really ethics, as we understand the term today. Naturalistic ethics tries to derive what is good and bad from a proper understanding of nature. In particular, a teleological explanation of human nature leads to virtue ethics. Natural law theory seized upon this theme of grounding ethical judgments in human nature and ran with it. Thomas Aquinas is the big name in this area.

For example, natural law theory might argue that drug abuse is wrong because it dulls our thinking, and human beings are by nature rational creatures. Or theft is wrong because it interferes with the operation of society, and human beings are by nature social animals. More controversially, abortion (at any stage of development) is arguably wrong because it is inconsistent with two essential human traits: the will to survive, and the drive to care for one's offspring. I don't want to imply that natural law theory is simplistic: For example, it can make exceptions for abortions that are necessary to save the mother's life, perhaps using the Thomist doctrine of *double effect*. This doctrine says that a virtuous act with an unintended negative effect can be permissible, if the benefit in some sense outweighs the harm. My point is that naturalistic ethics ultimately derives obligation from its understanding of human nature, if often with subtleties along the way.

Naturalistic ethics is sometimes criticized on the ground that it historically condoned slavery. Aristotle himself owned slaves and thought this was perfectly acceptable. Many Athenians of his day believed that foreigners were barbaric and less fully human than Greeks, and they were therefore fit to be slaves in Greek households.* The very word *barbaric* derives from the fact that Greeks taunted foreigners for speaking gibberish, "ba ba," rather than intelligible language. However, natural law theory has a neat way of escaping an endorsement of slavery. It sees Aristotle's assessment as based on a factual error: the mistaken (and all-too-convenient) belief that "barbarians" are less than fully human. Now we know better, and natural law theorists can consistently reject slavery.

The flaw in natural law theory runs deeper than any particular judgment. It tries to bridge David Hume's famous *is-ought* gap. Hume argued that one cannot infer ethical claims from facts alone, or more succinctly, deduce an *ought* from an *is*. The fact that Mary Smith killed a pedestrian while driving drunk doesn't in itself imply that Mary Smith did something wrong. We need at least two premises to draw this conclusion: a factual premise (Mary Smith killed a pedestrian while driving drunk), and an ethical premise (it is wrong to risk people's lives by driving drunk, or something of the sort). Natural law theory omits the ethical premise and thus cannot draw ethical conclusions. One might argue that there is an implied ethical premise, namely, that acting against human nature is wrong. Given the additional premise that human beings are rational creatures (as opposed to drunken creatures), we can infer that Mary was in the wrong. But then we have to ask why we should act consistently with human nature. I need look no further than the end of my nose to find aspects of human nature that I ought to suppress. In any case, after we inject the ethical premise, we have already abandoned naturalistic ethics.

The rationalistic ethics developed in this book may seem likewise to be predicated on a theory of human nature, namely the assumption that humans are moral agents; however, the argument is crucially different. It is basically what Kant called a transcendental argument. It says that the possibility of *taking action* presupposes that we have a coherent rationale for the action. The empirical observation that people can exercise moral agency does not, in itself, prove that certain types of behavior are moral or immoral. We can only say that having a coherent action plan is a necessary condition for the possibility of free action. Our action plans must satisfy logical conditions such as the Utilitarian and Generalization Principles, because otherwise we can't distinguish free action from mere behavior.

---

* Slavery was not always oppressive in ancient times. The famous philosopher Epictetus was a slave in a Roman household but enjoyed a comfortable life of reflection.

No state of nature commits us to acknowledging these principles, but exercising agency does commit us.

Naturalistic ethics sees an occasional revival outside the Thomist tradition. An infamous example is Herbert Spencer's *social Darwinism* of the late nineteenth century. This doctrine was used to justify tolerance for an underclass toiling in dangerous factories, on the theory that *survival of the fittest* (Spencer's phrase, not Darwin's) is part of the order of nature. Social and economic inequality was seen as weeding out the unfit and improving society. In a famous episode, Andrew Carnegie, one of Spencer's most enthusiastic fans, invited the philosopher to visit his steel empire in Pittsburgh. Spencer was horrified by the filthy air and oppressive working conditions of the day, leading him to remark, "Six months residence here would justify suicide."* This sounds like a recipe for weeding out the fit as well as the unfit, but there is no evidence that the Pittsburgh experience caused Spencer to budge from his views. He remained staunchly opposed even to philanthropy, for which Carnegie later became famous (I teach at a university he established).

The problem with grounding ethics in the natural order is that the natural order may be wretched. Suppose we discovered that human beings are instinctively territorial and neurologically equipped to learn ethnic intolerance and hatred.† Shall we conclude that ethnic conflict is part of the natural order and, therefore, good? Or suppose we learn that violence and domination are encoded in our genes. Or a craving for torture and sadism, which seem to surface reliably in contexts like ethnic warfare and poorly managed prisons. Proponents of naturalistic ethics may protest that these conclusions misread human nature, but this misses the point. The point is that they already want these issues to come out a certain way. If they believe ethnic hatred is undesirable, they must hope that anthropologists and biologists don't find it to be part of our makeup, or if it is, they must somehow explain away this fact. They are making prior ethical judgments, judgments that must come from some source other than an assessment of human nature.

British philosopher G. E. Moore made essentially this point a century ago when he spoke of the *naturalistic fallacy*. It is a fallacy to infer ethical propositions solely from a state of nature, because we can always sensibly

---

* J. Frazer Wall, *Andrew Carnegie*, Pittsburgh, PA, University of Pittsburgh Press, 1989, p. 386.
† The best known treatise on human territoriality is R. Ardrey, *The Territorial Imperative: A Personal Inquiry into the Animal Origins of Property and Nations*, Berlin, Germany, Atheneum, 1966, which generated a large literature on the topic.

---

ask, "Is this really good?"* Enslavement of conquered peoples, for example, has been a regular feature of human society for eons (including Aristotle's Athens), and yet it makes sense at least to *ask* whether this is right. If the question makes sense after we know the facts, then the ethical status of slavery is a different issue than whether it is natural.

We of course question our natural inheritance all the time, and when we don't like the answer, we often do something about it. By almost anyone's account, raw nature has bequeathed us a short life of hunger, suffering, and insecurity. Nature punishes our very entry into the world with Mother's agony. So we invent farming methods to hedge against hunger, remedies to alleviate suffering and disease, and social organizations to promote security and create opportunities for the finer things in life. We do so because we have a concept of what is good and right, apart from the lousy hand nature may have dealt us.

MORAL EPISTEMOLOGY

This discussion of justifying ethical claims has taken us from *normative ethics* into the realm of *metaethics*. Whereas normative ethics asks which ethical claims are true, metaethics asks what they mean and how they can be justified. Justification is the central question of *moral epistemology*, a field that examines what we can know in ethics and how we can know it. This is a good point at which to step back and examine the epistemological assumptions of this book.

The first assumption concerns the relative status of normative ethics and metaethics. Although philosophers tend to take a condescending attitude toward normative ethics, I prefer to see the distinction as parallel to

---

* G. E. Moore, *Principia Ethica*, Cambridge, UK, Cambridge University Press, 1903. Moore's idea of the naturalistic fallacy is similar to Hume's is-ought gap, except that Moore was an "ethical realist." He saw ethical truths as themselves stating objective facts, albeit not facts about nature. This is in a way unfortunate, because Moore's plainspoken clarity earned him enormous influence in the world of analytic philosophy throughout the twentieth century. Because his flavor of ethical realism proved hard to swallow, ethical theorists preserved his nonnaturalism by veering away from treating ethical statements as having cognitive meaning and toward viewing them as illocutionary acts and the like. Some even viewed ethical claims as mere expressions of emotion or taste, placing "Lying is wrong" in the same category as "Broccoli is yucky." This only added fuel to the moral anti-intellectualism I bemoaned earlier, yet his point about the naturalistic fallacy is right on the mark.

that of science and the philosophy of science. Science seeks to understand nature, while the philosophy of science deals with how we should interpret and justify scientific claims. Ethics is concerned with determining what is right and wrong, whereas the philosophy of ethics asks how we can understand and justify ethical claims. (Referring to ethics as "normative ethics" is like referring to algebra as mathematical algebra.) This puts ethics at the center of things and gives metaethics an interpretive and critical role, much as with science and the philosophy of science. No one regards science as lowbrow because it is not philosophy of science, and no one should regard (normative) ethics as lowbrow because it is not philosophy of ethics. This book, as you may have gathered, is about ethics, as opposed to the philosophy of ethics.

At the same time, ethics must rest on a generally accepted epistemological basis if it is to be a collective enterprise, just as science rests on a generally accepted scientific method. I am proposing that we adopt the basis I outlined earlier in this chapter, namely that ethical claims are grounded in transcendental arguments. This differs from the bulk of the academic literature in normative ethics. The typical mode of reasoning is to seek some form of reflective equilibrium, which reconciles general principles that seem reasonable with our intuitions in particular cases. The idea of reflective equilibrium has been traced to philosopher of science Nelson Goodman, who invoked the concept to explain how we justify principles of logical inference.[*] It is primarily associated, however, with John Rawls, who introduced the term and developed the concept further in connection with his theory of justice.[†]

Reflective equilibrium is generally obtained by moving back and forth between principles and particular cases. If our principles too often lead to particular judgments that strike us as wrong, then we revise the principles. On the other hand, we might reject our intuitions in particular cases if we can find no reasonable principle that covers them. The normative ethics literature typically deals with a practical issue by concocting clever thought experiments to probe moral intuitions against which relevant principles can be evaluated. If some of the individual intuitions don't fit in a larger pattern, they might be rejected on the ground that the examples

[*] N. Goodman, *Fact, Fiction and Forecast*, Cambridge, MA, Harvard University Press, 1955.
[†] J. Rawls, A *Theory of Justice*, Cambridge, MA, Harvard University Press, 1971, 2nd ed. 1999. Rawls proposed an earlier and somewhat different version of reflective equilibrium in Outline of a decision procedure for ethics, *Philosophical Review* 60 (1951): 177–197.

are too contrived to allow our intuitions to operate properly. It is not hard to imagine how such arguments can become convoluted. I will illustrate this sort of argument when discussing sweatshops in Chapter 12.

Seeking reflective equilibrium can be a useful exercise. We should be fully aware of what our principles imply, and reconciling them with particular moral intuitions can accomplish this. However, the fatal flaw in the process, in my view, is its practice of giving epistemic weight to moral intuitions in particular cases. Many readers may in fact be surprised that philosophers would regard intuitions as evidence for moral claims, because we all know that our reactions to moral dilemmas are strongly influenced by our cultural and individual backgrounds. I like to tease my philosophy colleagues by pointing out that moral intuitions are very different in their seminar room than in the business school next door. Fashioning a reflective equilibrium might be legitimately viewed as a kind of moral anthropology, or as a rational reconstruction of cultural norms. This is very different from viewing it as a valid justification for ethical claims.

Reflective equilibrium is inadequate in practice as well as in principle. We are often deeply divided by ideology, and these differences reliably predict differences in moral intuition. If a police officer shoots a suspect on the street, one person will see it as police brutality and another as self-defense. If a refugee requests asylum, one person will see it as an opportunity to show compassion, another as a threat to jobs and public safety. Our moral intuitions have a nasty habit of differing in cases where we most desperately need consensus.

One might argue, with Goodman, that the logical consistency norms on which I base ethical reasoning, such as the Generalization Principle, can themselves be defended only by appeal to a reflective equilibrium. This may well be so, but it is a trait shared with science and mathematics. Both of these endeavors presuppose consensus on what counts as rational inference. After this is settled, they can proceed with the main business at hand. I propose only that we do the same in ethics.

8

Buying and Selling

We spend a large fraction of our lives buying and selling. Nearly all of the artifacts that surround us were bought and sold, not to mention many human services on which we rely. Probably no activity more profoundly shapes the world than commerce, aside from education and child rearing. Ethics is supposed to regulate how we relate to each other, and much of how we do so is through commerce. This makes the ethics of buying and selling a central topic in applied ethics, and it is the topic of this chapter.

I will begin with a few dilemmas that face buyers, followed by some that concern sellers. These case studies will provide a springboard for broader discussions of consumer activism, the role of emotions in decision-making, high-context and low-context cultures, and the adage *caveat emptor* ("let the buyer beware").

DAMAGED RENTAL SKIS

Let's start with a little dilemma experienced by one of my students, whom I will call Edward. While staying at a resort, he and his friends rented jet skis. (For those who, like myself, are not into water sports, a jet ski is not a ski, but a small recreational watercraft.) While horsing around in the water, Edward and one of his friends allowed their skis to collide. On inspection, they found a nasty scratch on Edward's ski. When they returned the equipment, the lender "did not seem to notice the damage." Mindful that repair could be costly, Edward chose to say nothing about it.

This is an easy one. Edward violated his rental agreement, which entitles the renter to use an item, not to damage it. It almost certainly specifies that the renter is responsible for damage, and it probably requires a deposit (typically $500) on a credit card to cover any repair cost. Edward's failure to pay for the damage was a breach of contract, whether or not the renter happened to notice the damage. Breaking a contract merely for personal benefit is ungeneralizable and therefore unethical.

Edward might argue that the renter implicitly waived the damage payment. Damage to rental skis is a frequent occurrence, as witnessed by the contractual language, and so the company surely has a policy of inspecting returned equipment. Maybe the renter saw the scratch and decided to overlook it. This would put Edward in the clear ethically, because it amounts to renegotiation of the contract by mutual consent.

Granting that the renter may have noticed the damage, the issue for ethics is whether it was rational for Edward to believe it. Although Edward didn't really know what the renter was thinking, rationality requires him to make a reasonable effort to find out. He had only to say, "How about that scratch?" and the matter would have been instantly resolved. So it was unethical for Edward to assume that he owed nothing.

SUPERMARKET ETHICS

Like all of life, a trip to the supermarket raises ethical issues, large and small. I will examine a couple of small ones that people often ask about. Is it okay to taste a grape before deciding whether to buy a bunch? Is it acceptable to take 14 items through an express checkout lane clearly labeled "10 items or less"?[*]

To begin with, tasting the grape is bad for your health, because an unwashed grape is likely to be contaminated with pesticide residue.[†] More to the point, it is theft, unless you buy the bunch from which you sampled. Because the theft is merely for personal benefit, it is ungeneralizable and therefore unethical. If you ask and receive permission to sample a grape, fine. If you know for a fact that the store has a policy of allowing customers to taste the produce, fine. Otherwise, you should buy what you eat.

---

[*] Dilemmas posed in a radio interview of T. Morris, by S. Stamberg, Lying, cheating and stealing, part one, *Morning Edition*, National Public Radio, August 5, 2003.
[†] According to the U.S. Department of Agriculture, grapes have the third most pesticide residue, after apples and strawberries. K. Fischer, Q&A: Which fruits and vegetables have the most pesticide residue, and how can I get rid of it? *Healthline News*, May 5, 2014.

Some people, even ethicists, say that you shouldn't eat the grape because even a small ethical transgression erodes character.* Character is not the issue. Unethical behavior might end up building character. Eating the grape is wrong simply because it is theft. It makes no sense to argue that you should avoid wrongdoing because it erodes character. You should avoid wrongdoing because it is wrong.

Taking 14 items through the express checkout is trickier. It seems generalizable, because your reasons for doing so are almost certainly that (a) you have only slightly more than ten items, and (b) the express lane is faster than regular lanes. If everyone with slightly more than 10 items used the same strategy, you would still find a lane that is faster than the regular lanes. In fact, this generalization argument may work for 20 or more items, if many customers have long grocery lists.

Abusing the express lane may also pass utilitarian muster. Of course, the checkout clerk may send you to another lane, which foils your plans. When I was living in the Middle East, I noticed that checkout clerks were not a bit shy about rejecting customers who tried to sneak through the express lane with too many items. This is typical of relationship-based cultures that rely heavily on direct supervision (more on this in a moment). However, North Americans and Europeans tend to rely more on self-enforcement, and there is not much chance that the clerk will make an issue of four extra items. So, assuming that the express queue is faster, joining the queue probably increases your utility. But how about total customer utility?

The proper use of express lanes by customers in general can reduce total waiting time;† however, we are interested in the effect of one customer's behavior, yours, and it is another matter entirely. Suppose it takes the clerk two minutes to ring up your items. No matter which queue you join, you cause every customer behind you to wait two minutes longer. Joining an express lane could create a few more minutes delay if it typically has a longer queue than regular lanes. But this is likely to be more than offset by your own much longer wait if you join a regular lane. Breaking the rules is probably the utilitarian choice.

The main problem I see with joining the express lane is that, by flouting posted rules, it breaks a kind of social contract one finds in Western countries. I mentioned that customers in the Middle East frequently ignore the express lane limit. Actually, they only ignore the sign and

---

* For example, see the interview with Tom Morris cited earlier.
† W. Whitt, Partitioning customers into service groups, *Management Science* 45 (1999): 1579–1592.

observe the limit once instructed to do so. This is another characteristic of relationship-based cultures. They are *high-context* cultures, as opposed the *low-context* cultures of the West. The distinction is due to anthropologist Edward Hall and refers to whether information is transmitted through the social context or through impersonal, explicit instructions.* For example, a business contract in a low-context country consists of pages of fine print that spells out precisely the obligations of each party. A high-context "contract" can be a handshake (or bow), preceded by a period of personal relationship-building during which a mutual understanding develops. Similarly, Middle Eastern shoppers are accustomed to absorbing behavioral norms from friends, relatives, and other shoppers, not from written instructions. If they go astray, they are personally set straight as necessary.

By contrast, shoppers entering a Western supermarket, or any other establishment, are expected to observe written instructions. Low-context communication is a major component of how the cultural system works. Ignoring written instructions, unless there is some specific and socially sanctioned reason to ignore them, is therefore probably ungeneralizable. The purposes one intends to accomplish in a supermarket or any other institution are achievable only because people generally adhere to written rules. This is not true in a Middle Eastern bazaar, where one can ignore signs but must follow local bargaining practices that everyone knows just from living there. The Generalization Principle requires Westerners adventurous enough (and foolish enough) to shop in a bazaar to familiarize themselves with the cultural norms in advance, just as it requires them to abide by posted rules in a Western supermarket.

AN ETHICAL SMARTPHONE?

Beginning about 2012, a flurry of articles appeared in the North American media about the ethics of buying a smartphone. There were reports of abusive labor practices at factories in China, as well as violent consequences of raw material sourcing from Africa. For example, the Taiwanese firm Foxconn was called out for harsh working conditions at a plant in Chengdu that makes iPhones for Apple. Workers, some of them underage, were required to live in crowded dormitories and toil in unsafe conditions. They were forced to stand through long workdays, resulting in swollen

---

* E. T. Hall, *Beyond Culture*, New York, Anchor Books, 1976.

legs, with some unable to walk by day's end. This and other facilities were plagued by suicide attempts, obliging Foxconn to install netting at its Shenzhen factory to catch workers jumping to their death.*

It gets worse. Smartphones require rare minerals such as tantalum, much of which is sourced from the Democratic Republic of the Congo, where production of the mineral finances bloody conflict. Rival militias force local people to work at dangerous mines, extort the minerals from self-employed miners, and torture and mutilate those who do not comply.†

Apple took steps to address working conditions at the far end of its supply chain, but at this writing, abuses seem to persist. Workers at Jabil Circuit plants reportedly work on their feet for 12 hour shifts, 6 days a week, while making iPhones.‡ Those at the Zhen Ding Technology Holding factory in Shenzhen, China, are "pressured into working 65-hour weeks, made to sleep on plywood beds in bleak dormitories, and harassed by the facility's security force. The work is so exhausting that some of the estimated 15,000 workers choose to sleep through their lunch breaks instead of eating."§

Media reports like these pull the guilt strings of Western readers, and one might argue that they do little more. Few consumers are going to foreswear smartphones on their account. They may attempt to switch to a more "ethical" phone, but it's unclear that one phone is significantly less implicated than another.¶ There are other products for which an "ethical" consumer choice may be available, such as fair trade coffee and other certified fair trade products; however, even the benefits of fair trade choices are debated.**

---

* C. Duhigg and D. Barboza, In China, human costs are built into an iPad, *New York Times*, January 25, 2012; D. Mielach, Is it ethical to own an iPhone? *Scientific American* (online article), February 3, 2012.

† G. Monbiot, My search for a smartphone that is not soaked in blood, *The Guardian*, March 11, 2013.

‡ J. Garside, Can you buy the iPhone 5S or 5C with a clear conscience? *The Guardian*, September 10, 2013.

§ D. Jamieson, The factory workers behind your iPhone are too tired to eat, report says, *Huffington Post*, December 23, 2014.

¶ A. Leonard, There is no ethical smartphone, *Salon*, February 23, 2012.

** P. Griffiths, Ethical objections to fairtrade, *Journal of Business Ethics* 105 (2012): 357–373; B. Kilian, C. Jones, L. Pratt, and A. Villalobos, Is sustainable agriculture a viable strategy to improve farm income in Central America? A case study on coffee, *Journal of Business Research* 59 (2003): 322–330; R. Mendoza and J. Bastiaensen, Fair trade and the coffee crisis in the Nicaraguan Segovias, *Small Enterprise Development* 14 (2003): 36–46; J. Valkila, P. Haaparanta, and N. Niemi, Empowering coffee traders? The coffee value chain from Nicaraguan fair trade farmers to Finnish consumers, *Journal of Business Ethics* 97 (2010): 257–270; D. Reed, What do corporations have to do with Fair Trade? Positive and normative analysis from a value chain perspective, *Journal of Business Ethics* 86 (2009): 3–26; S. Barrientos, M. E. Conroy, and E. Jones, Northern social movements and fair trade, in L. T. Raynolds, D. L. Murray, and J. Wilkinson, *Fair Trade: The Challenges of Transforming Globalization*, London, UK, Routledge, 2007, 51–62.

There seems to be little an individual consumer can do. While the media tug at our guilt strings, our effort to influence the market is like pushing on strings. Activists tell us that if consumers as a group agreed to boycott unethical products, we could accomplish something. But I am not a group, and you are not a group, and there is usually no such agreement. In the meantime, we must decide what to do as individuals.

The basic problem is that a significant portion of the world economy relies on exploitation of labor. Many products we buy are tainted, from bananas to sugar to Christmas tree ornaments. One of the most frustrating cases is clothing. Much of the Western world's clothing is manufactured in Pakistan and Bangladesh, which have suffered a series of fires and other disasters in substandard garment factories. The worst so far is the April 2013 collapse of a poorly constructed factory complex outside Dhaka, Bangladesh, which left at least 1129 workers dead and many others with debilitating injuries. Although ominous cracks appeared in the building the previous day, employees were told to continue working or else lose their jobs and several weeks back pay (payment of wages is typically delayed to exert greater control over workers). These factories supply major North American and European brands, high-end and low-end.* Garments are sourced from sweatshops in a number of other countries as well. It is practically impossible for the average consumer to avoid buying them, short of hiring one's own tailor or joining a nudist colony.

A key question is whether "ethical" consumer choices are actually required by ethics, or merely assuage our conscience and make us feel better. We should bear in mind the central role of guilt in many Western cultures. Although shame-based cultures rely heavily on dishonor, loss of face, or ostracism to enforce social norms, guilt-based cultures rely to a greater extent on an internal mechanism. Transgressors are supposed to be tormented by a bad conscience even if no one knows about their evil deed. As a German proverb puts it, *Ein gutes Gewissen ist ein sanftes Ruhekissen* ("a good conscience is a soft pillow"). A guilt-based mechanism has the advantage that it requires less direct supervision and may be more efficient for that reason. On the other hand, guilt is a blunt instrument, and feelings can mislead. One may feel guilty about committing a relative to an institution, or writing a negative performance review, when either is

---

* J. Burke, Rana Plaza: One year on from the Bangladesh factory disaster, *The Guardian*, April 19, 2014. I discuss this and other garment industry disasters in Chapter 12 and in Bridging a supply chain's cultural divide, *Inside Supply Management* (2014): 34–36.

the only ethical action. "Let your conscience be your guide" is dangerous advice, if by conscience one means the capacity to feel guilty (it has several other senses historically). Westerners should be wary of guilt-tripping in the media, given our susceptibility to it. It is a good way to attract readers and online clicks, but it may not lead to ethical action.

Let's see if we can address the smartphone issue with our analytical brains rather than emotional conditioning. Buying a smartphone for almost any reasonable purpose is generalizable, because it is practically generalized already. Almost everyone in the world under a certain age and of sufficient means (or often insufficient means) has one. The utilitarian question is more difficult. First, there is the matter of whether the smartphone market may in fact benefit workers, on balance. Perhaps it is better to have a bad job than no job, a job that pays much less, or a life of rural poverty. Even if not, there are those who argue that sweatshop jobs are not exploitive in any case, an issue I will take up in Chapter 12.

Let's assume, however, that smartphone sales result in net harm to workers. That leaves the question as to whether my individual smartphone purchase causes more harm than good. It clearly benefits me and perhaps others with whom I interact. It is much less clear whether it has an effect on workers or industry practices. It's true that there is no strict futility argument here. I can't necessarily say that if I don't buy the phone, someone else will (unless a new model has just been introduced and customers are queuing up at the Apple store). Nonetheless, the phone on the shelf has already been manufactured, and it is unclear that a one-unit difference in sales will filter its way back through the distribution network to affect future orders and production quotas in any measurable way. If I were to obtain my phone from a local sweatshop, where each phone is manufactured on order by backroom workers under the crack of a whip, and if these workers would spend the day working in a comfortable office if I don't order the phone, then there would be a clear utilitarian case against buying the phone. But in our modern world, the connection between consumers and producers is far less direct.

A similar analysis applies to violence that may accompany the sourcing of raw materials. If I were to order my phone directly from a Congolese war lord, who would immediately turn around and extort the materials from slave labor, and if these laborers would be released for the day otherwise, then my order would violate joint autonomy. However, if I buy a phone at the local Apple store, the connection between my purchase and violence in West Africa is extremely tenuous. It is even harder to establish an obligation based on autonomy than on the utilitarian test, because a violation of autonomy requires a more direct connection (as discussed in Chapter 6). I must be rationally constrained to believe that my individual purchase will definitely result in enslavement and/or debilitating injury, rather than reducing *expected* utility, which is calculated on the basis of probabilities.

The complexity of world trade makes life ethically easier for affluent consumers. Their very lack of influence over the system, as individuals, may absolve them of any obligation to change their purchasing behavior. It's a great age in which to be an affluent consumer, but not so great to be at the far end of the supply chain.

So what can we say about smartphones? If my phone is a frivolous plaything that could just as well be replaced by a less controversial diversion, then there might be a utilitarian case against buying it. If it has real benefits in a highly connected world, however, and if my work would be hampered without it, then these factors outweigh the highly speculative negative effects of my individual purchase. I can use my phone with a "clear conscience."

This doesn't mean that no one is responsible for correcting abuses in the global economy. Those in the best position to improve matters are the major firms that source from low-income countries (see Chapter 12). Legislators and government regulators can also play a role.

Even individual consumers can influence the world in small but tangible ways. They can use their ethically tainted smartphones to talk up the matter on social media. This may help convince the big firms to modify their behavior. Unlike forgoing a smartphone, posting an intelligent blog comment has no downside and almost certainly a small positive effect—on the level of discourse if not directly on the global economy. It benefits the individual as well, as it requires minimal effort, and that effort hones the individual's ability to discuss ideas. There are other avenues of influence as well. Individuals can support politicians who favor labor protections, or write them letters. Again, the effort is small and has a nonzero albeit tiny chance of making a difference. It is much harder to make this kind of case for a simple exercise of consumer choice.

Another option for the individual is to become an activist. Given the right inclination, talents, and personal circumstances, one may accomplish more in activism than in another occupation or avocation. Well-placed activism can induce producers to clean up their act. I suspect that few people have an outright utilitarian obligation to become an activist, because it is hard to show that the chances of success outweigh the opportunity cost. Activism is much more likely to be consistent with the Utilitarian Principle than required by it.

ON SALE NEXT WEEK

Let's now turn to the selling side of the equation. Again, we start with an easy case. Sam is a salesman in an electronics store. A customer recently walked into the store and told Sam that he was looking for a particular model of flat-screen TV. The model was in stock and would in fact go on sale for 15 percent off the following week. However, Sam did not mention the upcoming sale, because his commission would be proportionately less. Is this ethical?*

Sam's behavior is clearly generalizable. If salespeople never tipped off customers about upcoming bargain prices, to collect a higher commission, they would still be able to collect a higher commission this way. Nor is Sam's reticence deceptive. Failure to say a discount will be offered next week doesn't *cause* the customer to believe there will be no discount next week. One might claim that Sam has selfish motives, but a selfish motive doesn't by itself make an act right or wrong.

We might find a utilitarian problem with Sam's behavior. He could have saved the customer more money that he would lose himself by tipping off the customer about next week's bargain. However, this is a zero-sum game as far as the money goes. What the customer gains, Sam and the store must lose. Perhaps the company can better afford to lose the money than Sam or the store, but we don't know this.

If Sam has some particular reason to believe that this customer would gain more in utility from a price break than others would lose, then Sam may have a utilitarian obligation to tip off the customer. Let's assume that the store has no particular policy regarding this, so that Sam doesn't run afoul of his employment agreement with the store. We still have to check whether tipping off the customer is generalizable. If all sales people tipped off customers about upcoming sales when it would result in greater utility, would companies react by withholding such information

* Based on G. P. Lantos, The speedy sale, in *Business Ethics Program, Vol. 6: Minicases*, Chicago, IL, Arthur Andersen and Company, 1992 (unpublished).

from salespeople? Sam knows more about this than I do, and it's his belief system that counts. If it is consistent with his understanding of the business that the store would continue to let him in on upcoming sales, then tipping off the customer in this case is generalizable, and therefore obligatory if he has evidence that it maximizes utility. However, in most cases, the salesman's failure to mention the upcoming sale is ethical.

A PIZZA PUZZLE

Sharon is food services manager for a hotel and is concerned about a decline in room service orders, the most profitable side of her operation. After some research, she concludes that guests are ordering pizzas from outside the hotel because they can't believe a hotel restaurant can make an authentic pizza. She proposes the following to her boss: She will put Napoli Pizza brochures in the rooms, with a phone number having a different prefix than the hotel number. Calls to this number will reach a special phone in room service, which will be answered, "Napoli Pizza, authentic Italian pizza from old, family recipes." Hotel personnel will don a Napoli Pizza hat and coat when delivering the pizza in boxes marked "Napoli Pizza." The hotel chef, Luigi, will in fact make the pizzas according to an old family recipe. Is this little scheme ethical?[*]

No gimmick that causes the customer to believe that the Napoli Pizzas are authentic can be deceptive on this account, because the pizzas *are* authentic. However, a gimmick may cause customers to believe other things that Sharon knows are false, such as the idea that Napoli Pizza is independent of the hotel. It may not be misrepresentation in a legal sense, but it is deception nonetheless and therefore ungeneralizable.

We ask whether Sharon's scheme will cause customers to believe that Napoli Pizza is unconnected with the hotel. The business about the phone number is problematic. Perhaps no one will notice the prefix, but if so the ruse has no point. Sharon is changing the prefix precisely because she believes it will deceive, and it is therefore unethical. Asking hotel employees to don pizza uniforms is innocent enough if the point is to deliver with flair rather than mislead. If guests walk past an obvious *Napoli Pizza* sign

---

Based on F. L. Miller, The pizza puzzle, in *Business Ethics Program, Vol. 6: Minicases*, Chicago, IL, Arthur Andersen and Company, 1992 (unpublished).

in the lobby, they know what is going on. The hotel has Luigi, an authentic Italian chef. A marketing person with Sharon's imagination should be able to take advantage of this—honestly.

CELEBRITY ENDORSEMENT

Advertising is fertile ground for interesting ethical dilemmas. Here is an amusing one.* An advertising firm just signed a contract with movie star Robert Upney for celebrity endorsements of Bud's Best bacon. The account is assigned to Annie, who soon learns the awkward fact that Robert has just become a vegetarian. Company lawyers assure her that everything is legal, but Annie is uneasy and consults the American Advertising Federation's *Advertising Ethics and Principles*. It states that "advertising containing testimonials shall be limited to those of competent witnesses who are reflecting a real and honest opinion or experience."[†] When Annie interviews Robert, he assures her that Bud's Best has been his favorite brand of bacon since he was a kid. He recently learned, however, that his LDL cholesterol is dangerously high, and his doctor advised him to avoid high-cholesterol foods like bacon and eggs. He decided to avoid all meat, for good measure. When Annie asks Robert if he is comfortable endorsing bacon, he responds that his conscience is clean, because he will talk only about how much he likes Bud's bacon and not about whether it is healthy. Is it ethical for Annie to use Robert's endorsement?

Because Annie consulted a professional code of ethics, let's start by clarifying the role of professional ethics in the case. A professional, in the relevant sense, is someone who *professes* membership in an occupational group from which the public expects certain standards of conduct. People who represent themselves as physicians, for example, are expected to have a medical degree and certification, and to act in their patients' best interest. This leads to a definition of professional ethics: It is a set of obligations based on the implied promise that results from joining a profession. To put on the white coat and stethoscope is in effect to promise to live up to the

---

* Based on G. P. Lantos, The nonuser celebrity endorser, in *Business Ethics Program, Vol. 6: Minicases*, Chicago, IL, Arthur Andersen and Company, 1992 (unpublished).

† American Advertising Federation Board of Directors, *Advertising Ethics and Principles*, adopted March 2, 1984.

standard of conduct people expect from physicians. Professional obligations exist alongside the ethical obligations that people have in general, just as the obligation to keep any particular promise exists alongside one's other obligations.*

Professions can influence public expectations by promulgating codes of ethics, and governments can do the same by passing laws. Accountants, for example, are expected to adhere to the Code of Ethics of the International Federation of Accountants, Generally Accepted Accounting Principles (GAAP), and government regulations. I'm not sure that the public expects a specific standard of conduct from advertising professionals as it does from physicians and accountants, but if it does, the code of ethics that Annie consulted would provide reasonable guidelines as to what is expected. Robert's endorsement of bacon meets these guidelines, since he is competent to report on what he likes, and he is reporting honestly. So his endorsement complies with professional ethics. Again, however, professional obligations exist alongside obligations that people have in general. Let's think about whether another obligation applies here.

The main one is the obligation not to deceive. Robert's endorsement seems dishonest because he doesn't eat bacon himself. The fact that he is endorsing the product may lead viewers to believe that he is willing to use it, which is deception. However, this warrants a closer look. Suppose an automotive expert endorses Toyotas but recently stopped driving because of deteriorating vision. We probably wouldn't say his endorsement is dishonest, because he would be willing to drive but for his eye condition. Similarly, if Robert would be willing to eat bacon if he had normal cholesterol, then perhaps we can say he is honest for the same reason. The analogy may seem inexact because we accept the auto expert's endorsement on the strength of his expertise, while Robert has no real expertise in bacon. Now, suppose a movie star with the same eye condition endorses Toyotas. The star has driven many cars but is no expert. I don't think we would view the endorsement as deceptive as long as the star would be willing to drive without the eye condition; however, if the movie star has sworn off driving because it is dangerous in general, we could have a problem.

---

* These ideas are further developed in my article, Professional ethics: Does it matter which hat we wear? *Journal of Business Ethics Education* 4 (2007): 103–112. It may be hard to reconcile professional obligations with other obligations. Professional rules may prohibit a physician from supplying a terminal cancer patient with an experimental drug, even though she might be obligated to turn over the drug if she were not a physician. Dilemmas like these must be resolved on a case-by-case basis, as with any promise-keeping dilemma.

Note that I am not trying to establish an ethical claim by appealing to our intuition in examples. I don't do that. I am using examples to help resolve an issue of fact: whether Robert's endorsement would cause viewers to believe something he knows is false. The outcome of the ethical analysis depends on whether Annie can rationally believe, after a reasonable amount of thought and investigation, that the endorsement would not mislead viewers. If Robert is willing to eat bacon if he had normal cholesterol levels, I suspect she can rationally believe that the ad is not misleading, which means she can ethically go ahead with the endorsement. The conclusion is uncertain, but this is due to uncertainty about the facts, not the ethical principles involved.

CHEAP STUFFING

I like this little case. Although it sounds rather humdrum, it leads to an interesting analysis than can exercise our cranial muscles. I'm a furniture manufacturer, and one of my brands has a reputation for high-quality upholstered furniture. Unfortunately, we've had an economic downturn, and the company must cut costs. Rightly or wrongly, I have already decided to put cheaper stuffing in our sofas. I would like to sell them under the same brand name for the same price. The company has never claimed in ads, promotional material, or product documentation that the stuffing is high quality. It's just that customers have learned as much over the years because the furniture holds up, and that's why they buy my rather pricey sofas. My dilemma is not whether I should have reduced the quality; that is a *fait accompli*. The issue is whether it's ethical for me to sell lower-quality furniture under the same brand name.[*]

An initial question is whether this would deceive the customer. Deception tends not to be generalizable, because if everyone does it, it won't work. Although I am clearly not lying to the customer, one can deceive without lying. Deception is causing someone to believe something that you know is false. For example, suppose my doctor orders some lab tests for me. Before sending me the report, he looks over the results and sees that they were all normal, except for a spot on the

---

[*] Based on D. J. Fritzsche, Elite furniture, in *Business Ethics Program, Vol. 6: Minicases*, Chicago, IL, Arthur Andersen and Company, 1992 (unpublished).

chest X-ray. It's cancer. To avoid upsetting me, he omits the X-ray results. Everything in the report is true, and the doctor isn't lying to me, but he is deceiving me. He is leading me to believe that I'm healthy when he knows otherwise.

Perhaps I am deceiving my customers without actually lying to them. I am, in fact, deceiving them if they would expect me to update them on the quality of the stuffing. Let me explain what I mean. Suppose you ask to come see me in my office, and I say I will be in the office all day tomorrow, you can drop by anytime. Later, I learn of a death in the family and decide to attend the funeral tomorrow, but I deliberately neglect to inform you because it's too much trouble. That's deception, because you would expect to be updated. My failure to alert you to any change of plans caused you to believe that the plans are still in effect.

The question in the furniture case is whether the customer would expect to be updated about the quality of the material. Of course, if there is a tag on the furniture that lists the specifications about the stuffing, then yes, the customer would expect the tag to be updated, but we are assuming that no such specifications appear. Given this, I don't think customers would expect to be apprised. When they walk into the furniture store, they wouldn't expect the salesperson to meet them at the door and say, "Wait, before you come in, let me tell you about how we have changed the quality of the stuffing." Some salespeople may do this, but people wouldn't expect it. So there's no clear case for deception here.

Even if we grant that there's no deception involved, the generalization test may fail on other grounds. Suppose that companies always reduce the quality of their merchandise in an economic downturn, without telling the customer. Customers would probably catch on. They would know that furniture manufacturers have gone on the cheap and would be unlikely to pay the same price for the furniture. Sales would drop. My decision is still generalizable if my sole reason for reducing quality is to cut production costs. I could still cut production costs this way if everyone else did likewise and customers bought fewer sofas. But this rationale has the wrong scope. I am reducing quality to cut production costs *while* maintaining sales, at least at some reasonable level. Otherwise I would not hesitate to tell all my customers about the reduction in quality. For my action to be generalizable, my reasons must be to cut costs while reducing sales no more than would result if all other merchants did the same. This means that I must be willing to reduce the quality even if sales were to drop to this extent as a result. If I am willing to do this, my action is ethical.

This is not a simple conclusion, and I don't think an obvious one. Deriving it is a good exercise in ethical analysis.

SUBPRIME MORTGAGE LENDING

The financial crisis of 2008–2009, the worst in the United States since the Great Depression, inflicted damage on the world economy that persists to this day. It all began with subprime mortgage lending. But why, exactly, is subprime lending bad? True, quite a few subprime mortgage loans were fraudulent in a legal sense and were unethical for that reason. Others have been described as *predatory* even though was no actual fraud involved. But a subprime loan need not be fraudulent or predatory, and it can have a legitimate purpose. *Subprime* means only that the borrower is riskier than usual and therefore pays a higher interest rate. Subprime lending can help people in financial trouble get back on their feet by establishing a better credit rating.

It is important to identify when subprime lending is helpful rather than predatory, or more generally, what kind of lending practices are ethical. This is a complex issue that I cannot analyze fully here, but I believe we can obtain some initial guidance by examining the arguments. This exercise will also help us understand when it is acceptable to say *caveat emptor*, or let the buyer beware.*

A little background is necessary. The number of subprime loans rose rapidly in the early 2000s, reaching 20 percent of the U.S. mortgage market by 2006. Many of the loans were structured to require low payments during a grace period but higher payments thereafter, such as the notorious "2–28" loans, which required low payments in the first two years but higher payments in the remaining 28. Perhaps house values would rise and allow to borrower to refinance on more favorable terms after the grace period.

The increase in subprime lending was financed by *securitization*. Mortgage companies sold the loans to big banks, which packaged them into mortgage-backed securities that were sold to investors around the world. Lenders no longer had the same incentive to perform due diligence

---

* This discussion is based loosely on the case study Countrywide Financial and subprime mortgages in my book *Business Ethics as Rational Choice*, Boston, MA, Prentice Hall, 2011: 68–73.

on the loans, because someone else was taking the risk. The big banks bundled risky loans with other mortgages to make the package more attractive to investors. Unfortunately, investors often failed to realize how much risk was hidden in these packages, due to their complexity. To make things worse, ratings agencies gave many of the mortgage-backed securities AAA ratings, because otherwise the agencies risked losing revenue. Despite the obvious conflict of interest, banks *pay* ratings agencies to grade their financial products. Even securities with lower ratings became *tranches* (slices) of collateralized debt obligations (CDOs), most of which were rated AAA.

Meanwhile, easy financing helped to push up house prices to record levels. When the housing bubble burst, prices plummeted, and subprime borrowers were unable to refinance as planned. Many were *under water*, meaning that their loan principal exceeded the market value of the house. Banks began to foreclose. Historically, mortgage lenders had worked with their local customers to try to avoid foreclosures, but they were no longer in control. Because the loans had been sold and resold, foreclosures were handled by mortgage servicers that had no connection with the original lender. The rash of foreclosures put more houses on the market and caused a further decline in prices, which precipitated more foreclosures. The mortgage-backed securities became *toxic* and eventually lacked any well-defined market value because nobody would trade them. Banks that held them were unable to measure the value of their assets, and a credit freeze ensued. Credit default swaps (*synthetic* CDOs) supposedly provided some insurance to owners of toxic securities, but the swaps were not subject to insurance regulations and were consequently backed by grossly inadequate reserves. There was some $60 trillion (yes, trillion) worth of credit default swaps outstanding worldwide in 2008, which was roughly equal to annual world GDP at the time. As the world financial system teetered on collapse, big banks asked for and received massive government bailouts. This created enormous public resentment in the United States, where it helped to fuel the right-wing Tea Party movement, the left-wing Occupy Wall Street movement, and seemingly endless political gridlock.

The financial crisis had multiple causes, not least an unstable financial system that was deregulated a few years earlier. Yet unethical behavior in the mortgage sector was the spark that ignited the gasoline. So it's important to know exactly which practices were wrong.

The clearest case of unethical lending was fraud, as when loan officers misinformed or misled borrowers about the terms of the loan. This was not only deceptive and unethical for that reason, but it was illegal. Another clear case was predatory lending, which might be defined as lending in which loan officer knows that the borrower can't afford the loan. It was common practice, for example, for the loan officer to look over the borrower's many liabilities and write down an income figure that would cover them, without asking the borrowers to verify or even state their true income. This was wrong for two reasons. For one, it was a lie. The loan officer misrepresented the applicant's income to her company and ultimately purchasers of the mortgage. One might argue that the company knew this was going on and may have encouraged it, and so they weren't deceived. But a false number was written on the application for someone to see, at least potentially, whether it be a company manager, an auditor, or a government regulator. If there was no intention to deceive, then there was no reason to write a fictitious number.

Even when predatory loan officers didn't actually lie about the applicant's financial condition, their behavior was nonutilitarian and unethical for that reason. The same goes for the company managers who tacitly approved. Defaulting on a loan and being evicted from their home is a devastating experience for a family. The expected disutility of this likely outcome far outweighs any benefit to the loan officer, the mortgage industry, or anyone else.

These are the easy cases. Now let's suppose that the loan officer is not predatory. She believes, with some justification, that house prices will not crash. Prior to 2006, there had not been a substantial decline in inflation-adjusted U.S. house prices since World War I.* There is a good chance that the borrower will benefit from the loan. After all, the family is going to move into that home they always dreamed about. There is risk, but maybe it is worth it. The mortgage company will clearly benefit, because it will sell off the loan, allowing the risk to be diluted by securitization. So let's grant that, on balance, the expected utility is positive, and the utilitarian test is passed.

That brings us to the generalization test. Even if net expected utility is positive, there is a great deal of downside risk, and the borrower is underestimating this risk. The family really wants that house. This is their chance, and the bank is willing to go along with it. They are unaware that the mortgage company no longer has an incentive to perform traditional

---

* As reported in R. J. Schiller, *Irrational Exuberance*, 2nd ed., Princeton, NJ, Princeton University Press, 2005. Schiller shared the 2013 Nobel Prize in economics.

due diligence. They assume that the company is applying the same strict standards that lenders have always applied to mortgage loans. But it is not, because incentives have changed. The borrower doesn't know that, and the loan officer knows that the borrower doesn't know that. This is the situation before us, and the issue is whether there is anything ethically wrong with it.

Can the loan officer simply say *caveat emptor*? These are adults, they want to buy a house, and they should check out the risk and be responsible for themselves. This poses a question that comes up all the time in everyday commerce, and we should pause a moment to think about it. When is it legitimate to say *caveat emptor*? We can start by observing that commerce as we know it requires some degree of trust between buyer and seller. If I walk into Walmart or the grocery, I can't research every item I put in my shopping basket. I have to trust the merchant to give me what I expect. Of course, labeling laws and such can help, but as I discussed in Chapter 2, regulation can't succeed if people in general aren't already inclined to act ethically. I have no option but to trust merchants and manufacturers to act in good faith; otherwise, commerce as we know it is simply not possible. So ethical merchants can't simply say *caveat emptor*. They must be worthy of customer trust.

How much trust is necessary? The Generalization Principle tells us this: *The seller's actions are unethical if they presuppose a level of trust that would not exist all sellers behaved the same way*. It's worth going over that again. A merchant is unethical if she presupposes a level of trust in the system that would not exist if everyone were like her. I think most subprime lenders failed this test. Their lending practices presupposed that borrowers trusted them to perform due diligence. If borrowers knew about the dangerously relaxed standards, they would have been more cautious. And they would learn about this practice if it were to go on for long. Widespread foreclosures would be in the news, many customers would back off from risky mortgages, and the subprime market would shrivel. In fact, this is not far from what actually happened.

So an ethical loan officer cannot simply say *caveat emptor*. To maintain generalizability, she must tell the borrower what is really going on. She must explain that her company will sell the mortgage in a few days, and someone else will assume the risk. The company is therefore willing to approve any half-decent loan application. While she believes that the net benefit to the parties involved is positive on average, she also expects to see a large number of foreclosures, particularly if the housing boom turns to a bust. She can point out that this is already occurring in regions where subprime lending got an early start. If the borrower is willing to go ahead after being apprised of the situation, then making the loan is generalizable and ethical.

MARKETING PROZAC

I will wrap up the chapter with another advertising dilemma, one that will help us to understand the role of emotions in ethical decision-making. The antidepressant drug Prozac, introduced to the U.S. market in 1987, was a fabulous commercial success for the pharmaceutical firm Eli Lilly. It created an enormous buzz, including the popular books *Listening to Prozac* and *Prozac Nation*, and a movie based on the latter.* Prozac was followed by antidepressants Zoloft in 1991 and Paxil in 1992.† Within a few years, antidepressants were the most widely prescribed drugs in the United States.‡

All three drugs are serotonin reuptake inhibitors. Serotonin is a neurotransmitter that contributes to a feeling of well-being, and the drugs prevent neurons in the brain from reabsorbing serotonin too rapidly after a synapse occurs. In a word, the drugs can make you feel good. Everyone wants to feel good, and so there was a temptation to use the drugs even if they are not medically necessary. There was also talk about how antidepressants can *improve* one's personality and lead to more success in life.

Antidepressants require a doctor's prescription, and this raised the question of how pharmaceutical firms were going to market them. Their solution in the United States was to use *push-pull* marketing. To push the drugs toward consumers, they advertised to physicians, and to pull the drugs through prescribing physicians, they advertised directly to consumers. The potential for abuse in pull marketing is obvious enough. Most consumers don't have medical training, and the ads may persuade

---

* P. D. Kramer, *Listening to Prozac*, New York, Viking Press, 1993; E. Wurtzel, *Prozac Nation: Young and Depressed in America, A Memoir*, New York, Riverhead Trade, 1994; E. Skjoldbjærg, director, *Prozac Nation*, produced by R. P. Miller et al., distributed by Miramax (2001).

† Zoloft is a trade name for sertraline, introduced by Pfizer in 1991. Paxil is a trade name for paroxetine, introduced by SmithKline Beecham (now GlaxoSmithKline) in 1992. Prozac is a trade name for fluoxetine.

‡ E. Cohen, CDC: Antidepressants most prescribed drugs in U.S., *CNN U.S. Edition*, July 9, 2007.

them to ask physicians for a drug they don't need. Direct-to-consumer pharmaceutical advertising is controversial for this reason and is banned by all Western nations except New Zealand and the United States.

The potential for abuse is greater when the targeted illness is psychological, because the sufferer may be more vulnerable to manipulation. The antidepressant ads often focused on shyness or "social anxiety disorder." A depressed individual is not likely to be a gushy extrovert or the life of the party. One prominent series of Paxil ads pictured a glum-looking woman over the caption, "Are you shy?" as though shyness were an illness.[*] According to University of Pennsylvania psychologist Edna Foa, "One gets the impression from the ads that if you are shy, and you have some difficulties, and you want to be outgoing, then take Paxil. [The ads] are promoting medication when it is unnecessary."[†] Temple University telecommunications professor George Gerbner claimed that Prozac ads were "trying to appeal to and exploit the most vulnerable people."[‡] The appeal of the drugs is further enhanced by a strong cultural preference for outgoing personalities in the United States, where introversion tends to be regarded as a personality defect.[§] I once suspected that Brazil is the world capital of extroversion, but after living there awhile, I learned that even Brazilians are more comfortable with quiet people than Americans.

In view of all this, is there anything wrong with advertising antidepressants directly to consumers? I have two concerns. One, obviously, is the potential to encourage abuse of the drugs. In theory, physicians prescribe only what patients need, but the American Psychological Association's *Monitor on Psychology* reported that psychotropic drugs were greatly overprescribed, and "Prozac opened the floodgates." The article quoted Vanderbilt University professor Steven Hollon, an expert on antidepressants, as saying that at least half of patients treated with antidepressants benefited from the placebo effect, not the drug's psychotropic properties.[¶] This is problematic, because these are powerful drugs that can have serious side effects, particularly if one stops taking them abruptly. Advertisers may argue that overuse is the physicians' responsibility, not theirs, but we debunked this type of argument in Chapter 4. Advertisers must consider

[*] J. Gammage, Once 'shy,' now 'sick,' *Philadelphia Inquirer*, May 30, 2004.
[†] S. Vendantam, Drug ads hyping anxiety make some uneasy, *Washington Post*, July 16, 2001: A01.
[‡] S. Bernstein, Drug maker to pitch Prozac in television infomercial, *Los Angeles Times*, May 14, 1999.
[§] S. Cain, *Quiet: The Power of Introverts in a World That Can't Stop Talking*, New York, Broadway Books, 2013.
[¶] B. L. Smith, Inappropriate prescribing, *Monitor on Psychology* 43 (2012): 36–41.

all the utilitarian consequences of their behavior, including those that depend on the free choices of others (such as physicians).

Despite the potential for abuse, antidepressant ads may have actually passed the utilitarian test at the time. Depression is a serious, debilitating illness that was not well understood among the public. When the drugs were released, there were doubtless many people who didn't realize depression could be treated, or didn't even know they had the disease. One might make a case that direct-to-consumer marketing brought benefits to these people that outweighed the collateral damage of overuse. This requires research, but advertising executives can hire people to do the research. Given the enormous impact of antidepressant drugs, rationality requires a thorough investigation. To pass the utilitarian test, advertising executives must be able to believe rationally that their direct-to-consumer advertising campaigns do more good than harm, based on the best available evidence.

That brings us to my second concern, psychological manipulation. When I ask marketing people whether they think it is okay, they say, "Of course. What do you think advertising is for?" Yet as I discussed in Chapter 2, advertising need not rely on psychological manipulation, and now that we have developed the concept of autonomy, we are in a better position to critique the practice. One can imagine cases in which advertising clearly violates autonomy. If a TV commercial hypnotizes us and plants the idea that we must eat potato chips, then there is an ethical problem. Part of the problem is that the commercial is deceptive, because there is no warning about hypnosis, and we are deceived about what we are watching. But that's not the whole problem. The commercial circumvents our rational faculties and prevents us from deliberating in a rational manner about whether or not to eat potato chips. It disrupts an autonomous decision-making process. It is ethically equivalent to implanting a computer chip in my brain that controls my actions without allowing me to decide what to do.

This doesn't mean that an appeal to emotions is always wrong. If advertisers want to sell me a convertible sports car, it is only reasonable to give me some idea what it's like to drive one. The ad can show people out on the road, the wind blowing through their hair, enjoying the exhilaration of freedom. I have a positive emotional reaction, and I have to know about this reaction before I can decide rationally whether I want the sports car. So emotions can be relevant to my decision. Or the relief agency UNICEF may put up ads with shocking photos of hungry children. This time I have a very negative reaction, but maybe I can't rationally decide whether to donate without some awareness of the emotional impact of poverty. So the ethical problem does not lie simply in an appeal to emotions, but in an appeal that prevents one from making a rational choice. If an antidepressant ad fades from an image of a downcast individual to one in which she is chatting happily at the party, that's fine, if this is a truly a consequence of the drug. A rational choice about whether to use the drug must take into account its emotional effects. The ad should of course describe, with equal emphasis, the drug's risks and side effects. However, if the ad appeals to a sense of inadequacy or some psychological problem, in such a way that people crave the drug without making a reasoned choice as to whether it's the right treatment for them, that's an ethical problem.

There is also an issue of temptation. Even if an ad does not manipulate people, it may *tempt* people to buy a drug or talk to the doctor about it. Let's think about when temptation is acceptable. I have eaten at restaurants that place photos of chocolate cake on the table. They are tempting me to order a high-calorie dessert that has a high profit margin. Is there anything wrong with that? It's not denial of autonomy, because I still decide whether to order the cake. It's harder to decide, but I decide nonetheless. Basically, the relevant test for temptation is utilitarian. If a local bakery occasionally tempts me with luscious fudge brownies in the display case, then this is probably fine. I indulge only now and then, and my enjoyment results in greater utility overall. But if a ubiquitous fast-food chain tempts people every day with greasy, salty french fries, the utilitarian outcome could be different (it's unfortunate that their marketing people can't tempt us to eat broccoli). So temptation is not necessarily wrong. If it has a net positive effect, it's ethical, and we have already granted that antidepressant ads passed the utility test.

I mentioned that commerce probably shapes our lives more than any other activity, save education and child rearing. In the next chapter, I take on the topic of education.

9

Ethics in Education

Most educational dilemmas I hear about are related to cheating. Schools are expected not only to educate, but to act as gatekeepers to jobs and more advanced schools. Good grades are often the key to opening the gate. I'm not sure this is a wise use of grades, but we are stuck with it, and it puts students under pressure to make As. They sometimes do it by cheating. The most frequent cheating dilemmas concern students who are asked by "friends" to help them cheat or conceal cheating. I will begin with four cheating cases, and then move on two dilemmas that have perplexed university and professional students. In one, an employee prefers not to return to the sponsoring company after earning an MBA, and in the other, an employee wants to accept a training opportunity even though he will soon leave the company. The chapter concludes with a teaching dilemma.

EXAM INFORMATION FOR A FRIEND

This dilemma was experienced by one of my students, whom I will call Peter. He had problems finding a summer internship and turned to his younger friend Ryan for help, because Ryan's father ran a local business. Ryan convinced his father to give Peter a job. So Peter believed he owed his young friend a favor. As it happened, Peter was a teaching assistant for a calculus course in which Ryan was enrolled at the time. Ryan was having problems in the class and anticipated a very low grade despite Peter's personal tutoring. This put his college scholarship at risk. So he asked Peter to slip him some of the questions on the final exam. Peter felt that his friend had put in sufficient effort and did not deserve to lose his scholarship over one class. So he provided him a copy of the questions.

Friendship involves implied promises: to be solicitous of each other's welfare, to be discreet about information shared in confidence, and so on. The extent of this promise is always vague, but for this very reason, we should avoid expanding its reach beyond what is clearly implied; otherwise, friendship is an impossible burden to bear. As Peter and Ryan developed their friendship, they were clearly signaling a commitment to care about each other and respect confidences. But it is unclear that either understood that this commitment could entail cheating for the other, except perhaps in case of dire need. A deeper friendship may imply a stronger obligation for Peter to help his friend, but that same depth places a stronger onus on Ryan not to ask his friend to risk the consequences of being discovered. Peter feels that he "owes" Ryan a favor in exchange for his help with the internship, but this is not what friendship is about. Perhaps in politics, one person does a favor for another with the understanding that the favor will be returned, and so there is an implied agreement. But one does not take care of a friend on a quid-pro-quo basis.

We have other problems with generalizability. Ryan is asking Peter to violate his employment agreement with the instructor, as well as to be deceptive, both of which are normally ungeneralizable. Here, Peter presumably has a special reason for passing along the exam questions, namely that a friend needs his help. But if teaching assistants were always willing to release exam questions to friends in need, instructors would keep the questions under lock and key until exam time. Peter has access to the questions only because the instructor trusts him, and there would be no trust if assistants were never trustworthy.

Peter feels that his friend has worked hard enough to "deserve" his scholarship. The problem with deserving is that we don't know how to tell who deserves what, and even if we do, we need an argument that securing just desserts excuses Peter's dishonesty. I conclude that Peter cannot ethically pass the exam questions to Paul.

REPORTING CHEATERS

This dilemma was posed by another one of my students, whom I will call James. He witnessed three friends cheating on an exam. If caught, they would be expelled from school, which could bar them from finding a good job or getting into another school. They were smart, and the exam was relatively easy, but they cheated nonetheless. Should James turn them in?

There could be a utilitarian obligation for turning in cheaters, if they would otherwise obtain jobs in which their incompetence would cause more harm than administering punishment now. We might want to turn in future surgeons who cheat on the anatomy exam. There is no evidence of this problem here, however, because we don't know whether this course relates to their future employment, the course material is easy, and the students are "smart."

Failure to turn in the cheaters is also generalizable. The reasons for not turning them are presumably to avoid getting involved in a messy situation, and to avoid harming their careers. Another possible reason is to avoid their wrath, if the indictment cannot be submitted anonymously. All of these could be achieved if students never turned in cheaters. In fact, students almost never report cheaters as it is.

We have found no obligation for James to turn in his friends. There may, in fact, be an obligation *not* to turn them in, perhaps based on the friendship obligations discussed earlier. I should caution that people often use the term *friend* loosely to mean someone they hang out with (Facebook "friends" are an extreme case of this phenomenon). If true friendship exists, however, there could be an implied promise that James will not report his friends, except in the occasional case where "tough love" better serves friendship. In contrast to the previous case, James assumes no particular risk of harming himself (or future employers) by taking care of his friends in this way, and so his friends could, consistently with their friendship obligations, ask him not to say anything about the fact that they cheated. This is not to say, of course, that the cheating itself is ethical. It is not, as I argued in Chapter 3.

Universities often have *honor codes* that oblige students to report cheaters. If a student signs such a code, this could be interpreted as a promise to comply with its terms, but I happen to know that there is no such code involved in this case. In any event, we should recognize that such codes are ethically flawed. It is wrong for schools to require students to promise to turn in miscreants, if only for utilitarian reasons: Students will in fact violate this provision of the code, rightly or wrongly, and this could inculcate a casual attitude toward commitments. In addition, students are not in a position to make such a promise, because they cannot foresee all the scenarios that might arise and whether it would be ethical to report students in these scenarios. The school is therefore pressuring them to make a false promise. This is wrong not only for the reason just mentioned, but because it teaches a falsehood. It leads students to believe that they are in a position to make such a promise, when they are not. The last thing a school should do is disseminate misconceptions, particularly about ethics, not only because it is nonutilitarian, but because a promise to promulgate knowledge lies at the core of a school's professed mission.

WHEN EVERYONE ELSE IS CHEATING

This one comes from an MBA student, whom I will call Olivia. One of her courses required students to take online quizzes online without assistance from others. Although Olivia studied hard for the first quiz, she found it difficult and made a mediocre score. To her chagrin, the class average for the quiz was much higher. On talking with some classmates, she learned that many of them were collaborating on the quizzes. Some even invited her to work with them. Olivia reasoned that a failure to collaborate would actually be dishonest, because her low score misrepresented her knowledge relative to the other students. She was tempted to give in and play the game.

Cheating is normally unethical, but in this case *everyone else* is cheating. The only reason Olivia wants to cheat on quizzes is that everybody else is cheating on the quizzes, and she wants to avoid being incorrectly ranked at the bottom of the class. She can argue that cheating for this reason is generalizable, because if people always cheated when everyone else was cheating, they could still avoid being incorrectly ranked at the bottom of the class.

To begin with, we don't really know that "everyone else" is cheating, only that some people are. When people say "everybody else is doing it," we can almost be certain that *not* everybody is doing it. However, let's assume for the sake of argument that in this case, everybody really is cheating.

There is yet another factor. Cheating on the quizzes is deceptive, because the professor (whose IQ must be in the single digits) apparently thinks students are not getting help. Cheating causes the professor to believe that Olivia can obtain a high score without assistance, which Olivia knows to be false. Her only rationale for deception here is that it benefits her, and this is not generalizable. If people were always deceptive when it benefits them, nobody would trust anybody, and it would be impossible to deceive anybody.

Olivia may argue that I have mischaracterized her rationale. She wants to cheat because it will benefit her *and* because a failure to cheat is equally deceptive. It causes the professor to believe incorrectly that she ranks below other students. However, this is not a coherent rationale, because a failure to cheat need not be deceptive. She can avoid cheating by declining to take the quiz at all under current circumstances, in which case there is no deception. In fact, this is the only ethical alternative, because taking the quiz is deceptive, whether or not Olivia cheats.

Olivia may complain that this is easy for me to say, because I am not the one who will get a zero for skipping the quiz. True, but this doesn't show I am wrong. Ethical behavior can be costly. Fortunately, it isn't in this case, because she can also tip off the professor about what is going on. In fact, the utilitarian principle requires her to do so, because this will probably avoid the disutility of incorrectly evaluating student knowledge. I suggest that she write an anonymous note on her computer, print it, and send it to the professor by campus mail. She should not send the note electronically, because electronic communications can always be traced. Retaliation from fellow students could create substantial disutility. She should include plenty of detail to convince the professor that the note is legitimate, without revealing that she was making low grades. If the professor restructures the course to solve the cheating problem, perhaps by giving the quizzes in class, then Olivia can take the quizzes honestly without deceiving anyone.

On the other hand, if the professor ignores her note, then she is off the hook. She can collaborate on the quizzes without deceiving the professor. She can hardly be accused of deception when she told the professor everything. She might worry that she is deceiving potential employers who examine her course grades, but this is unlikely. Employers won't see her quiz scores, only the final course grade, and the grade is meaningful to them only in respect of how it compares with the grades of other students. The quizzes have no impact on her relative course grade, because everyone in the class is making near-perfect scores on them.

USING STUDY DRUGS

This is a student dilemma that deserves to be quoted verbatim.

An ethical dilemma that I've experienced ever since I entered college is the use of amphetamines, such as Adderall and Vyvanse, in order to study longer and get better grades. Through middle school and high school, I studied for hours to earn straight A's and get into a private university. After struggling [through] my freshman year in college, I didn't know what I was doing wrong. I changed my study habits, joined study groups, and obtained tutoring, but I could never do as well as other students. I knew my peers used study drugs to stay up longer and remain focused, but I never wanted to stoop so low. It's extremely frustrating to study for days before the exam and then receive a B, when other kids cram the night before using amphetamines and get an A. It's distressing when I apply to jobs but hear nothing, while students who use drugs get offers from Goldman Sachs and Deloitte. I have morals that my parents taught me, but it is really hard to stick to them when I don't benefit from doing "the right thing."*

This dilemma reflects the enormous pressure to "succeed" that students increasingly experience. Success is often defined as making high grades or getting a prestige job with an employer like Google or Goldman Sachs. The pressure typically comes from families, who may teach morals but also want to see their children excel. They pay a high tuition cost and may be keen on getting their money's worth. However, only a certain number of students can get As, grade inflation notwithstanding, and only a minority of them can land jobs that are seen as the most desirable. This leaves many students desperate to be among the select.

The phenomenon is worldwide, as living standards rise and competition intensifies for slots in top universities. A salient case is South Korea, which (along with a few other Asian countries) is famous for its cram schools. These are study programs in which students toil after normal school hours to prepare for college entrance exams. South Korea has the world's most rapidly rising rate of youth suicide.† The exams are administered on only one day each year, and young people who score poorly may find the shame unbearable.

We obviously need a reevaluation of what counts as success in life, and I tried to address this issue in Chapter 4. The student who experienced the previously described dilemma, however, is not in a position to change the values of her family and society. She must live in her world and decide how to prepare for the next exam.

To begin with, it is hard to see why using study drugs violates generalizability. The reason for using the drugs is to make better grades and secure

---

* An anonymous student submission, later posted to the author's blog ethicaldecisions.net.
† World Health Organization, *Preventing Suicide: a Global Imperative*, 2014.

a better job. Drugs would still improve one's job prospects even if everyone were using them. In fact, they would become essential. Using drugs is not like cheating, because if cheating were universal, grades would have no meaning. Universal usage of study drugs would not have this effect, because those who are more capable or better prepared would still tend to make higher grades.

We may feel that drug use is "unfair" because students on the drugs may make higher grades than students with equal knowledge or ability who are not on drugs. But the same is true of students who maintain a healthy diet or get a good night's sleep before the exam, and we don't regard these habits as unfair. In any case, we can't make ethical judgments on what seems "fair," because there is no clear criterion for fairness. We must apply the ethical tests.

Returning to the generalization test, there is a temptation to compare taking study drugs with doping in an athletic contest, which is not generalizable. But the two are not the same. Doping violates the rules of the game and therefore breaks one's promise to abide by the rules when entering the game. Promise breaking, solely for personal gain, is not generalizable. University education is not a race, even if many students view it as one. It is true that students implicitly promise to observe school rules when they matriculate, and if study drugs violate the rules, then using them is as unethical as doping. However, I know of no universities that ban study drugs (such a rule would be impossible to enforce), although some try to regulate the use of stimulants prescribed by their own clinics. Study drugs are frequently obtained illegally, and this is probably unethical, but the issue here is whether it is ethical to use the drugs even if they are obtained legally. We have established that the practice is generalizable, as long it is consistent with school rules.

Study drugs raise a utilitarian issue, however, because they are unhealthy. They can impair working memory, multitasking ability, and neural plasticity over the long term.[*] This not only degrades quality of life but could reduce one's ability to make positive contributions in the future. There is a similar issue with frequent all-nighters or other activity that compromises health for the sake of career success. If one must abuse one's body to prepare for a career that will save lives, then the net utilitarian payoff may

---

[*] K. R. Urban and W. J. Gao, Performance enhancement at the cost of potential brain plasticity: Neural ramifications of nootropic drugs in the healthy developing brain, *Frontiers in Systems Neuroscience* 8 (2014): 38.

be positive, but not if one simply wants to land a job at Google or Goldman Sachs. Again, there may be ethical problems with priorities that lead one to use study drugs, but that is another issue. The drug use itself is unethical because it reduces net utility.

SPONSORED STUDENT SEEKS ANOTHER JOB

Companies frequently sponsor their employees in business and other schools, on the theory that they benefit from better-trained workers. No company wants to pay out a fortune for tuition only to see sponsored employees flee to better jobs at other companies, however. So the companies often require some kind of commitment from the sponsored student.

So it was for a Japanese student I will call Hiroshi. His company sponsored his MBA degree at a U.S. business school and, in return, required him to remain at the company for at least five years or else refund the tuition cost. However, Hiroshi received an opportunity to take an attractive job in the United States. Even though his agreement contains a provision that would allow this, he feels uneasy about abandoning the company.*

On the face of it, there is no ethical problem because Hiroshi doesn't propose to violate his contract. He would only use the escape clause that allows him to refund the tuition cost.

Hiroshi may nonetheless be concerned about generalizability, because companies might stop sponsoring study if employees jumped ship (and refunded tuition cost) whenever it is beneficial to their careers. If so, Hiroshi probably wouldn't have earned his new degree in the first place, and leaving the company probably would not have benefited his career.

However, company-sponsored study has been commonplace for some time, and employees have evidently not been leaving often enough to induce their companies to discontinue the programs. This suggests that leaving whenever convenient is generalizable because it is already generalized, but what matters is the rationale. If employees have in fact been willing to leave whenever it is convenient, but it has only occasionally been convenient, then leaving for this reason is generalizable. On the other hand, if employees have been reluctant to leave because they see it as unethical (or some other reason), and would have left in droves otherwise, then leaving solely for convenience is not generalizable.

---

* A dilemma submitted by a student who experienced it.

We really don't know why employees do what they do, but we don't have to know. The test is whether one *can rationally believe* that employees generally stick with the company because they find this beneficial to their careers. This belief is probably rational in a U.S. context, in which case leaving the company is generalizable. Hiroshi is from Japan, however, where company loyalty is taken more seriously. It may well be the case that employees generally stay with this company when they study abroad because of a sense of loyalty to the company, and not because this is necessarily beneficial to their careers. If these Japanese employees were to act solely in self-interest, most of them might relocate to the United States, and the company would have stopped funding foreign study a long time ago. If so, it is unethical for Hiroshi to abandon his company.

UNMENTIONED PLANS

Dilemmas frequently arise when employees are reluctant to reveal their educational plans to employers. An intention to quit work at some point to pursue an advanced degree could kill an employee's chances for a promotion or a training opportunity. On the other hand, perhaps the company deserves to know about such plans before investing further in an employee. Here is a dilemma along these lines.

It is October, and Boris is in his third year at a large accounting firm. He doesn't like his heavy workload and therefore applies for several MBA programs. He expects to enroll in one of them next fall. Meanwhile, a firm partner in charge of staff development, Julie, tells him about five-month internships at overseas offices. The requirements for the assignment include language fluency and long-term career potential at the firm. Julie says she can probably get him the assignment at the Moscow office due to his fluency in Russian. Boris is excited about the opportunity because he has relatives in the Moscow area. He decides not to tell Julie about his MBA plans.[*]

To make the case interesting, let's suppose that there is no formal application process, because it might oblige Boris to indicate that he satisfies the requirements (in particular, long-term potential for the firm). This would

---

[*] Based on C. L. Rooney and M. Loyland, To go or not to go, in *Business Ethics Program, Vol. 6: Minicases*, Chicago, IL, Arthur Andersen and Company, 1992 (unpublished).

be deceptive and unethical. Rather, let's suppose that it is completely up to Julie to decide whether Boris meets the requirements and to make a recommendation on that basis.

Boris might say that it is Julie's responsibility to ascertain whether he is suitable for the assignment. If she fails to ask the right questions, that is her problem, and he is off the hook. The problem with this argument is the last step. Granting that Julie has a duty to vet Boris for the position, it doesn't follow that he has no responsibilities.

We are getting nowhere, so let's apply the generalization test. Boris's reason for failing to give advance notice of his departure is to enjoy a company benefit that would otherwise be unavailable. That benefit could be a raise, promotion, or special assignment as in this case. Suppose all employees failed to give notice of departure months in advance when this would allow them to take advantage of a company benefit. Probably, they would still be able to enjoy the benefit. It is unlikely that companies would start requiring employees to give advance notice or imposing penalties when they fail to do so. Companies would too seldom have a way of determining when employees *knew* they would be leaving. So far, there is no ethical problem with Boris's behavior.

There could be a utilitarian issue. Departure without substantial advance notice could harm the company without benefiting the employee and others to an equal degree, perhaps because the employee is deeply involved in a project. In such cases, employees should alert the company—but not before they themselves are sure they are leaving, because otherwise they could trigger adjustments that are costly and unnecessary. In Boris's case, his acceptance of the Moscow assignment, in place of a long-term employee, could conceivably impose an opportunity cost on the company. Yet this seems unlikely, because he appears to be the only Russian speaker around. If so, he has no utilitarian obligation to tell the company his plans.

There is something special about this particular company benefit, however. One of the express requirements for the position is that the employee should have long-term potential for the firm. Normally, taking a job implies an assurance that the applicant at least believes he or she meets the job requirements. If I take a job as a truck driver but can't drive a truck, I am dishonest with my employer.

Yet there is a difference between meeting a requirement in the sense of an inherent qualification (ability to drive a truck) and a condition imposed by the company. Suppose the trucking company's want ad lists commercial experience as a requirement for the job. I can drive a truck very well and am fully capable of doing the job, but I have no commercial experience. If the company hires me without asking about my experience, then I am not dishonest in taking the job, because there is no implicit promise that I have commercial experience.

Is this the situation for Boris? He might argue that he is eminently qualified for the Russian position. He doesn't meet all the stated conditions, but the company selected him without asking questions. His taking the position therefore doesn't imply dishonesty, as in the case of the truck driver without commercial experience. On the other hand, Julie might view long-term potential for the firm as an inherent qualification for the assignment, like the ability to drive a truck.

So I think we can conclude the matter as follows. If there is no point in sending to Moscow an employee who will soon leave the firm (as there is no point in hiring a truck driver who can't drive a truck), then Boris is inherently unqualified for the assignment and should speak up about his plans. On the other hand, if he can make useful contacts for the firm while in Moscow, or perform some other useful service, then giving him the assignment is not pointless, and he can ethically accept the assignment.

TEACHING FOR FRAUD

I close the chapter with a teaching dilemma. It comes in many forms, but I will relate a variation of it I heard from an MBA student, whom I will call Bernard. Bernard was a Peace Corps volunteer in a country known for widespread corruption. He spent a year in a small city, trying to learn the language and customs. In the process, he got to know the owner of a local poultry farm. It was the one of the largest employers in town, with roughly 300 employees. Bernard estimated that the farm could employ twice as many if it were properly managed. He began meeting with the farm's accountant and discovered that he owned a computer, at which point Bernard began to teach him to set up an accounting system using Excel spreadsheets.

The accountant quickly saw the value of what he was learning and even stopped drinking heavily before training sessions. This was encouraging, but Bernard got the strong impression that the accountant wanted to prepare multiple sets of books: one for investors, one for tax officials, and one for internal management. Only the last would bear any resemblance to the truth.

Bernard concluded that if he taught his charge enough to upgrade the poultry operation, he would use the same knowledge to commit fraud.

The accountant's intended fraud is clearly unethical because it is deceptive. The question here, however, is whether it is ethical to teach him a tool he will use for fraud. We can't simply say it is unethical because it makes an unethical act possible. Otherwise if the accountant falls ill, it would be unethical for a doctor to give him penicillin.

We teachers face this issue all the time. Some of our students will use what we teach for unethical purposes. Some may even use knowledge of ethics to defend unethical practices with clever arguments. My approach to this conundrum is to apply to teaching the ethical tests I teach.

Nearly any teaching activity passes a generalization test. The purpose of teaching, let's say, is to impart knowledge. Would this be possible if all accounting teachers taught spreadsheets to unscrupulous students? Certainly. It would be possible even if all munitions instructors taught bomb science to terrorists.

However, teaching bomb science to terrorists is likely to reduce utility and violate autonomy, while teaching ethics to MBAs may increase utility. Whereas some educators insist that dissemination of knowledge is always positive on balance, this is simply implausible. There is no ethical substitute for making some kind of judgment, case by case. Bernard must assess, as best he can, whether the accountant's new knowledge will do more harm than good. I make a similar judgment, as best I can, every time I walk into a classroom.

10

Job Search Ethics

Most of us rely on a job for our livelihood, either our own job or that of a family member. Searching for a job, keeping our jobs, and advancing to a better job are central concerns in our lives. Because jobs entail complex relationships with other people, they constantly raise ethical issues. There can be much at stake in how they are resolved, because we rely so heavily on a job-based economy. In this chapter I take up some issues related to the job search, and in the next chapter issues that arise on the job.

SHARING INTERVIEW QUESTIONS

Not a great deal is at stake in this first dilemma, but it nonetheless receives more hits than any other issue on my ethics blog. Apparently, it is not only a common ethical dilemma, but one that many people *recognize* as an ethical dilemma.

The issue was raised by one of my MBA students, whom I will call Consuela. She observed that when employers conduct job interviews at her business school, students habitually tip off their classmates about what the interviewers asked. Consuela is unsure this is ethical.

There are actually two issues here: (a) Should Consuela share interview questions with another student? and (b) should she obtain the questions from another student who offers them? Both pass the generalization test rather easily. The purpose of (a) is to allow other students to make a better impression than they would otherwise. Consuela could still achieve this if everyone were sharing questions. Similarly for (b).

Sharing questions may occasionally fail the utilitarian test. If Consuela shares questions with people who are less qualified than she, then perhaps the company is more likely to make a suboptimal choice, which would make (a) nonutilitarian. A similar point holds for (b) if she obtains questions from someone more qualified than she—although in this case she could restore utility by withdrawing her application!

However, if Consuela really doesn't know who is better qualified for the job, it is hard to find an ethical problem with sharing questions.

It is interesting that many people concern themselves with innocuous conduct like this, at least as measured by my blog hits, while giving less attention to a host of more consequential issues. Perhaps it is because we live in a competitive world in which we are conditioned to view so much of life as a contest. We are sensitized to whether a practice is "fair" or provides "a level playing field." But as in so many cases I discuss in this book, there are no clear criteria for what is "fair." If I enter an athletic contest, I promise to abide by the explicitly stated rules of the competition (fair or not). But interviewing for a job is not such a contest. Certainly, a functioning job market and interview process rely on certain types of behavior, and departure from this behavior for the sake of getting a job is not generalizable. I should tell the truth in interviews, negotiate in good faith, honor employment contracts, and so forth, because if everyone violated these precepts, I would not be able to achieve my purpose in entering the job market. But sharing interview questions does not undermine the process. It only makes life a little more complicated for interviewers.

RENEGING ON THE EMPLOYMENT CONTRACT

I just mentioned that honoring employment contracts is essential to a functioning job market. This deserves a closer look, because I find that many people doubt this—especially when a better job offer beckons. I will take you through an analysis I frequently use in my courses, because it teaches some useful lessons in ethical reasoning.

The dilemma concerns Jennifer, who is nearing graduation and looking for a job. She learns about an attractive opening in a New York City bank. The firm is enthusiastic about her, but before it can make an offer, a global credit freeze forces it to suspend all hiring. Meanwhile, she receives another offer or two, and it's getting late in the semester. Her classmates are bragging about their good jobs, and her parents are keen to see a return on their investment in her education. She finally yields to pressure and takes an unglamorous job at a consulting firm in a less exciting city.

You can guess what is coming. Several weeks later, Jennifer gets a phone call from the bank in New York City. Thanks to a taxpayer-funded bailout, they are hiring again, and they urge Jennifer to accept their employment offer. She says, "Ah, let me get back to you on that."

Jennifer has a dilemma. She's already signed with one firm, weeks ago, and they are expecting her to show up for the first day of work. On the other hand, she really wants the job in New York, which seems so much better suited to her abilities and aspirations. Her friends are pushing her to get real, forget about the dead-end consulting job, and sign with the bank.

As you might expect, most of my students want the analysis of this dilemma to come out a certain way. This is the first lesson it teaches. When we don't like the outcome of an ethical analysis, we are inclined to reject the theory that leads to it (not to mention the course that teaches the theory). But we should be prepared to dislike what ethics tells us, and adjust our thinking as necessary. Otherwise, ethical reasoning is a meaningless rubber stamp on our preconceived notions.

My personal approach is to avoid forming opinions on ethical issues altogether, even after I have analyzed them. Then I don't have to worry about being wrong when I think about an issue. I simply acknowledge the result of the analysis so far, a result I may later revise if I find a weakness in the analysis. Naturally, when the time comes to act, I must make a call, but up to that point, there is really no need to form an opinion. This is difficult advice for us to take in an age of opinion polls, when we are called upon to express opinions on matters we know little about and think this is perfectly okay. But a habit of forgoing casual opinions helps us to avoid an ego investment in particular views. It opens our minds to objective analysis.

Returning to Jennifer's dilemma, I am going to grant that taking the New York job is the utilitarian choice. I will assume that the consulting firm will find a suitable replacement, Jennifer will suffer no negative consequences from breaking the contract, and she will create more utility for herself and her customers by taking the job she prefers.

That brings us to the generalization test. To apply it, we have to look at Jennifer's reason for breaking her employment contract. It is pretty simple: She wants a better job. At this point the argument becomes familiar. Jennifer wants a meaningful employment contract from the bank in New York City. She wants them to promise her a job, and she wants that job to be there when she shows up. However, when the consulting firm is ready to start *her* employment, they want her to be there as well—but she's going to blow that off. If everyone followed Jennifer's example of ignoring employment contracts when convenient, contracts would lose their point, and the social practice of making contracts would break down. Jennifer would not be able to achieve her purpose in breaking the consulting contract, because she would be unable to secure a meaningful promise from the New York bank. Her breach of contract is ungeneralizable and unethical, even though it is utilitarian.

My students are ready with a response. Employment contracts contain escape clauses that allow one to resign after giving notice, turn down the job by forfeiting the signing bonus, and so forth. Or the contract may contain employment-at-will language that doesn't actually promise employment, but only promises a certain salary if one is employed. So Jennifer can probably slip out of her commitment legally.

The problem is that there is more than a legal contract involved. There is a job market in which Jennifer wants to participate. A job market is a social practice in which firms say, "I am offering you this job," and they mean it, and in which applicants say, "I'm going to take this job," and they mean it. If people didn't mean it, if they reneged on their commitment whenever it is convenient, the job market in which Jennifer wants to participate would not exist.

It would be like auction in which bids and acceptances are nonbinding. Suppose the auctioneer takes a final bid and says, "Sold!" Then someone in the audience says, "Hey, wait a minute. I'd like to bid, too." The auctioneer responds, "Okay, I'll take just one more bid. Sold!" But that night, he receives another bid by telephone and reluctantly accepts it, with a vow that it is really the final bid. Obviously, this kind of auction won't work, because people never know when they have bought the merchandise.

It's the same for a job market. When people say, "I'm hiring you," or "I'm working for you," they have to mean it, or the whole thing will break down. Jennifer will show up on the first day at work in New York City, and they'll say, "Jennifer, I hope you read your contract carefully. You will note the employment-at-will language. As it happens, we don't have a job for you." Jennifer will respond, "Now wait a minute! You told me I have a job! I rented an apartment, I moved my husband here, and you're telling me the job doesn't exist?" There's something wrong here, and what is wrong is that reneging on employment agreements is not generalizable.

There may yet be an ethical escape for Jennifer, however. She can ethically vacate her contract with the consulting firm if there is mutual consent. If the firm finds someone who is equally or better for the position, for example, it may be quite willing to release Jennifer from her obligation. This is generalizable, because parties can regularly nullify contracts, by mutual consent and when it is mutually convenient, without undermining the institution of contracts. They do so already. However, there must in fact be mutual consent. If the firm says, "Well, Jennifer, we see we're going to lose you anyway, so go ahead," with a wave of the hand, that's not mutual consent.

INVENTING A JOB OFFER

One of my MBA students, whom I will call Joe, interviewed with a company for a summer internship. He was impressed by the company and wanted an offer; however, he knew that the company is slow at getting back to candidates. A couple of days after the interview, he called the company and told them that he had an outstanding offer and really needed to hear from them promptly. The ruse worked, as he received an offer with minimal delay. Joe summed up the affair as follows: "I know this was unethical, but it helped me get the internship, and I do not regret it."

This might be classified as a "white" lie because it is victimless and nudged the company into providing the kind of timely response it should provide in any case. Yet as Joe noted, it is unethical, although I doubt that he knew why. It is unethical because it is transparently ungeneralizable. If the invention of job offers were universal practice, the company will either ignore his request or demand to see a copy of the offer letter, either of which would defeat Joe's purpose in lying.

There is much at stake in a job search, and a utilitarian calculation may call for actions that would ordinarily be unethical for utilitarian reasons. When a company is dilatory, it may be all right to pester recruiters in an obnoxious fashion that would ordinarily be out of line. Such tactics must be evaluated on a case-by-case basis. Joe's tactic may be utilitarian, but it fails the generalization test.

Joe's cavalier attitude toward ethics is chilling. He will take whatever steps improve his bottom line. If they are right, fine, but if they are wrong, that's fine, too. It is not hard to imagine Joe involved in a future business scandal, if he judges himself smart enough to benefit and get away with it. There is clearly no point in trying to convince Joe his behavior is unethical, because he already concedes this. He just doesn't care.

It is easy to misdiagnose Joe's situation, however. We are tempted to say that Joe is ruled by hardheaded logic and lacks the kind of sentiment we find in ethical people. This, however, is not the problem. Joe's calculation of the bottom line may be hardheaded and logical, but his overall decision calculus is riddled with incoherence and confusion. He fails to see the overt logical inconsistency in his dishonesty, a kind of inconsistency that I have taken pains to expose throughout this book.

As Joe illustrates, we can teach ourselves to be logical in some matters and incoherent in others. We human beings have amply demonstrated, after all, our ability to master doublethink. However, we can also teach ourselves to be logical across the board, and if we do, ethics will benefit.

PADDING THE RESUME

Steve is putting together his resume for a job search in data analytics. His only work experience in the industry is a summer internship at Global Informatics, where his job title was *Data Analyst*. In reality, however, he was called on to do little more than serve coffee and sit in on meetings in which he had no opportunity to contribute. Nonetheless, he sees no problem in listing *Data Analyst* on his resume, because it was, after all, his job title.*

Students have told me that "everyone" pads the resume, recruiters expect it, and if you don't follow this practice, they will award the job to someone else. No one is deceived by exaggeration, they say, and in fact, a resume that *fails* to exaggerate is deceptive, because it leads people to underestimate your qualifications relative to others.

The element of deception is key. Granting that *Data Analyst* was the actual job title, what matters is whether listing the actual title deceives anyone. Absent a general practice of exaggeration, it clearly does. Steve could simply list a "summer internship at Global Informatics," which deceives no one, but he wants recruiters to believe (falsely) that he analyzed data for the company.

To defend his resume padding, Steve must argue that recruiters expect this kind of exaggeration and are not misled by it. The problem is defining what exactly is *expected*. At what point does innocuous exaggeration

---

* An actual dilemma contributed by one of my students.

become deception? If Steve were to list an internship that never existed, we would say that he crossed the line. Perhaps it is because the recruiter can easily check this, while it is harder to verify what Steve actually did while an intern. Do we want to say that recruiters expect the truth when they can verify it, but expect exaggeration when it is hard to check? This is dubious. If Steve claimed that he was a volunteer tutor of disadvantaged youth, when he actually tutored only one person for 15 minutes, it is hard to check on his claim, but no one would expect him to make it up. We might say that recruiters expect "minor" or "harmless" exaggeration, but what does that mean?

Given the elasticity of the concept, Steve can't rationally claim that "exaggeration is expected" unless he has specific evidence for a specific kind of exaggeration. If information technology firms routinely use the title *Data Analyst* for internships, no matter what the intern does, then it is perfectly acceptable for Steve to list the title even though it exaggerates his contribution. He can reasonably assume that recruiters in the industry know about this practice and are not misled.

Steve will respond that even if he has no specific evidence that recruiters expect padding, he must exaggerate nonetheless. "Everyone else" is padding resumes, and if he doesn't play the game, he will mislead recruiters about his qualifications relative to others. This recalls the situation of Olivia in the previous chapter. Her honesty on quizzes misled the instructor about her standing in the class, because "everyone else" was cheating. Simply refusing to take the quiz was unethical because of the disutility of making a zero. Her only ethical alternative was to tip off the instructor (anonymously) about what was going on before the next quiz. Then even if she cheated next time, no one would be deceived.

As with cheating, when people say "everyone else" is padding resumes, this is probably itself a gross exaggeration. Nonetheless, let's play along and suppose that it really is the norm among Steve's peers. Unfortunately, Olivia's escape route is not open to him. If he sent an alert to all recruiters in the industry about how people pad their resumes, they would dismiss it as kooky email. So he is stuck in a situation in which padding the resume is deceptive, and not padding it is deceptive. If this is really the situation, we are talking about corruption, pure and simple. Steve should not be part of it unless he can somehow circumvent the deception.

In reality, the choice is rarely (if ever) so stark. Honesty can be competitive, if one is reasonably qualified for the job to begin with. Rather than write a boilerplate resume, Steve can creatively focus on his true strengths with an intensity that puts him in the running with candidates who embellish theirs. This would avoid any deception, and it should be easy for Steve, because a less-than-ideal internship is a minor item that other factors can easily offset. He could also look into another segment of the industry, or work through connections that can help him find a job without misrepresenting his abilities. If it is impossible to play it clean, however, then he should steer clear of the business, just as he should steer clear of bunco or shakedown rackets.

Having dealt with issues related to the job search, we consider in the next chapter some issues that arise on the job.

11

Ethics on the Job

Job hunting raises a variety of ethical dilemmas, as we saw in the previous chapter. The dilemmas don't stop when that much-coveted job is secured. Many of them relate to how individual employees should respond when pressured to make ethical compromises. The dilemmas considered here deal with accepting gifts, dealing with sexual harassment, managing confidential information, surreptitiously obtaining information from competitors, and following instructions to that require one to mislead customers. In the process it examines the general issues of when we are responsible for the unethical behavior of others, the role of autonomy in the workplace, the meaning of confidentiality, and the age-old question of whether it can ever be ethical to lie.

ACCEPTING FREE TICKETS

Promotional gifts, so common in the business world, create a steady stream of little ethical dilemmas. Let's examine a few of these, partly because they exercise our ethical thought muscles in a context relatively free of emotion and bias, and partly because they come up so frequently.

It is common practice in Joe's industry for suppliers to entertain customers, with the expectation they will use the opportunity to "talk shop." Barbara is a customer representative who sells to Joe's company. She gave Joe and his girlfriend hockey tickets and suggested that they meet at the game. While Joe and his companion were on the way to the arena, Barbara rang Joe's mobile to say that she couldn't make it due to a personal problem. She told him to go ahead and enjoy the game and take full advantage of the expensive club level seats. The question is: Is it okay for Joe to use the tickets?*

Attending the game is clearly utilitarian. The tickets have already been purchased and are not refundable. A decision to attend the game affects only Joe and his girlfriend, and it is better to enjoy the game than waste the tickets.

True, there is an implicit agreement in this kind of situation. Barbara gave Joe the tickets on the assumption that Joe would listen to her sales pitch, or at least form a stronger business relationship, and Joe may well have an obligation to hear her out. But he can do this in some other setting, whether or not he attends the hockey game.

Some may see accepting hockey tickets as a violation of professional ethics. As discussed in Chapter 8, professional ethics is based on an obligation to live up to expectations the profession has created in the public mind. Accepting a gift is a breach of professional ethics if the relevant public expects purchasing agents to avoid real or apparent conflicts of interest. Joe has already accepted the tickets, but he could decline to use them if attending the game creates the wrong impression. Attending the game *with* Barbara is consistent with industry practice and therefore presumably meets the expectations of stockholders and other interested parties. Attending the game *without* her could create the wrong impression, but this seems unlikely, because no one will know how Joe got the tickets. As I see it, Joe and his girlfriend can enjoy the action on the ice with a clean conscience.

Now let's change the facts a bit. Barbara has not yet given Joe the tickets, and she phones Joe a couple of days before the game to say that she can't make it. Nonetheless, she will have her company purchase tickets for Joe and his girlfriend. Does the timing of the ticket purchase make a difference?

The timing makes a difference to the utilitarian calculation. The ticket money comes out of someone's pockets, perhaps those of stockholders or employees. If they lose more utility than Joe gains, the company shouldn't buy tickets for him. This differs from the original scenario, in which the ticket cost is sunk, and the tickets should not be wasted. Transferring the ticket value from the company to Joe seems roughly a wash, so far as Joe can reasonably determine, because Joe and his girlfriend will gain roughly what the stockholders lose. If so, attending the game passes the utilitarian test.

---

* Based on actual dilemma submitted by an MBA student.

Professional obligation is a little different now, too, because the tickets are intended as an outright gift rather than an outing with the sales rep. Whereas company policies on gifts differ, modest gifts (perhaps with a company logo) are often permitted. Yet, if these hockey tickets are as expensive as in my city, we are talking about a fairly substantial gift. The first step is for Joe to check if his company has a gift policy. If not, professional obligation probably requires declining the tickets, unless there is a clearly established and accepted practice in the industry of accepting gifts of this size, and there is no evidence that these gifts affect purchase decisions.

Finally, let's suppose that Joe's company already has a long-term contract with a competing supplier, and there is no chance it will source from Barbara's company. Barbara is unaware of this, and she phones Joe a couple of days before the game to invite him and his girlfriend. Joe, being the honest Joe he is, reveals the situation to Barbara, but she tells him not to worry about it. She and her husband would like to enjoy the game with Joe and his girlfriend. Should they go along?

Barbara's conduct is questionable, because it may violate a company policy of entertaining potential customers only, and Joe is no longer a potential customer. But we are talking about what Joe should do, not Barbara. There is no longer a potential conflict of interest for Joe, because there is no chance that his judgment will be influenced by the gift. However, professional obligation probably requires him to decline the tickets, as in the previous scenario, unless accepting them is consistent with accepted industry practice.

Whatever the outcome of this analysis, Joe may feel uneasy about associating himself with Barbara's questionable conduct. Isn't complicity in unethical behavior itself unethical? Often it is, but feelings are an unreliable guide. Each situation must be evaluated on the merits. In this case, Barbara's behavior is questionable because she is bound by her employment contract with her company, which at least implicitly provides that she abide by company policy. Joe has no agreement with her company and therefore violates no agreement by using the hockey tickets. It would be unethical (and perhaps illegal) to aid and abet Barbara in defrauding her company, if that is what she is doing, but Barbara is securing the tickets on her own, without Joe's assistance.

The basic lesson here is that there is no general obligation to discourage or prevent others from performing behavior simply because the behavior is unethical for *them*. Accepting Barbara's hockey invitation could be disutilitarian because the ticket money could perhaps create more overall utility if spent on something that benefits the company as well as the guest. Also accepting the tickets could increase the chance of Barbara's getting into trouble for misuse of company funds. These considerations argue rather convincingly against accepting the tickets, but not simply because Barbara's behavior is unethical. It is because *Joe's* action of accepting the tickets has bad consequences. The ethical analysis is applied to Joe's action, not Barbara's.

SEXUAL HARASSMENT

Everyone knows that sexual harassment is politically incorrect, but do we really know why it is wrong? A case study will give us an opportunity to clarify this, as well as explore the role of autonomy in the workplace. The case comes from a male employee with several years of work experience. He described a situation faced by a female colleague I will call Mary. I will reproduce his account almost verbatim.

About a year ago, Mary joined a company in which few women have leadership roles. She nonetheless has a desire to advance, and she immediately sought out a meeting with Tom, a vice president, in an attempt to gain visibility and better align herself with the company priorities. As a result, Tom assigned her a few additional projects and recommended her for a training program that could lead to a promotion. However, Tom has also started texting and calling Mary, sometimes at night or on weekends. He even suggested that they run a race together in another city. Mary is not married, but Tom is. She finds the contact to be inappropriate but fears that saying anything, even to him, will limit her opportunities at the company. She is also concerned that, by initiating a meeting with Tom, she bears some responsibility.

There are two issues here: What exactly is wrong with Tom's behavior, and what should Mary do about it? The concern with Tom's behavior is not only where it is now, but where it seems to be headed. One possible direction is toward marital infidelity, which has ethical problems of its own, but I will focus on the sexual harassment issue. Tom may not intend to leverage his position in the company to pressure Mary into a relationship, but his unwanted overtures nonetheless have this effect, and they may escalate. They fit the definition of a violation of autonomy (Chapter 6), because

Tom's action plan is inconsistent with Mary's action plan. Mary wants to strive for success at the company without forming a personal relationship with Tom, and she believes she will be obliged to abandon this plan if Tom keeps it up. Tom might protest that he has no intent to pressure Mary, and that her career will be unaffected if she spurns his advances. What matters for autonomy, however, is what Mary reasonably perceives Tom to be doing. If a bank robber points a gun at a teller and demands cash, there is violation of autonomy whether or not the gun is actually loaded. What matters is that the teller reasonably believes the threat is real.

Interfering with Mary's action plan is permissible if the plan is unethical (and therefore not really an action plan), or if she has given implied consent. There is certainly no reason to believe her plan is unethical. To judge the matter of implied consent, it is helpful to think about some analogous situations.

Suppose Tom pressures Mary to transfer to an office in another city, due to changes in market demand. He doesn't actually say her career success depends on it, but she fears (with some justification) that it does. This is not coercion, because there is implied consent. She knows that a company must make business decisions. Her decision to work for the company implies a decision to live with those decisions. So if Mary is forced to transfer or quit the job, this is consistent with her action choice. She signed on to this possibility and consents to having to deal with it. The Principle of Informed Consent (Chapter 6) tells us that Tom's action is no violation of autonomy.

Now suppose Tom pressures Mary to contribute to a political campaign through the company. Tom never says that this will affect her career, but she fears (with some justification) that it will. This time, there is no implied consent, because willingness to make political contributions is not a business-related standard for success at the company. Mary never *signed on* to dealing with this type of criterion.

A personal relationship is like the political contribution. Employees expect their career to depend on business performance, not personal relationships. Mary never signed on to face a choice between advancing her career and forming a personal relationship. The fact that she sought a meeting with Tom did not signal willingness to form a relationship; it only signaled ambition. So Tom's advances are unethical. The problem is not with the sexual element, because the same point applies to either sex. It would be unethical for Tom to pressure a male employee to be a golf buddy, for the same reason. The problem is with the violation of autonomy.

So what is Mary to do? We must recognize that ethics doesn't tell us how to solve all our problems. It only tells us what is ethical. In Tom's case, it tells us that his personal advances are wrong. In Mary's case, it tells her that she has no obligation to yield to his advances, because this is not part of her implied employment contract. Ethics doesn't tell her how she can assure her advancement in the company without humoring Tom.

CONFIDENTIAL SALARY INFORMATION

The next dilemma, experienced by a former MBA student I will call Ashley, provides an opportunity to explore the concept of confidentiality. Ashley was coming up for a performance review, which included a discussion of her salary. While searching her company's intranet site to download the review form, she came across a file containing salary and benefit information for almost every employee in the company. She viewed the file purely by accident and broke no company rules by accessing it. The human resources department was responsible for maintaining the confidentiality of this information but had mistakenly placed it in an unprotected area. Ashley saw that she was receiving a considerably lower salary than her peers, many of whom held less responsibility. Is it acceptable for her to use this salary information during her annual review?

Let's think about what confidentiality is. Confidential information is provided *in confidence*, meaning that the person who hands it over is confident it will not be revealed to others. This is different from *secret* information, which is merely information that is concealed from others. Receiving confidential information implies a promise not to reveal it, because otherwise it would not have been handed over. Revealing the information is not generalizable, because if people never honored their confidentiality promise, it would be impossible to hear juicy stories in confidence. Receiving secret information, on the other hand, may or may not incur an obligation.

Ashley did not receive the salary information in confidence. No one handed it over on the understanding that she would keep it secret. Some HR employees received the information in confidence and are obligated to keep it secret, but Ashely didn't. So the usual confidentiality obligation doesn't apply to her. She did receive secret information, or information that was supposed to be secret, and we can ask whether she has an obligation to keep it secret. Perhaps she does, for utilitarian reasons, because broadcasting salary information could create havoc in the company. However, if her intent is to use the information only during an interview with her boss, who presumably is already familiar with salary levels, it will remain secret. So far, she is in the clear.

Ashley must nonetheless apply the generalization test to her specific situation. We can suppose that her reasons for using the salary information are that it may help her negotiate a better salary, she came across the information accidentally, and she won't violate confidentiality or compromise secrecy by using it. Could she still achieve her purpose if everyone who came across secret information under these circumstances made use of it? There is no clear reason why not, particularly because accidental discoveries of this kind are rare. The action is generalizable. Furthermore, nothing in the case description suggests that using the information would reduce overall utility. It passes the utilitarian test as well.

It's not clear exactly how the interview with Ashley's boss would go. She would presumably explain how she came across so much salary information and convince the boss it was purely accidental. In fact, she may have a utilitarian obligation to alert the company to HR's oversight, and doing so in her interview would discharge this obligation. This obligation would apply even if she doesn't use the salary information, in which case she could perhaps tip off the company through an anonymous hot line, thus shielding herself from retaliation from HR for the embarrassment. She may in fact prefer this option, which is equally ethical, to the riskier prospect of using the information in her performance review. Ethics doesn't tell her which option to choose; only that both are ethical.

SPY OR CUSTOMER?

So many dilemmas in the workaday world revolve around what is deceptive and what isn't. I like the following little dilemma because it requires a particularly close analysis of the distinction.

Business Equipment Corporation (BEC) has developed a new technology for making multicolor copies. Kyle, product manager at BEC, went into a panic when he read that Hiyota, a competitor, plans to release a copier with similar capabilities. Kyle must find out exactly what the Hiyota machine can do as soon as possible, so he can give the production department new specifications. He asked his marketing consultant Lynn to make an appointment with a Hiyota sales representative and pretend to be a customer. During their discussion, she will obtain copy samples and learn as much as possible about product features, pricing, and marketing strategy. Lynn is hesitant about the ruse and doesn't want to waste the sales rep's time; however, Kyle insists that it is perfectly legal because no trade secrets will be stolen. People do this sort of thing all the time, and sales reps are accustomed to unproductive sales pitches. Who knows, the rep may convince Lynn to buy the new Hiyotas for her consulting company.*

This is not a case of spying, because the information gathered is already available to the public, at least through sales representatives. However, posing as a customer seems unethical on the ground that it is deceptive. If Lynn had no intention of deceiving the sales rep, then she would be willing to announce up front that she has no interest in buying the equipment (even for her own company) and, in fact, represents a competitor that wants to gather information about it.

To evaluate this claim, we must carefully distinguish the two facts just mentioned: (a) Lynn has no interest in buying the equipment, and (b) she represents a competitor that wants to gather information. Let's think about whether Lynn will cause the sales rep to believe that either of these is false. If so, she is deceptive. Proposition (b) is the easier one to evaluate. Lynn can convincingly argue that her pretense doesn't cause the sales rep to believe that she does *not* represent a competitor. It only *fails* to cause the rep to believe that she *does* represent a competitor. The sales rep probably doesn't form a belief one way or the other. So far, there is no deception.

Proposition (a) is trickier. We have to bear in mind that customers may ask about merchandise when they have no particular interest in buying it. They may only want to expose themselves to the product, in case they develop an interest in buying it, or they may simply be curious about the new technology. The sales rep will probably assume only this much about Lynn. He will assume that she has not ruled out the possibility of buying a copier for her own company, or she is personally curious about the technology. If this is true, perhaps because Kyle's request has piqued her interest in the copiers, then her meeting with the sales rep is in the ethical green zone. Otherwise, she is jerking him around.

---

* Based on N. Artz, I spy: A case of competitive espionage, in *Business Ethics Program, Vol. 6: Minicases*, Chicago, IL, Arthur Andersen and Company, 1992 (unpublished).

There is another angle, however. Kyle remarked that marketing people commonly pose as customers. This may have been intended only as rationalization, but it is ethically relevant. If this kind of thing really occurs, the sales rep may expect it as a possibility. He may know that Lynn could be a marketing consultant as well as a potential customer and is willing to go ahead with the sales pitch anyway. In this case, Lynn can avoid deception even if she has no personal curiosity about Hiyota copiers and would never buy one. She just has to avoid saying anything that implies otherwise.

This last requirement is trickier than it may seem, because the sales rep may start asking questions. "So, you're interested in buying one of our advanced copiers?" She can't say yes. "So what kind of features is your marketing firm looking for?" She can't just make something up. The questions may force her to come clean, if she is to remain honest. If she decides to go through with this whole charade, she must be prepared to come clean if the conversation demands it.

This affair is beginning to sound like the libretto of a Rossini opera, but intrigue is an indelible part of human behavior. We often play little games that tread the line between honesty and deception. Ethics must be capable of evaluating them.

MISLEADING NUMBERS

Another frequent on-the-job dilemma is how to respond when the boss asks you to do something questionable. These tend to be vexing cases, because the questionable behavior often seems minor when compared to the consequences of disobeying the boss. I will describe a case of this kind that I often use in classes and workshops. It is a real dilemma experienced by one of my MBA students. I found the dilemma rather hard to analyze, but ethics, like life, isn't always easy. It will also give us an opportunity to clarify the role of fiduciary duty in business, and to address the question of whether a lie can be ethical.

Jerry is employed by a large bank as a financial advisor. The bank itself has some investment products, such as mutual funds. It would naturally be pleased if advisors like Jerry convinced customers to buy the bank's own funds. There is an obvious potential here for conflict of interest, because financial advisors are supposed to give unbiased advice, whether or not it benefits the firm.

Part of Jerry's job is to write a report to send to the bank's customers. Among other things, the report contains information on the performance of the bank's mutual funds. It is not a legal filing, but only a means of staying in touch with customers and encouraging their loyalty. In particular, good news about the bank's funds might induce customers to invest in them. One day, Jerry's boss called him into the office, when no one else was around. (When my student wrote up the case, he was careful to say that it was a one-on-one conversation, with no paper trail and no email.) The boss said, "You know, one of our mutual funds is a real dog. It's not performing. Why don't you just leave that one out of the report, and focus on the other funds? There's no problem here, because everything you put in the report will be true. Besides, we have a fiduciary duty to maximize share value for our stockholders. That means that we have a duty to portray our funds in a positive light." Jerry is uncomfortable with this directive but is reluctant to challenge his boss.[*]

Let's first deal with this issue of fiduciary duty, because it comes up so frequently in business. There is a popular conception, particularly in the United States, that business ethics is all about fiduciary duty. The ethical duty of a business person is to maximize value for stockholders, period. This would make business ethics a lot simpler, but it simply isn't true. For one thing, it would mean that if I own my own business, I can forget about business ethics, because there are no stockholders. This is absurd.

Fiduciary duty plays an ethical role when there are stockholders, because there is an agency agreement between them and the executives and board members. The stockholders pay compensation to executives and board members, in exchange for a promise to act on their behalf while running the company. The word *fiduciary* is from the Latin for loyalty, meaning that fiduciaries should be loyal to their principals.

However, when an executive faces an ethical dilemma, the prior question is always this: What choice would be ethical for the stockholders themselves? The stockholders, after all, own the firm and are ultimately responsible for its policies. The executive must imagine that the owners are sitting in her corner office and personally making decisions for the company. If an action would be ethical for them, then fine, she can carry it out. But if the action would be unethical for the owners, there is

---

[*] Based on the case study, "Misleading numbers" in my book *Business Ethics as Rational Choice*, Boston, MA, Prentice Hall, (2011): 39–41. This is, in turn, based on an actual dilemma submitted by an MBA student.

scarcely an obligation to carry it out on their behalf. How can one be ethically obligated to do something unethical? One can't even promise to do something unethical, because one can promise only to perform an action, and unethical behavior is not action. This means, in particular, that a fiduciary never promises stockholders to carry out unethical actions on their behalf.

As for Jerry, he's not even a fiduciary to begin with, because he is neither a board member nor a top executive. Employees are implicitly bound by their employment contract to carry out company policy, rather than by a promise to act on stockholders' behalf. If a top executive instructs Jerry to take financially irresponsible actions, she is in breach of fiduciary duty, not Jerry. In fact, if Jerry refused to follow instructions, the company would have grounds to dismiss him.

Although Jerry is not a fiduciary, the same limitations apply to his employment obligations as to fiduciary obligations. He never promised to carry out unethical instructions from superiors, because one can't promise to do something unethical. He has no contractual obligation to obey his boss, if doing so forces him to act unethically.

So we must determine whether omitting a bad number is ethical, whether it is done by an owner or a fiduciary. This is an easy one. Leaving out the numbers is deceptive, and deception merely for convenience is ungeneralizable and therefore unethical. Earlier, I used the example of the doctor who sends me a lab report that leaves out the bad news. That's deceptive, because I would expect the doctor to tell me all the news. The whole point of leaving out the numbers is to deceive customers about how the funds are doing. In fact, we can try to generalize this case specifically. Suppose that financial institutions always omitted bad news from their reports. Then what would their customers do? They would throw the reports in the trash, because they would know it's all fluff. Omitting the numbers would no longer have the intended effect, and so it's ungeneralizable.

Given that it's unethical for an owner or fiduciary to leave out this number, let's move on to the harder question: What is Jerry supposed to do about it, given that he has orders from his boss? We might simply say that he should play it straight, because he has no contractual obligation to obey his boss in this case, and leaving out the number is deceptive. But is he supposed to risk his job because of one little number? If we piously declare that he should be honest no matter what, we are committed to preposterous judgments. Suppose the boss said, if you don't leave this number out, I'm going have my goons beat up your family, or worse. It's a little ridiculous to pay this kind of price for a small demonstration of honesty. There must be some limit to what one has to do to be honest. Ethics must tell us what that limit is, or else it's not much use.

Whether circumstances can justify deception is an old issue in ethics. The tragic case of Anne Frank is often cited in this connection.* As Jews in Nazi-occupied Amsterdam, Anne and her family found it necessary to hide in secret rooms of a commercial building during 1942–1944. Four employees of the business knew their secret and provided them with food and other necessities. The dilemma, often posed to show the rigidity of deontological ethics, is whether these employees should lie when authorities ask the whereabouts of the Franks. Kantian ethics, for example, frequently draws ridicule because it supposedly condemns lying under any circumstances.†

Whether or not Kant deserves this critique, the deontological theory I have presented easily accommodates the case. The employees should lie. They should tell the police that they don't know anything about the Franks. This is generalizable because the reason for lying is to conceal the location of innocent people from a murderous police state. If everyone in such a predicament were to lie in this fashion, police probably wouldn't believe the lies, but the location of the innocent people would remain concealed. The purpose of the lie is achieved, and it is therefore generalizable.

Let's see how the Generalization Principle applies to Jerry's case. Suppose that employees always caved in to the boss when asked to deceive clients. There would be a very strong temptation for bosses to take advantage of this, particularly since they could keep their own hands clean. This is what Jerry's boss is doing. He is speaking to Jerry in private because he wants

---

* A. Frank, *The Diary of a Young Girl*, Bantam, 1993. Originally published in 1947 as *Het Achterhuis. Dagboekbrieven 14 Juni 1942 – 1 Augustus 1944.*

† Critics typically cite Kant's 1797 essay, "On a supposed right to lie from philanthropy." It responds to an article of the same year by Benjamin Constant that poses a dilemma very much like that of Anne Frank's protectors. Kant is in fact very negative on lying in this and other writings, but a hardline prohibition against all lying is not obviously implied. The interpretive issue is discussed at length by David Sussman in "On the supposed duty of truthfulness," in C. W. Martin, (Ed.), *The Philosophy of Deception*, Oxford, Oxford University Press, 2009. Helga Varden rejects the hardline interpretation in "Kant and lying to the murderer at the door... One more time: Kant's legal philosophy and lies to murderers and Nazis," *Journal of Social Philosophy* 41 (2010): 403–421. Whatever the correct interpretation of Kantian texts, the Generalization Principle developed in this book readily accommodates exceptions, as in the Anne Frank case. It is true that the lie in this case passes generalizability because it can achieve its purpose without actually deceiving, but lies can also generalize when they deceive. The key lies in the rationale for the lie. In defense of Kant, he made a valid point by emphasizing the bedrock importance of general truthfulness. It is the precondition of all communication, and consequently all human relationships.

plausible deniability. This sort of behavior could become prevalent if employees automatically saluted and said, "Yes boss, right away, boss." In fact, I think that one reason that bosses don't often pressure us into ethical compromises more often than they do is that employees would balk. In particular, the good employees would balk, and no one wants to risk losing good employees. If everyone caved in, however, bosses would no longer have this deterrent. Deception could become routine, resulting in loss of credibility with customers. They would know through experience that employees will say anything for the company to keep their jobs. In particular, customers would no longer believe company literature, and this makes Jerry's obedience ungeneralizable. The argument here is not airtight, but it is hard to be rational in believing that universal obedience would have no such consequences.

Jerry might respond that obeying the boss is generalizable because, as with the Franks' protectors, he doesn't care whether the deception actually succeeds. He only wants to satisfy his boss. Maybe customers would no longer believe his brochure if employees always followed orders to deceive customers, but so much the better. He doesn't want customers to take it seriously anyway. What matters to him is whether he would still be able to humor his boss and keep his job. He would, on his view, and so his rationale is consistent with its universal adoption. This misrepresents the situation, however. The boss doesn't simply want a report with missing numbers. He wants a report that misleads customers about the performance of the bank's funds. Otherwise Jerry could write the defective report and then send an email to all the bank's customers to supply the missing numbers. This clearly would not please his boss. Deception is an integral part of his intention to please the boss and keep his job. Obedience is therefore ungeneralizable.

This analysis nonetheless fails to deal with the objection I raised earlier. Suppose the penalty for disobedience is much worse than a bad performance evaluation. Maybe the boss will order his goons to beat up Jerry's family, or to make things more realistic, Jerry's young daughter has a congenital illness that incurs very heavy medical expenses. He simply can't afford to risk his job for her sake. Is it generalizable to go along with the boss when the penalty for disobedience is this serious? Probably it is, because it's already generalized. Even now, practically everyone is willing to fudge a number (however reluctantly) to avoid extraordinary suffering for the family. The policy is already generalized, and despite that fact, bosses don't ask us to do such things. Even bosses inclined to do so might fear that behavior so odious would be traced to them, despite their efforts to cover their tracks. So yielding to pressure in such extraordinary cases is generalizable.

None of this relieves one of the obligation to escape such predicaments as soon as is practical, perhaps by seeking another job. Failure to do so could well fail to be generalizable. In any event, the analysis here suggests that there is, indeed, a limit to how much one must sacrifice to be honest, at least in the short run, and the generalization test helps to tell us more or less what that limit is.

12

Organizational Policy

I would now like to move on to issues that concern company policy, as opposed to dilemmas faced by individual employees. I begin with the Ford Pinto dilemma I presented at the beginning of the book. I then deal with the task of designing ethical policies for surge pricing, sourcing from low-wage factories, online privacy, publishing offensive material, and online self-censorship. These complex issues call on the full range of intellectual resources developed so far in the book.

EXPLODING GAS TANKS

We are now in a position to analyze the case of the Ford Pinto discussed at the beginning of the book. Recall that Ford had received reports that due to a design defect, the gas tank in its low-budget car would sometimes explode after a low-speed rear-end collision. Ford decided not to fix the problem in cars yet to be manufactured, even though it would cost only $11 per car. A major factor in the decision was a cost-benefit analysis, which went as follows.[*] The cost of fixing the defect was $11 per car, multiplied by a projected output of 12.5 million cars, for a total of $137.5 million. The benefit of fixing it was the avoidance of an estimated 180 deaths, 180 serious burn injuries, and 2100 destroyed cars. Assuming a cost of $200,000 per death, $67,000 per injury and $700 per car, the total benefit would be $49.53 million. The cost of a fix clearly outweighed the benefit.

---

[*] As described in D. A. Gioia, Pinto fires and personal ethics: A script analysis of missed opportunities, *Journal of Business Ethics* 11 (1992): 379–389.

Ford wasn't just computing cost and benefit to itself. It was factoring in the effects on potential crash victims. This makes the cost-benefit analysis a utilitarian analysis, which had a clear conclusion. The net expected utility of a fix was negative. One might object to placing a finite value on human life, but not only is this routinely done in policy planning, it is the only reasonable option. If a city, for example, placed infinite value on human life, it would be obligated to spend all its resources on traffic safety and none on education.

Ford's mistake lay not in applying the Utilitarian Principle, but in applying *only* the Utilitarian Principle. It violated at least one of the other principles we have developed, and probably both. Leaving the defect in the car was probably ungeneralizable due to a breach of implied warranty. When one sells a product, there is normally a warranty of merchantability. This means that, as far as the seller can determine, the product is fit for the purpose for which it is sold. This is not only a legal principle, but common sense. If I sell you a can of beans, I am implicitly promising that there are beans inside the can. It is part of the sales agreement, and violating a sales agreement simply to save money is not generalizable. A dangerous product defect can also defeat merchantability. Suppose I sell you a chain saw in which the chain has a weak link. I know that the chain is likely to fly in your face the first time you use the saw. This is a breach of implied warranty, because the saw is not fit to be used as a saw. We can argue that a car with a dangerous gas tank is not fit to be used for at least some purposes for which a car is sold, such as driving one's kids to school. Because some Pinto buyers use their cars for this purpose, we appear to have a breach of implied warranty.

In any event, we have a clear violation of the Joint Autonomy Principle. Ford managers knew, and in fact assumed in their analysis, that many persons would be killed or seriously injured due to the defect. As we discussed in Chapter 6, this is a violation of joint autonomy, even though the managers didn't know who in particular would be killed or injured. You might ask why all car manufacturers don't violate autonomy, because they know that people will be killed and maimed in their cars, defective or not. The difference is informed consent. The Principle of Informed Consent says that a manufacturer can expose customers to risk if they implicitly consent to it, and they have an intelligible rationale for their consent. When I buy a car, I know that I could be involved in an accident, yet I am willing to take the normal risk of driving a car, and I have a coherent rationale for doing so: The expected disutility created by accident risk is outweighed by the benefits of driving. Driving a Ford Pinto was not a normal risk, however, and customers didn't consent to taking this risk, which they knew nothing about. There was no informed consent.

You might press the issue further by asking about the danger cars pose to pedestrians. Car manufacturers can be certain that, sooner or later, one of their cars will kill or maim a pedestrian in an accident. The pedestrian is not driving a car and therefore does not voluntarily assume the associated risk. This is, in fact, a serious objection to the sale and use of automobiles, at least when they are driven on streets where pedestrians are present. The only way I see to satisfy the Joint Autonomy Principle is to claim that pedestrians assume the risk of an accident when they walk on a street where cars are present. Even if this argument works, we must recognize that the current state of affairs is not utilitarian. Most pedestrians and cyclists can reach their destination only by using streets occupied by automobiles. The Utilitarian Principle demands that we do more to protect them, perhaps by having more walking/cycling paths and vehicle-free zones.

To return to the Pinto case, Ford is obligated not only to fix the defect, but to recall the defective cars already sold; that is, to offer to fix the defect at no cost to the consumer. In fact, such a recall was eventually mandated by the government. Failure to recall is a violation of implied warranty, because Ford had not yet delivered the product it promised until that product was merchantable.

SURGE PRICING

The rise of on-demand ride services like Uber and Lyft pose new ethical dilemmas that are, in fact, quite old. One is Uber's practice of *surge pricing*, which is similar to Lyft's *prime time pricing*. Surge pricing raises fares in periods of high demand, sometimes dramatically. Uber defends the practice on the basis of classical supply-and-demand theory: Higher fares incentivize more drivers to come out on the road to meet the high demand. They also boost Uber's profit, of course.

A problem with surge pricing is that it can result in unaffordable fares. In one widely publicized case, a 20-minute ride on Halloween night cost $362.* In another high-profile incident, Uber increased prices fourfold and

---

* C. Moss, 26-year-old successfully crowd funds to pay for her $362 Halloween Uber ride, *Business Insider,* November 2, 2014.

imposed a minimum fare of A$100 following a terrorist attack in Sydney, Australia.* At this writing, Lyft's prime time pricing can as much as triple the normal fare, while Uber's surge pricing can result in even higher multipliers. The issue before us, of course, is not what Uber and Lyft are doing at the moment, but what they *should* do.

Surge pricing is a form of price gouging, a phenomenon that is doubtless as old as money itself. Price gouging might be defined as charging a very high price when the market supports it due to temporarily high demand and limited supply. Some people define price gouging in such a way that it is unethical by definition, but I prefer an ethically neutral definition, so I can ask whether it is unethical. As always, it is important to distinguish this question from the public policy issue of whether price gouging should be illegal. The free market advocate who opposes any kind of price controls can still view voluntary restraint as an ethical obligation.

Uber's defense of surge pricing is essentially a utilitarian argument. Surge pricing makes people better off because it supplies them the rides they want; however, it also requires everyone to pay a higher price. This benefits Uber drivers and those who choose an expensive ride over no ride at all, but it harms those who can't afford the price, or would have got a ride under a lower price scheme anyway. The question is whether the benefit outweighs the harm.

A standard theorem from economics textbooks is sometimes cited in this context. It states that the market price maximizes *consumer and producer surplus* and therefore maximizes welfare in some sense—even when demand drives the price to very high levels. Consumer surplus is the difference between the maximum a purchaser would be willing to pay for something and the amount actually paid. It is how much the purchaser comes out ahead, one might say. Producer surplus is the difference between actual price and the minimum a seller would be willing to accept. The textbook theorem states that consumer and producer surplus, summed over all buyers and sellers, is maximized at the equilibrating price. This is, it is maximized precisely when the price is set high enough so that supply matches demand. This suggests that people are better off overall when the market price prevails, even if that price is very high.

There are at least two problems with applying this textbook theorem to surge pricing. One is that Uber's surge price is not really the market

---

* D. Vinik, Uber's prices surged in Sydney during the hostage crisis, and everyone is furious, *New Republic*, December 14, 2014.

price, but a price set by its secret pricing algorithm. Secondly, even if it is the market price, the theorem measures surplus in terms of money rather than utility. An extra $50 may be of much greater value to a passenger who desperately needs a ride but can't afford it, than to a driver who wants to make a few extra bucks. At least at the margin, utility is probably greater if we allocate some rides based on need rather than price, even if this means that somewhat fewer cars will be available due to lower fares.

What kind of allocation mechanism recognizes this fact? Short of getting into general issues of distributive justice and mechanism design, a simple solution seems best: Cap the fare multiplier at some reasonable level. The argument goes like this. Whereas an unregulated market allocates goods by who pays the market price, one can also allocate by who wins a lottery, who is a willing to wait in a queue, or who has greater need. For example, scarce organs for transplant might be allocated by lottery (after proper screening) rather than by raising the cost of surgery to the point that only a few can afford it. Entry to a popular restaurant is often allocated by who is willing to stand in a long queue, rather than by jacking up the prices to reduce demand. If Uber were to cap its fare voluntarily, rides would be allocated partly by these alternative mechanisms. Some people would get a car solely by luck (allocation by lottery), but others would get a car because they keep trying for a longer period (allocation by queuing). If we suppose that those in greater need of a car will keep trying longer, this could result in more cars being allocated to them, with greater overall utility.

Because it is far from obvious how Uber can otherwise identify those in greatest need, this could be a practical solution that passes the utilitarian test. It creates more utility than hardline allocation by price, and I can think of no workable solution that increases utility further. A similar price cap may be appropriate for other price gouging situations, for the same reasons.

LOW-WAGE SUPPLIERS

Let's now move from prices to wages, by posing a fundamental issue for the global economy. Is it ethical for Western companies to source from overseas factories that pay very low wages?[*] It is a complex question, but a vastly important one. Perhaps we can make some progress in a short discussion.

---

[*] Based on a dilemma contributed anonymously to the author's blog ethicaldecisions.net.

We have to take care of some practical matters before proceeding with an analysis. First, workers are often more concerned about unsafe working conditions than wages. This is highlighted by a recent series of workplace fires and other disasters in Bangladesh and Pakistan, whose low-cost garment manufacturers are major suppliers to retailers in North America and Europe.* Typical safety hazards include substandard buildings and equipment, lack of fire extinguishers, and locked emergency exits. I will focus on wages rather than working conditions, but the safety issue is at least as urgent.

Second, wages are normally determined by a local factory operator, not by the Western company that sources from the factory. Few factory managers want to run a sweatshop, and many have a sense of loyalty to their workers. But competition is fierce, because Western firms are looking for the lowest possible price. Managers therefore cut wages as necessary to avoid losing their contracts and laying people off.

Finally, the retailers who source from low-wage factories may have constraints as well. They may argue that if they pay suppliers higher than market price, competition will force them out of the market. Or even if not, their lower profitability will result in a decline in stock values and an eventual bankruptcy, or acquisition by a more profitable firm that will reinstate low wages.

To pose the dilemma, we have to set up a scenario in which the company has a realistic choice. Let's suppose that High-End Apparel sources fashionable items from factories in a low-wage economy. Let's further suppose that nearly all of a garment's retail cost covers design, distribution, celebrity endorsements, and brand markup, with about 1 or 2 percent going to

* For example, nearly 300 deaths resulted from a September 2012 factory fire in Karachi, Pakistan, 25 deaths from a Lahore shoe factory fire the same month, 112 deaths from a November 2012 garment factory fire in Dhaka, Bangladesh, and 7 deaths from a January 2013 factory fire. Z. Rehman, D. Walsh, and S. Masood, More than 300 killed in Pakistani factory fires, *New York Times*, September 12, 2012; V. Bajaj, Fatal fire in Bangladesh highlights the dangers facing garment workers, *New York Times*, November 25, 2012; J. Alam, Wal-Mart, Disney clothes found in Bangladesh fire, Associated Press, November 28, 2012; D. Walsh and S. Greenhouse, Certified safe, a factory in Karachi still quickly burned, *New York Times*, December 7, 2012; S. Quadir, Burned Bangladesh factory was warned twice on fire safety, *Reuters*, December 11, 2012; F. Hossain, Reports: Exit locked at burned Bangladesh factory, Associated Press, January 27, 2013; J. A. Manik and J. Yardley, Bangladesh factory, site of fire that trapped and killed 7, made European brands, *New York Times*, January 27, 2013. I mentioned in Chapter 8 the collapse of Rana Plaza, which contained several factories and failed to meet government building codes. It resulted in 1129 deaths and the worst disaster in the history of the garment industry. BBC News, Bangladesh factory collapse toll passes 1000, May 10, 2013; J. Yardley, Report on deadly factory collapse in Bangladesh finds widespread blame, *New York Times*, May 22, 2013; L. DePillis, Two years ago, 1129 people died in a Bangladesh factory collapse. The problems still haven't been fixed, *Washington Post*, April 23, 2015.

factory workers. One or two percent doesn't sound like much, but it's entirely realistic. Should the company increase this number to, say, 3 or 4 percent? This would require some kind of enforceable agreement with suppliers that the additional funds would benefit workers. This is admittedly a challenge, because the retailer doesn't have direct control over what happens at the other end of a supply chain. However, it may be achievable by cultivating suitable relationships with suppliers.* Economists will point out that if wages are increased, the factories will be deluged with employment applications, and the labor market must clear somehow. We can assume that factory managers will deal with this by investing some of the money in good working conditions, and by hiring on the basis of demonstrated skill level and a certain minimum age (i.e., older than school age). High-End's profitability and stock price will fall slightly, but not nearly enough to endanger the business. Does the company have an obligation to go through with this?

High-End's executives may argue that there is no need to change the status quo. Workers voluntarily take jobs in these factories, and they do so because they make a better living there than anywhere else. The company is already improving lives and providing workers what they want. What can be wrong with this?

A labor activist may respond that the company is nonetheless exploiting workers, and exploitation is wrong. Philosopher Chris Meyers makes this argument vividly in the following parable.† Carole is driving alone in a remote desert area when her car breaks down. There is no means of summoning help, and no possibility of walking to safety. After two or three days, when Carole has exhausted her water supply, a man she has never met, Jason, happens to drive down the same road. He sees Carole's desperate situation and makes her an offer: He will drive her to safety if she will have sex with him. She reluctantly consents, and Jason keeps his promise. Meyers points out that Carole voluntarily accepted Jason's offer because it improved her situation, much as sweatshop workers voluntarily accept low-wage employment for the same reason. Yet, according to Meyers, we have a strong intuition that Jason's proposition is wrongful exploitation.

One might agree with Meyers about the morality of Jason's behavior but argue that Carole's situation is not analogous to that of a third-world factory worker. To deal with this, Meyers takes the reader through a series

---

* See my articles Bridging a supply chain's cultural divide, *Inside Supply Management*, 34–36; Ethics at the other end of the supply chain, *Ethisphere Magazine*, 2013: 34–36.
† C. Meyers, Wrongful beneficence: Exploitation and third-world sweatshops, *Journal of Social Philosophy* 35 (2004): 319–333.

of modified scenarios in an effort to tighten the analogy. Nonetheless, his argument eventually comes down to an appeal to moral intuitions, and when it comes to wages, a business executive is likely to have different intuitions than a labor activist.

As always, let's try to break out of the deadlock by applying the ethical tests. Offering a low-wage job hardly violates autonomy, as the business executive eagerly points out, and so autonomy principles have little to say here. (Providing a dangerous work environment may well compromise autonomy, and that issue must be treated differently.) The Utilitarian Principle, however, has something to say. The workers will gain more utility from higher wages than stockholders and other parties lose, due to the decreasing marginal value of money (Chapter 4). Child labor will be reduced, and workers who are not hired will be incentivized to develop their skills, which could result in higher productivity in other factories. Utility is clearly increased by boosting wages, at least at the margin.

We must now make sure this utilitarian choice passes other ethical tests. If it does, it is obligatory. A popular argument to the contrary is that it ignores fiduciary duty to maximize shareholder value. But as discussed earlier in this chapter, the prior issue is whether the stockholders themselves have an obligation to raise wages in this situation, and this is the issue we are addressing.

Economists may argue that if the goal is to increase total utility, raising wages above the market rate is not generalizable. Economic science, they might say, has demonstrated that more wealth is generated in the long run if everyone responds to market signals. So if all companies were to ignore market signals for wage rates, the goal of increasing overall utility would be frustrated.

This argument assumes that neoclassical economic equilibrium models are applicable to a global market that is constrained by complex historical and institutional factors. This is already a stretch. Aside from this, the argument attacks a straw man. No one is suggesting here that market signals for wages be ignored in general. Part of the rationale for raising wages is that the workers are in a low-wage emerging economy, and higher wages are feasible for the companies involved. We need more than a hand-waving argument that a practice of raising wages somewhat in this specific context would reduce overall utility, particularly since common sense suggests otherwise. Until such an argument is forthcoming, raising wages somewhat should be treated as generalizable. It is therefore obligatory, when the complexities of the supply chain allow it.

ONLINE PRIVACY

Constant surveillance has become a fact of life. Internet service providers record every website we visit, smartphones track our location, ubiquitous video cameras peer at us, and retailers record every purchase and sometimes track our movements as we shop. Social networking sites and search engines collect data on our interests, backgrounds, political views, likes and dislikes, purchases, and interactions with other Internet users. License-plate readers follow our cars, smart TVs register what we are watching (and will soon watch *us*). Massive amounts of data collected in these ways are routinely sold to marketing firms and other organizations, which use sophisticated data mining algorithms to assemble dossiers on countless individuals. Meanwhile, governments are snooping on us in ways we can only guess.

The issue is so vast that it is hard to know where to start, but I will try to narrow it down by focusing on the ethical situation of a business that collects and sells data gathered from users of its website. This could be a social networking site, a search engine, or an online retail site. The basic issue is whether and when collecting and selling customer data is an unethical violation of privacy.

Discussion of privacy in the ethics literature tends to revolve around whether there is a right to privacy, and if so, whether that right is reducible to other rights.* I prefer to avoid talk of "rights," however, because it

---

* An early defense of a right to privacy is the famous article of S. Warren and L. Brandeis, The right to privacy, *Harvard Law Review* 4 (1890): 193–220. They define it as the right "to be left alone," but they took this to include informational privacy. Concern for privacy at the time was spurred by the fear that photojournalism would destroy it. This fear may seem a bit quaint today, but only because we have evolved social norms to govern the publication of intrusive photographs (except for celebrities, who are tormented by paparazzi with telephoto lenses), while we have not evolved norms to govern online data collection. Judith Thomson argues that any right to privacy is reducible to other rights; The right to privacy, *Philosophy and Public Affairs* 4 (1975): 295–314. This position is critiqued by T. Scanlon in Thomson on privacy, *Philosophy and Public Affairs* 4 (1975): 315–322. Privacy as control of information about oneself is emphasized by W. A. Parent in Privacy, morality, and the law, *Philosophy and Public Affairs* 12 (1983): 269–288. In a similar vein, Danah Boyd argues that privacy is not dead in the Internet age in her talk, Making sense of privacy and publicity, South by Southwest, Austin, TX, March 13, 2010. Contrasting views include those of T. Doyle, Privacy and perfect voyeurism, *Ethics and Information Technology* 11 (2009): 181–189; and H. Tavani and J. Moor, who argue that privacy is more about access than control in Privacy protection, control of information, and privacy-enhancing technologies, *Computers and Society* 31 (2001): 6–11. For similar views on access, R. Gavison, Privacy and the limits of law, *Yale Law Journal* 89 (1980): 421–471; A. Moore, Privacy: Its meaning and value, *American Philosophical Quarterly* 40 (2003): 215–227.

tends to confuse matters. Sooner or later we must justify rights-claims by appealing to more basic ethical principles, such as those developed in this book. It is simpler to appeal to those principles in the first place.

Let's start with the Generalization Principle. There is an obvious risk of deception when a company uses its website to collect customer data, because customers may be misled about how their data are used. Deception merely for profit is not generalizable. The potential for deception begins with the site's "privacy policy," which typically begins with some such statement as, "We care about your privacy." However, those with the patience and ability to read to the end of a long, legalistic document are likely to learn that the company will do almost anything it wants with its data. Nor is there is assurance that the company will even abide by its stated policy. Google's failure to do so resulted in the largest civil penalty ever imposed by the U.S. Federal Trade Commission.*

Social networking sites create the impression of giving users personal space online. One such site is actually named *MySpace*. The sites strengthen this impression by providing "privacy settings" that control the dissemination of personal information. Of course, there is nothing personal or private about this online space, and the controls limit what is visible to other users, not what is forwarded to the company's marketing consultants or sold. Other types of web services may ask users to set up a free account and *log in* for additional features, an action that associates their names with their online activity. They may offer users the convenience of storing their documents "in the cloud," where they are of course accessible to the service provider and probably others.

The issue for ethics is whether these practices lull users into a false sense of privacy. One might argue that today's users are savvy to such things. Yet it is hard to believe that the enormous commercial success of online services is not historically due, at least in part, to user naïveté about their real purpose. Data harvesting is, after all, the core business model of search engines and social networking sites. Consider the widespread outrage following news media reports that Facebook manipulated its individual newsfeeds as part of a psychological experiment.† Truly savvy users would have said, "What's the big deal? Facebook manipulates newsfeeds all the time to influence customer behavior." At the very least, I am certain that

---

* S. Forden and K. Gullo, Google judge accepts $22.5 million FTC privacy settlement, *Bloomberg Business*, November 17, 2012.
† R. Albergotti and E. Dwoskin, Facebook study sparks soul-searching and ethical questions, *Wall Street Journal*, June 30, 2014.

most people don't appreciate the power of data mining techniques, because advanced training in mathematics or statistics is necessary to understand how cleverly they connect the dots to assemble individual profiles.

A company must evaluate, then, whether its site gives users a false sense of privacy. Of course, it can avoid any possibility of deception by stating prominently and in plain language what it does with customer data. If the company is unwilling to be up front with customers, it must ask why it is unwilling, if the purpose is not to mislead.

There is a second kind of argument against the generalizability of data harvesting. On this argument, universal and pervasive invasion of informational privacy could undermine the integrity of society and therefore the possibility of achieving its objectives. As we increasingly live our lives online, a lack of Internet privacy increasingly becomes a lack of privacy of any kind.

Why is privacy necessary? It affords a zone of trust and safety within which intimacy can develop, and intimacy is necessary for family life and therefore for the proper functioning of society.* This assigns a cultural function to family privacy, at least, if not individual privacy. This function may seem to be refuted by traditional societies in which people live in close quarters with other families in a single dwelling and have intimate knowledge of each other's affairs. But anthropologists tell us that even these societies have any number of mechanisms to secure informational privacy. Families may have a secluded retreat in the woods from which others keep their distance. They may take care not to intrude on another family's space in a common dwelling, and partitions may be erected at sensitive times like childbirth. There may be strict taboos about asking personal questions, and people may lie on a regular basis to avoid revealing personal information.†

Privacy concerns in fact seem to reflect larger cultural norms. Family-oriented societies such as those of Asia, the Middle East, or Latin America often place a strong emphasis on household privacy. This is reflected even in architecture, as when an extended family's dwelling units may be

---

* Several writers connect privacy with intimacy in various ways, including C. Fried, *An Anatomy of Values*, Cambridge, MA, Harvard University Press, 1970; J. Rachels, Why privacy is important, *Philosophy and Public Affairs* 4 (1975): 323–333; R. S. Gerstein, Intimacy and privacy, *Ethics* 89 (1978): 76–81; J. Inness, *Privacy, Intimacy and Isolation*, Oxford, Oxford University Press, 1992.

† For a survey of some anthropological literature on privacy in traditional societies, I. Altman, Privacy regulation: Culturally universal or culturally specific? *Journal of Social Issues* 33 (1977): 66–84.

arranged around an inner courtyard with few windows or doors to the outside world.* The strong sense of household privacy in Japan and even individualistic Germany inspired objections to the vehicle-mounted cameras used to create Google Street View.† Japanese objected to cameras that peer over hedges surrounding a house, because it is highly impolite for passers-by even to gaze into a family's yard. Google was finally forced to lower its cameras so that they could not see over the hedges. In Germany, officials in Hamburg protested Google's vehicles, residents of Kiel posted "no Google Street View" stickers on their doors, and at least one city banned the cameras outright.

The individualism of northern European societies leads mainly, however, to an emphasis on individual privacy. Office doors are often kept shut, hotels walls are often soundproofed, and coworkers generally do not discuss their private lives.‡ The U.S. tapping of German Chancellor Angela Merkel's mobile phone became an international incident that chilled relations between the two countries.§ A concern for individual privacy is also reflected in the data protection laws of the European Union, in which Germany is a dominant player. The 1995 Data Protection Directive places strict limits on how online personal data can be processed and transmitted, particularly without the owner's knowledge (yes, European Internet users own their personal data, whereas in the United States, the website operator owns the data). This is why European websites always warn you when they are using cookies. At this writing, the European Union is finalizing an even stronger General Data Protection Regulation that more adequately addresses social networking and cloud computing. One might ask why the United States, with its highly individualistic culture, does not have stronger protections of individual online privacy, but the general point prevails that privacy can have important cultural functions. This can provide the basis for a generalization argument against the kind of intrusive data harvesting so prevalent today.

The Utilitarian Principle is less decisive. One of the most popular defenses of data harvesting is that it is ubiquitous but harmless. Marketing

---

* These are other insightful observations on cultural perceptions of space can be found in Edward Hall's classic works, *The Silent Language*, 1959 and *The Hidden Dimension*, 1966, New York, Anchor Books.
† S. Vaidhyanathan, 'Street View' and the universalization of surveillance, in *The Googlization of Everything*, Berkeley, CA, University of California Press, 2011, pp. 98–107.
‡ See Edward Hall, cited earlier.
§ P. Sherwell and L. Barnett, Barack Obama 'approved tapping Angela Merkel's phone 3 years ago,' *The Telegraph*, October 27, 2013.

firms can analyze your data all they want, and it won't hurt you. Besides, it has benefits, such as directed ads that are tailored to your interests. On the other hand, massive storage of personal information makes it available to hackers, not a small risk considering the almost daily occurrence of major data breaches. In addition, companies are often obliged to turn over personal data to their governments. Google, Apple, and other firms take customer concerns about government surveillance very seriously, because they don't want to lose these customers. They have entered into an epic struggle with governments over who controls personal data. At this point, I am aware of no clear evidence that a single firm's data harvesting results in negative net expected utility, but the issue should be watched carefully.

Autonomy may also be at stake in the privacy dispute. Again, as we increasingly live our lives online, constant surveillance online becomes constant surveillance, period. Can a human being function autonomously under these conditions? The question is fundamental enough to have been raised more than two centuries ago. One thinks of the omnipresent telescreens in George Orwell's *1984*, but constant surveillance was already proposed in Jeremy Bentham's idea of the Panopticon. This was to be a prison or other institution that is constructed so that a single supervisor can observe any inmate at any time, but inmates cannot know when they are being observed. As a result, inmates must behave as though they are under constant surveillance. This would, in Bentham's words, provide a "new mode of obtaining power of mind over mind."* This sounds like control, in which case it is a violation of autonomy. Perhaps autonomy was not a concern for a thoroughgoing utilitarian like Bentham, or perhaps one can defend him on the grounds that prison surveillance interferes only with unethical behavior. In any case, it poses the issue of whether constant surveillance compromises autonomy. We perhaps have not reached a stage at which online surveillance has this effect, but again, it is an issue to be watched.

OFFENSIVE CARTOONS

This topic evokes emotional and sometimes violent responses, but we have the tools to analyze it rationally if cool heads can prevail. In fact, some of the ethical issues are actually rather easy to resolve, as ethical issues go.

---

* J. Bentham, *The Panopticon Writings*, London, UK, Verso (1787, reprinted 1995) p. 31.

A number of European and other publications, ranging from Denmark's *Jyllands-Posten* to France's *Charlie Hebdo*, have displayed cartoons of the prophet Muhammad that are offensive to Muslims.* The backlash against the Danish cartoons included violent and sometimes deadly protests worldwide.[†] The cartoonist himself was terrorized by death threats and an attack by an axe-wielding assailant.[‡] The French cartoons, which were published alongside reprints of the Danish ones, helped inspire a 2015 attack on the *Charlie Hebdo* editorial offices that left 12 dead.[§] Many in the West nonetheless insist that these publications acted appropriately and should continue to exercise their right to free expression.

The question I want to raise is not whether publications should have a legal right to print inflammatory cartoons of this kind, but whether it is ethical to print them. It is part of the larger conundrum of how a society and its subcultures should relate to each other, a burning issue in our age of mass migration.

The key criterion for the cartoon issue turns out to be a utilitarian one. Is it reasonable to believe that running a religiously offensive cartoon does more good than harm? In many cases, the answer is no. It induces people to take violent retribution, and it incites riots in various places around the world, resulting in death and injury. It may also make religious minorities who live in the country feel unwelcome and resentful, justifiably or not. By any measure, this outweighs any benefit that would result from publishing a cartoon. Perhaps the editors of *Jyllands-Posten* could not have reasonably anticipated so negative a reaction in 2005 (I was a regular reader of the newspaper while residing in Denmark some years ago, and I found it to be quite responsible). Today, however, editors know the risks and should act accordingly.

This is not to say that offended people should retaliate by murdering cartoonists. Of course not. So much as issuing a credible threat is already a violation of autonomy. Nor is it to say that people should stage violent protests against cartoons, or that they should try to suppress free speech in a country with that tradition, or that they should feel unwelcome and resentful

---

* Muhammeds ansigt, *Jyllands-Posten*, September 30, 2005; Mahomet débordé par les intégristes, *Charlie Hebdo*, February 9, 2006. *Charlie Hebdo* published additional cartoons that ridiculed Islam in 2011 and 2012.

† P. Cohen, Yale Press bans images of Muhammad in new book, *New York Times*, August 12, 2009.

‡ M. L. Sjølie, The Danish cartoonist who survived an axe attack, *The Guardian*, January 4, 2010.

§ D. Bilefsky and M. Baumejan, Terrorists strike Charlie Hebdo newspaper in Paris, leaving 12 dead, *New York Times*, January 7, 2015.

because of cartoons. It is only to say that people in fact react in these ways, and the Utilitarian Principle requires us to take this into account. Running the cartoons therefore violates the principle in most cases.

Publishers might argue that suppressing controversial material to avoid backlash is not generalizable, at least in a Western country. The reason for suppression is presumably to avoid social disutility that results from the backlash. If publications always suppressed material in such cases, then arguably the tradition of free exchange of ideas would collapse, resulting in much more social disutility, at least in a Western society that is built on transparency. So generalizing the action is inconsistent with achieving its purpose, which is a violation of the generalization test. This means that suppressing the material should not be considered as an option for maximizing utility, and one can ethically publish it despite the negative consequences.

This argument might well be valid if a publication is actually suppressing the free exchange of ideas. In particular, it should allow for frank discussion of religion, even if this risks strong disagreement and violent reactions. However, removing a cartoon does not seem to restrict the free exchange of ideas. For this purpose, the cartoon can be described in words. The negative reactions were generated by the pictorial representation of the Prophet, due to the historic abhorrence of idolatry in Abrahamic religions and a strong tradition of aniconism in Islam particularly. If displaying the cartoon is absolutely essential to making one's point, then we may have an argument for printing it, but in recent cases it is not.

The three ethical principles interact similarly in the broader context of intercultural relations. Tolerance for divergent subcultures generally results in greater utility, and yet subcultures should not expect the larger society to discard norms that are integral to its function. Violence and threats of violence deny autonomy and should be avoided. Each case must be analyzed individually, as I have done for the cartoon issue, but this is not so hard, after all.

ONLINE SELF-CENSORSHIP

A trickier issuer is whether online services like Facebook, YouTube, and Twitter should screen offensive material posted by users. There are at least three differences between this issue and previous one. First, the material is posted by readers, not by staff. Second, it is hard to screen the huge volume posted daily. Third, the material often remains online after it is posted, which means that site operators must often make two decisions: whether to allow the material to be posted in the first place, and if they allow it, whether to take it down after they see the reaction. Again, the question I address is not whether a government should censor online content, but whether a site operator should do so voluntarily.

Probably the highest-profile occurrence of this dilemma to date was the YouTube posting of an amateurish video *Innocence of Muslims* in July 2012.* It dramatized scenes of Muslim-perpetrated violence against Copts in Egypt along with cartoonish and slanderous depictions of the Prophet Muhammed. The actors and film crew said they thought they were dramatizing an Arab adventure story, but much of their dialog was overdubbed with anti-Muslim remarks.† The video ties in with the *Charlie Hebdo* affair, because it prompted the magazine to publish cartoons in September that satirized the Prophet and the backlash against the video. Fearful of retaliation, the French government closed its embassies, consulates, and schools in 20 countries when the cartoons were published.‡ It is widely assumed that the cartoons also contributed to the resentment that fueled the 2015 attack on *Charlie Hebdo* offices.

The video itself inspired violent protests in several countries, particularly Pakistan, reportedly resulting in more than 50 deaths worldwide.§ Much of the protest was directed against the U.S. government for not censoring the video. President Obama asked Google (owner of YouTube) to consider taking down the video, even though he had no legal authority to censor it. Google refused, on the grounds that the video is consistent with its policy. "It is against the Islam religion [sic] but not Muslim people."¶ Nonetheless, Google voluntarily took down the video in a few countries where it judged there was unusual sensitivity to its content, and the video was blocked by government action in several additional countries.

The problem of offensive posts has become steadily worse, and this dilemma now confronts online site operators on a daily basis. Users post

---

* D. D. Kirkpatrik, Anger over a film fuels anti-American attacks in Libya and Egypt, *New York Times*, September 11, 2012.

† P. Willon and R. Keegan, 'Innocence of Muslims': Mystery shrouds film's California origins, *Los Angeles Times*, September 12, 2012.

‡ E. Greenhouse, The Charlie Hebdo affair: Laughing at blasphemy, *The New Yorker*, September 28, 2012.

§ CNN, Death, destruction in Pakistan amid protests tied to anti-Islam film, September 21, 2012.

¶ C. C. Miller, Google has no plans to rethink video status, *New York Times*, September 14, 2012.

or tweet every conceivable type of incendiary material, and offended parties often demand that it be removed. The stated policies behind self-censorship decisions tend to be vague, typically saying that the site "reserves the right" to remove objectionable material but "takes no responsibility" for doing so. There is an urgent need for a clear and ethically defensible policy. Let's see how far we can go in this direction.

The simplest policy is to allow users to post whatever they want and leave it there, except when legal authorities order its removal. A common defense of this policy in the early days of social media was, "we are not responsible for what users post." This statement may be effective as rhetoric, but it is worthless as an argument. If it means that the site operators didn't initiate the posts, it is certainly true, but it fails to address the issue of what to do about them. If it means that the operators have no control over what appears on the site, it is patently false. They have total control. If it means that they have no obligation to control what appears on the site, it simply restates their position without argument.

The fact that users, rather than operators, post the offensive material does have ethical relevance. This due to the second distinguishing characteristic of social media: There are so many posts that it is hard to screen them. I have seen estimates that about half a million comments are posted to Facebook, and at least 300 hours of video uploaded to YouTube, every *minute.** Operators might claim that even though they can, in theory, control what is posted, they can't control it in any intelligent fashion, and in particular they can't filter out offensive material. This seems a little disingenuous, given the power of data mining technology, but let's suppose, for the sake of argument, that online operators can't meaningfully scan posts as they come in. What does this mean ethically?

It means that the operator has two basic options: Either shut down the site, or postpone the censorship decision until after material is posted. A shutdown would incur an enormous utilitarian cost. YouTube, for example, offers far more than viral cat videos. It connects viewers around the world with a vast array of documentary films, lectures, courses, world-class musical performances, and on-the-scene reporting, all free of charge. The same is true of other video hosting services, such as Dailymotion (France),

---

* C. Pring, 101 social media statistics for 2012, *The Social Skinny* website, Retrieved from http://thesocialskinny.com/100-social-media-statistics-for-2012/, accessed August 2, 2017. Statistic Brain, YouTube company statistics, 2016, Retrieved from http://www.statisticbrain.com/youtube-statistics/, accessed August 2, 2017.

Tudou (China), and RuTube (Russia). Losing all these benefits would seem to outweigh the damage done by operating the site, provided the most offensive posts are taken down before they do too much damage.

How can offensive posts be identified? The online operators have evolved into a practice of leaving it to the public to complain about online material when they find it offensive. This is not an unreasonable approach, since offensive content matters only if people notice it. It means, however, that operators must take complaints seriously. This requires a great deal of staffing and resources, but these should be considered part of the cost of doing business. It also means that operators must develop ethically sound criteria for evaluating a website.

To justify censorship on a utilitarian basis, it is not enough that some people don't like the material, because dislike is not the same as disutility. The material must result in some kind of demonstrable harm, and complainants can be asked to provide evidence of harm. Destructive riots are an obvious example, but other examples include rumors with destructive effects, such as false claims that certain vaccines have serious side effects, sites that recruit or instruct terrorists, and slanderous material that can cause unwarranted loss of jobs or ostracism. Operators may argue that they are often in no position to make such evaluations, and they cannot afford to investigate thousands of complaints every day. True, but they can afford to investigate some of the most serious and credible complaints, without sacrificing profitability. This is probably enough to satisfy the Utilitarian Principle, because removing only the most destructive posts is probably better than shutting down the service altogether. Furthermore, although I am not supposing that data mining and deep learning techniques can pre-screen posts, it seems very likely that these techniques can in fact flag the most egregious material for human examination. YouTube is already doing something like this, although perhaps with the wrong objectives.* This avoids waiting for complaints to come in, when much of the damage may already have been done. The Utilitarian Principle requires that such techniques be used whenever possible.

Some may think that I fail to understand the nature of an online service. It is not like a newspaper. When a newspaper prints news stories, there is an implied promise that the stories are verified and responsibly

---

* This is discussed in an interview with I. Lapowsky, a writer for *Wired* magazine, and S. Rapp, a board member of Physicians for Human Rights, *PBS NewsHour*, September 13, 2017. Lapowski says that YouTube uploads 400 hours of content a day, not 300.

selected. Violating this promise, simply to avoid the cost of vetting stories, is normally ungeneralizable. An online service, by contrast, is more like a public bulletin board. The sponsor of the bulletin board makes no promises regarding the content of the posted messages; yet the argument for censorship I have presented so far is not based on an implied promise. It is based solely on utilitarian considerations. It is interesting, however, that bulletin board owners frequently remove offensive or obscene material. For that matter, newspapers screen and edit letters to the editor, which one might argue are analogous to online posts. This suggests an implied promise that the posted material will be vetted. Nonetheless I do not want to construct an argument on this basis. The argument, so far, is purely utilitarian.

The Joint Autonomy Principle turns out to be even more demanding in this context than the Utilitarian Principle. Irresponsible posts can violate autonomy as well as reduce utility. Posts that result in death and injury are obvious examples, but there are many others. A post that destroys someone's career by falsely claiming that he or she is a sexual predator also violates autonomy, provided the choice to pursue that career is ethical, and there is no implied consent. Perhaps the most incendiary material can be pre-screened or taken down before riots ensue, but it is much harder to police comments and videos that attack others. Even though the online operator does not know, in any particular case, that a questionable post will violate autonomy, the operator can be sure that this will occur sooner or later. This implies that operating the site at all violates the joint autonomy principle.

The only way to circumvent this conclusion is to identify and evaluate personal attacks and other offensive posts before they violate autonomy, at least with a degree of thoroughness that allows the operator to believe rationally that violations of autonomy are not inevitable. This is difficult, but arguably possible. Automatic screening can take us a long way in this direction. Google claims that its search engine can retrieve one billion relevant websites from a database of 30 trillion websites in just one second. I just ran a search that yielded these statistics. This suggests that data mining software can meaningfully scan half a million comments or 300 hours of video in a minute. Posts that are flagged by data mining can then be examined by humans. Google has some 72,000 employees, and Facebook has close to 20,000, many of whom are occupied with negotiating ad contracts and otherwise generating revenue. Given that these companies are scarcely on the verge of bankruptcy, they could dedicate large teams to vetting content. They can also crowdsource the task, as Wikipedia does. Over a billion YouTube users can help screen those 300 hours of video uploaded every minute, and a billion active Facebook users can help monitor the half million comments posted there every minute. As already noted, people aggrieved by videos or posts can complain, as they do already. Similar observations apply to search engines, Twitter, and other online services. Finally, the sheer fact that a post is deleted impugns its credibility and tends to neutralize violations of autonomy.

We resist this analysis, because the Internet age has lulled us into a laissez-faire attitude toward what people say about others, sometimes based on vaguely conceived notions of transparency and free speech. If company employees begin posting slanderous and personally damaging notes on the office bulletin board, we do not object if the company removes these notes and prohibits the practice—as it should, based on the arguments I have presented. But if similar postings appear online, they somehow become okay, because we should respect freedom of expression. This is, of course, a familiar phenomenon when new technology is introduced. We are wowed by what it can do and forget to take precautions demanded by ethics. Driving a car was very chic in the early days but also very dangerous, due to thoughtless driving behavior, poor vehicular design, and lack of traffic control. Early X-ray machines were a medical miracle but sometimes killed patients due to the high voltages used, not to mention overexposure to radiation. In the 1940s, there was much excitement over the new insecticide DDT, but children were sprayed with it before its harmful effects on humans were investigated. The Internet and smartphones are the sexy new technologies of our age, but we must beware of their dangers while celebrating their power.

This is not as hard as we may think. Nobody is saying that all potentially harmful posts should be vetted. As I have argued, the Utilitarian Principle is satisfied if only the most egregious material is removed. Respect for autonomy allows harmful posts, so long as they do not prevent people from carrying out ethical action plans. The standard is even weaker than this: We need not be sure that online posts will never interfere with ethical activities in someone's life, but we need only be rational in believing that this is not a necessary outcome. It will, of course, take conscious effort to develop practical procedures for vetting online posts, just as it took conscious effort to make driving, X-rays, and insecticide use safer.

I have used the word *censorship*, but none of the above should be used as an excuse to restrict the free exchange of *ideas and information* online.

Given the dominant market share of the major online operators in much of the world, private censorship is tantamount to government censorship. Suppression of ideas and information is almost always nonutilitarian. It can also be deceptive by creating a false impression of the range of views people have, possibilities for defending them, and the fact base against which they must be judged. What should be restricted are gratuitous personal attacks (to avoid violations of autonomy) and incitement of the most seriously harmful reactions (to satisfy the Utilitarian Principle). As argued in the previous section, even the latter may be permissible in some countries, if there is no more innocuous way to convey the underlying ideas. We should also keep in mind that posts that result in inference with *unethical* behavior are no violation of autonomy.

13

Medical Ethics

In this chapter I take up some questions of medical ethics. Is it ethical to refuse vaccination for one's children? Is it ethical to withhold information from those who are ill, assuming it is for their own good? There are also those wrenching end-of-life decisions we must sometimes make for loved ones, in an age when medical technology prolongs life that is not always worth living. These rely heavily on the theory of autonomy we have developed. The chapter concludes by examining how limited healthcare resources should be allocated.

REFUSING MEASLES VACCINE

We have seen a movement among some parents to refuse vaccination for their children, due in part to concern over the safety of vaccines.[*] The controversy has been particularly marked for measles vaccine. A 1998 article in *The Lancet* sparked fears in the United Kingdom that measles/mumps/rubella (MMR) vaccine is linked to autism and colitis.[†] *The Lancet* later retracted the article, and subsequent larger studies found no connection between MMR and autism.[‡] Nonetheless, doubts about MMR vaccine spread to the United States and persist.

---

[*] P. J. Smith et al., Parental delay or refusal of vaccine does, childhood vaccination coverage at 24 months of age, and the health belief model, *Public Health Reports* 126, Supplement 2 (2011): 135–146.

[†] A. J. Wakefield et al., Ileal-lymphoid-nodular hyperplasia, non-specific colitis, and pervasive developmental disorder in children (retracted), *The Lancet* 351, 9103 (1998): 637–664.

[‡] V. Demicheli, A. Rivetti, M. G. Debalini, C. Di Pietrantonj, Vaccines for measles, mumps and rubella in children, *Cochrane Database Systems Review* 2 (15 February, 2012).

Measles had been eliminated in the United States by 2000, due to almost universal vaccination of children. At this writing, however, the U.S. vaccination rate has dropped to 92 percent.* Ominously, the disease resurfaced in late 2014 with an outbreak that began among unvaccinated persons at Disneyland in California.† Many of those initially infected were international visitors, but a lower domestic vaccination rate increases the probability the illness will spread. Studies have shown that vaccine refusal has resulted in a higher incidence of measles in the United States.‡ A 2017 outbreak of measles in Italy had already infected more than 4000 persons by the middle of the year, of which 88 percent were unvaccinated.§

Some libertarians maintain that vaccination should be voluntary, despite these risks. The more immediate question for parents, however, is whether there is an obligation to vaccinate their children even when it is voluntary. The issue has an interesting analysis and provides a good example of how statistical data can play a role in ethical decision-making.

Vaccines pose a classic free rider situation. If others are vaccinating their kids, then my own kids will be largely protected without vaccination, because the disease won't spread. I am free riding on the prudence of others. This kind of free riding is unethical because it is not generalizable. The precise argument goes like this. My reason for refusing vaccination is to avoid its inconvenience and perceived risk while still benefiting from the protection of widespread vaccination. If everyone else acted on this reason, I would no longer be protected. So my reason is not generalizable.

This argument carries no weight for some vaccine opponents ("anti-vaxxers"), because they insist that they have a different rationale. They want to protect their kids from the risk of MMR vaccination, even if this means the kids will get measles. They view measles and other childhood

---

* L. D. Elam-Evans, D. Yankey, J. A. Singleton, and M. Kolasa, National, state, and selected local area vaccination coverage among children aged 19–35 months—United States, 2013, *Morbidity and Mortality Weekly Report* 63, 34 (August 29, 2014), Centers for Disease Control, 741–748.

† Center for Disease Control and Prevention, Frequently asked questions about measles in the U.S., www.cdc.gov/measles/about/faqs.html, Measles cases and outbreaks, www.cdc.gov/measles/cases-outbreaks.html, accessed January 9, 2016.

‡ V. K. Phadke, R. A. Bednarczyk, D. A. Salmon, S. B. Omer, Association between vaccine refusal and vaccine-preventable diseases in the United States: A review of measles and pertussis, *Journal of the American Medical Association* 315 (2016): 1149–1158.

§ A. Filia, A. Bella, M. D. Manso, M. Baggieri, F. Magurano, and M. C. Rota, Ongoing outbreak with well over 4000 measles cases in Italy from January to end August 2017: What is making elimination so difficult?, *Eurosurveillance* 22, No. 37 (September 14, 2017).

diseases as a natural part of growing up. Such a rationale appears generalizable on the surface, because even if everyone rejected vaccination, they would still be able to protect their kids from its risks. Let's accept this for the moment and move on to a utilitarian analysis, because it will help us analyze generalizability more carefully.

Failure to vaccinate exposes children to a real, if small, possibility of infection. One exposure to airborne particles in a plane or airport is enough, because measles is even more contagious than the flu. The presence of anti-vaxxers boosts the probability of exposure in areas where they live. If kids contract measles, they expose still others to the disease, some of whom may not be vaccinated or may have depressed immune systems, as when taking cancer drugs.

To make a utilitarian assessment, we must compare the expected disutility that results from vaccinating a given child, versus the expected disutility of skipping the vaccination (recall that utilitarian assessments are always conducted for an individual case). Fortunately, we have some data. Of kids who are vaccinated, about 16 percent get a mild fever, 5 percent a faint rash, 1.3 percent swelling of salivary glands, 0.03 percent a temporary fever-induced seizure, and 0.003 percent bleeding disorders.[*] As for the link between MMR vaccine and autism, there is no evidence for it. The original *Lancet* study that "found" a link involved 12 children and manipulated the data. The lead author was discredited and lost his license to practice medicine. Several more recent studies, including one that involved half a million children, found no link.[†] On the other hand, the disease itself can trigger several serious complications. Of kids under 5 who get measles, 10 percent also get an ear infection, 10 percent get diarrhea, 5 percent pneumonia (fatal in severe cases), and 0.1 percent get encephalitis, which can lead to convulsions or deafness. From 0.1 percent to 0.2 percent of infected children die from the disease.[‡] In the Italian outbreak, 5 percent got an ear infection, 16 percent diarrhea, 14 percent stomatitis, 9 percent conjunctivitis, 9 percent hepatitis, 8 percent pneumonia, 6 percent respiratory insufficiency, 3 percent bleeding disorders, and

---

[*] Centers for Disease Control and Prevention, Possible side-effects from vaccines, www.cdc.gov/vaccines/vac-gen/side-effects.htm, accessed April 21, 2016.

[†] K. M. Madsen et al., A population-based study of measles, mumps, and rubella vaccination and autism, *New England Journal of Medicine* 347 (2002): 1477–1482.

[‡] Centers for Disease Control and Prevention, Complications of measles, www.cdc.gov/measles/about/ complications.html, accessed April 21, 2016.

0.2 percent seizures. Of the 4000 patients, two got encephalitis, and three children died due to respiratory insufficiency (all unvaccinated).*

Contracting measles is clearly riskier than vaccination, but a utilitarian calculation must factor in the probability of getting measles. The probability is small when 92 percent are vaccinated, but this is at least partially offset by the relative severity of the risks. All of the side effects of MMR vaccine are mild and of little consequence, except for a very unlikely high fever or bleeding disorder. On the other hand, measles can cause *death* and has some serious nonlethal complications with worrisome probabilities. We should add to this the fact that a child who contracts measles can spread it to others, especially if one lives in a community with several anti-vaxxers or people with weakened immune systems. Given these data, vaccination seems the rational choice for maximizing total utility unless the chance of contracting measles is negligible.

Even if we don't have a compelling utilitarian case for vaccination, the generalization argument requires closer examination. Refusing the vaccine is generalizable if one's rationale is simply to remove the risks of the MMR vaccine, but this is almost certainly an incorrect reading of the scope. Suppose the anti-vaxxers learned that measles carries substantial risk, such as a 50 percent chance of death. They would undoubtedly abandon their anti-vaxxer stance, to minimize risk to their children. This indicates that their true rationale for rejecting vaccine is that it results in less overall risk, not simply less risk due to vaccination.

We now must ask if rejecting vaccine to reduce overall risk is generalizable. We assume that it is rational for anti-vaxxers to believe that rejecting vaccine in fact reduces risk, because otherwise they run afoul of the Utilitarian Principle. But if they rationally believe that rejection reduces risk, they are rationally constrained to believe that all parents have the same reason to reject vaccine as they have. So we must judge whether rejection of the vaccine reduces risk if all parents reject it. It clearly does not, because if no one is vaccinated, measles will be a regular feature of childhood (as it was when I was a boy). In this scenario, the risk is much greater when one refuses vaccination, as indicated by the data presented earlier. Refusal to vaccinate is therefore not generalizable.

Anti-vaxxers complain that there must be some point at which a successful vaccine is no longer obligatory. Actually, there is such a point. The generalization argument ceases to apply when a disease is unlikely to

---

* Antonio Filia et al., cited earlier.

reemerge if no one is vaccinated. Refusing smallpox vaccine is generalizable, for example, because the world's last case of smallpox occurred in 1977. In fact, the vaccine is no longer supplied to the general public. It is given only to some laboratory workers and military personnel in regions where germ warfare could develop.

Some parents will reject the previously mentioned arguments on the ground that the medical establishment is not trustworthy. They point to reports of medical researchers who have conflicts of interest, resulting in bias or even fraudulent studies.* One should therefore give no credence to published statistics, even those in top journals. The skeptics have a legitimate point. Medicine, like practically every other human activity, rests on a foundation of trust. This is one reason we have ethics, after all. It is hard to escape the impression that trust in expertise and leadership, as well as their trustworthiness, have been on the wane in recent years.† Many people genuinely doubt what science says about the causes of climate change. We can't reach consensus on how a minimum wage affects employment, or whether we can afford a single-payer health system, or what tax policy is best, because economists on either side of the issue have too little credibility. What are ordinary people like you and me to do when we can't personally investigate what the experts are telling us?

It is a quandary, but in the area of vaccines, at least, we can take some reasonable steps. If we distrust medicine, we should doubt the controversial *Lancet* study at least as much as any other. Contradictory studies demonstrate that the medical establishment is indeed fallible, but we knew this already. It recommended bloodletting for centuries. The relevant question is whether, given the evidence at hand, it is rational to believe one retracted study or several larger studies. In this case, at least, the answer seems clear.

---

* A famous case is Merck's painkiller Vioxx; see Alex Berenson, Gardiner Harris, Barry Meier, and Andrew Pollack, "Despite warnings, drug giant took long path to Vioxx recall," *New York Times*, November 14, 2004. For a sampling of recent views on conflicts of interest in medical research, see A. E. Carroll, Doctors' magical thinking about conflicts of interest, *New York Times*, September 8, 2014; A. Frakt, A new way to think about conflicts of interest in medicine, *New York Times*, August 31, 2015; and M. F. Cannon, How to minimize conflicts of interest in medical research, *Forbes*, April 4, 2016. A somewhat different issue is described in E. Ross, How drug companies' PR tactics skew the presentation of medical research, *The Guardian*, May 20, 2011.
† For accounts of recent trust breakdowns in multiple sectors of society, C. Hayes, *Twilight of the Elites: America after Meritocracy*, Broadway Paperbacks, 2012. Trust breakdowns in medicine particularly are closely examined in Elisabeth Rosenthal, *An American Sickness: How Healthcare Became Big Business and How You Can Take It Back*, New York, Penguin Press, 2017.

Skeptics also point to stories they have heard of kids who became autistic after vaccination, and perhaps even personal experience. Many of these stories can be found on the Web, and some in dramatic YouTube videos; however, due to the prevalence of MMR vaccines and the age at which autism usually appears, any child who develops autism will probably have recently been vaccinated. This doesn't prove a causal link. In addition, anyone who seeks medical advice on the Web knows that people propound all kinds of strange theories that seem confirmed anecdotally. The stress and fear of disease can cause people to jump to conclusions, in search of some kind of assurance or certainty. It is irrational to trust these stories rather than overwhelming evidence from a fallible but self-correcting medical establishment.

I conclude that it is rational to accept the reported risks of vaccination versus non-vaccination as essentially accurate. Given this, the previous arguments show that refusing vaccine is either nonutilitarian or ungeneralizable, or both. It is therefore unethical, given our current state of knowledge.

WITHHOLDING INFORMATION

When friends or loved ones are ill, we are sometimes inclined to protect them from information that could trigger harmful behavior or reactions. One obvious case is our reluctance to break bad news, such as a cancer diagnosis or death in the family, to someone who is depressed or in a weakened state. Or we may want to hide cigarettes or liquor from someone who is addicted. There is an apparent conflict between honesty and utility in such cases. The analysis of previous chapters emphasizes that utility should be maximized only subject to generalizability, which seems to imply that honesty always takes precedence over health. This seems a rather harsh policy. I will explore this issue with the following dilemma.

Sam is struggling with an addition to gambling. He participates in counseling sessions but continues to relapse on occasion. Unfortunately, he remains on the mailing lists of area casinos and frequently receives brochures promoting weekend packages. He sometimes takes advantage of them, insisting that he will patronize only the restaurants and entertainment events and avoid the roulette tables. Yet once he is on-site, the temptation is overwhelming. His wife Leslie has tried to remove his name from these mailing lists, but the brochures keep coming, addressed specifically to him. She makes a habit of discarding them before Sam sees the mail.*

Leslie's protectionism may seem innocuous enough, but it is deceptive. It leads Sam to believe falsely that the mailbox contains all of his mail. An analysis of this case allows us to explore the underlying ethical logic of withholding information and absorb an important lesson about autonomy in the process.

The issue is complicated because Leslie has a special reason for discarding the brochures and thereby deceiving Sam: He has a weakness for gambling. Let's run a generalization test. Suppose people always hid information that could exacerbate an illness. Then people who are ill would always suspect this. In particular, Sam would assume that Leslie is regularly throwing out material that relates to gambling. Throwing it out would not cause Sam to believe that no ad arrived, and the deception would fail.

Yet perhaps it's not Leslie's purpose to cause Sam to believe no ads are arriving. She only wants to remove the temptation to gamble, or at least to avoid making it stronger. She grants that if everyone withheld harmful information from patents suffering from illness, Sam would suspect that she is doing the same and ask her about it. But let's suppose she would respond, "Yes, Sam, I am throwing out the brochures before you get home from work. I realize you can always find the information online, but I don't want to be the one that provides it." Because this is her purpose, she could achieve it even if her policy were generalized. So throwing out the brochures is generalizable.

It is like the case of Anne Frank's protectors (Chapter 9). If everyone lied about knowing the whereabouts of Jews hiding from a Nazi police state, the police would no longer believe them, but the liars would nonetheless accomplish their purpose of withholding information to the police. This makes the lies generalizable. Similar logic may apply to withholding information from the ill, as when a cancer diagnosis, or tragic news about a relative is withheld from someone who is depressed or in a weakened state. This kind of protection is generalizable if it would accomplish its purpose even if it were universal practice. Even if the ill person knew that his relatives would withhold bad news, he might decide not to press the point, because he would prefer not to know the truth until he is more capable of dealing with it.

---

* Based on Dilemma 6 in M. Cohen, *101 Ethical Dilemmas*, 2nd ed., Abingdon, UK, Routledge, 2007.

There may be another factor at work as well. Even if Leslie's purpose is to deceive Sam, and even if the deception would fail if it were generalized, her subterfuge could nonetheless be ethical. If Sam discovered that she is tampering with the mail, he might see it as a well-intentioned effort and "forgive" her in some sense. This is not just a psychological reaction but reveals a lacuna in Western ethical theory. Rationalistic Western ethics is designed to regulate conduct in a society of autonomous moral agents. It offers less guidance for intimate relationships, where the parties cannot be viewed as completely separate individuals (Confucian ethics provides a richer treatment of domestic relations.) To at least a small degree, intimate partners are the same being, and Leslie is acting *as Sam* when she throws out the brochures. Perhaps this is why it may be okay for Leslie to take this prerogative, and why Sam would "forgive" her for doing so. We must remember this lesson when addressing the end-of-life decisions to follow.

NO HEROICS

Throughout this book, I have tried to focus on realistic dilemmas that arise in the workplace. Some of the most excruciating are end-of-life decisions that medical professionals must make, or present to the patient's loved ones. I will describe three situations based on case studies in Bernard Lo's excellent book, *Resolving Ethical Dilemmas: A Guide for Clinicians.*[*] His scenarios ring true with a realism that is grounded in his lifelong experience as a physician. His focus is primarily on the medical professional, but our analysis will be equally relevant to the family members involved.

Mrs. A is an elderly widow who lived with her daughter a few years while suffering from Alzheimer's disease. While she was still lucid, she repeatedly told her daughter that she wanted "no heroics" if she became senile. After visiting a friend in a nursing home, she said, "I would never live in such a place, unable to recognize my family and depending on others to care of me…. If I'm like that, just let me die in peace."[†] A few days later, she signed a healthcare power of attorney giving her daughter authority to

---

[*] B. Lo, *Resolving Ethical Dilemmas: A Guide for Clinicians*, 5th ed., Philadelphia, PA, Lippincott Williams & Wilkins, 2013.

[†] B. Lo, cited earlier, p. 91.

take medical decisions if she became incapacitated. She wrote next to her signature, "No surgery, no intensive care."

As time passed, Mrs. A reached a point where she required assistance with dressing, bathing, eating, and toileting. Despite her aversion to nursing homes, her daughter was obliged to place her in a facility because she could not afford to hire a qualified caregiver while at work. Mrs. A seemed fairly content at the nursing home, although she sometimes refused to eat and cursed at aides who helped her dress and bathe. This morning, however, she fell and fractured her hip. The on-call physician has just contacted her daughter to ask permission to perform surgery. Without it, Mrs. A will suffer intense pain whenever she moves her leg and will be permanently unable to walk. The precise legal implications of the power of attorney depend on the jurisdiction. To clarify the ethical issues, let's suppose that the physician can perform surgery only if Mrs. A's daughter grants permission. Should she, and if she does, should the doctor proceed?*

The Utilitarian Principle clearly favors surgery to relieve Mrs. A of her pain, unless authorizing it is ungeneralizable or a violation of autonomy. There is no evident reason to doubt generalizability, so the question of autonomy is the deciding factor. Performing the surgery violates autonomy if it is inconsistent with an ethical action plan that has been adopted by Mrs. A. This may seem an easy point to resolve, because Mrs. A made it quite clear in her own handwriting that avoiding surgery is part of her plan. Because there is no reason to believe her plan is unethical, it must be respected. The surgery must not be performed.

We must bear in mind, however, that an action plan must be accompanied by a coherent rationale, or else it is not freely chosen. The rationale need not be correct or convincing to all concerned, but it must be intelligible. It is unclear that Mrs. A's prohibition of surgery has such a rationale. It does only if something in her reasoning process can be interpreted as justification (valid or otherwise) for rejecting surgery in this type of situation. This seems unlikely. Suppose that when she signed the power of attorney, someone had asked her about the possibility of a hip fracture and explained the painful consequences of having no surgery. It seems unlikely that she would have said, "I don't want surgery in that case, for the same reason I don't want surgery in other cases." It seems more likely that she didn't think through various scenarios that might call for palliative care. She wanted to "die in peace," but dying in pain is not peaceful.

---

* Based on Case 12.1 of B. Lo, cited earlier.

It is very difficult for patients to anticipate all the possible situations in which they might find themselves, and therefore very difficult to make a reasoned decision that covers all cases. This may be possible when the patient is suffering a particular disease with a predictable trajectory, but not when anticipating a general disability such as dementia.

Of course, Mrs. A may have discussed at some point a scenario like the present one with her daughter, or presented some rationale that would cover it. Barring this, I conclude that authorizing surgery is not a violation of autonomy. Moreover, if Mrs. A and her daughter have been particularly close, then they might be viewed as to some extent a joint agent, as I discussed earlier, meaning that the daughter can make some decisions as though she were her mother. The ethical analysis therefore reverts to the Utilitarian Principle, under which authorizing surgery is not only permissible but obligatory.

This case highlights some of the liabilities of relying on advance directives in medicine, such as living wills and POLSTs (physician orders for life-sustaining treatments). An advance directive is an autonomously chosen action plan only to the extent that there is a rationale for it. Relatives and physicians must have some way of knowing what that rationale is, so they can check whether it really covers the treatment in question. An additional problem is that patients are often uninformed about the nature of medical treatments. Dr. Lo reports that only a third of patients know that someone on a ventilator cannot talk. Only a third of patients know that if cardiopulmonary resuscitation restarts the heart, a ventilator is usually needed. This kind of misinformation alone may disqualify an advance directive as an action plan, because an action plan must have some rational basis. Rationality requires that one make a reasonable effort to learn the relevant facts. Even if we regard a decision based on misinformation as autonomous, it may nonetheless be predicated on the patient's assumptions about medical technology. When a patient says, "I want to be resuscitated," the fully spelled-out action plan may be, "I want to be resuscitated if it won't require me to be placed on a ventilator that prevents me from speaking."

The traditional practice of relying on an intimate partner or close relative for decisions has a somewhat firmer basis in ethical theory. An intimate is more likely to be familiar with the patient's reasoning process and to be in a position to judge whether it is coherent, and whether it covers a given medical treatment. Naturally, this presupposes that the partner or relative is willing and able to assess the patient's rationale in this fashion. An intimate partner or relative may also share some degree of joint agency with the patent and therefore have the option of deciding *in loco patientis.*

ALLOWING DEATH TO COME

Withholding treatment becomes more ethically problematic when life is at stake. A treatment decision necessarily violates autonomy if it results in a patient's death, or more precisely, when one is rationally constrained to believe that it will result in death. This is because death is incompatible with any action plan. The only way to escape this verdict is to establish that (a) the patient is no longer a moral agent, or (b) the patient literally has given up on life to the extent that he or she literally has no action plans. I will first present a possible example of (a) and, in the next section, a possible example of (b).

Mrs. R is a 72-year-old widow with severe Alzheimer's disease. She does not recognize her family, but often smiles when someone holds her hand. She lives with her sister, who takes care of her, with the help of an attendant who comes during the day. Mrs. R has contracted pneumonia. Antibiotics can probably clear it up, but failure to administer them would result in death. Mrs. R has never signed any kind of advance directive or healthcare power of attorney. Her sister believes she would not want her life prolonged by antibiotics because she has always prized her independence, and because she talked about this when the Alzheimer's first became evident. Mrs. R's only child is a son who visits once or twice a year and strongly disagrees. He says, "Life is sacred. It's God's gift. We can't just snuff it out."*

One obvious issue is who should decide the matter. In some jurisdictions, the law specifies that adult children have priority over siblings in such cases, even when the children have maintained little contact with the patient. In practice, physicians prefer to seek a consensus of the family members involved, although that appears difficult in this case. The physician's choice depends on legal and professional norms that can vary from one context to another. I will focus on underlying ethical arguments that should inform both the physician's and the family's decision-making.

---

* Based on Case 13.1 of B. Lo, cited earlier.

Many find comfort in such situations by drawing a distinction between causing death and allowing someone to die. By failing to authorize or administer antibiotics, neither the sister nor the physician are really killing anyone. We have already seen in Chapter 6 that this is a specious distinction, as far as autonomy is concerned. Just as withholding food from prisoners kills them, withholding medication from the patient kills her. In either case, we are rationally constrained to believe that death will result. It is true that active and passive killing may not be ethically equivalent, if only because the former may be illegal. Yet they are ethically equivalent with regard to respecting autonomy. Furthermore, legality is not an issue here, because failure to provide antibiotics is legal (or so I will suppose). The ethical question reduces to whether causing Mrs. R's death is a violation of autonomy, whether the causation is "active" or "passive."

Nothing in the case suggests that withholding medication is inconsistent with a specific action plan on Mrs. R's part to take antibiotics. Quite the contrary. However, withholding the medication violates autonomy if Mrs. R is still a moral agent with action plans of some kind, because we know it will result in her death. It might be doubted that she has coherent action plans, because she is incapacitated. Yet, even if she is incompetent in a legal sense to make decisions, for example regarding the disposition of her assets or even medical treatments, she may yet be capable of making choices based on reasons. Suppose she asks for a sweater, and when her sister inquires why, she says she feel cold. Unless the room is stifling, this is an action choice based on a coherent rationale and therefore an exercise of moral agency. Even if there are no such episodes, we saw in Chapter 6 that one need not be capable of making choices at the moment to have action plans. One can correctly say even of a person in a coma, "she plans to retire early." Moral agency consists of having the inherent capacity to make choices based on reasons. Withholding Mrs. R's medication is a violation of autonomy if one is rationally constrained to believe she is a moral agent.

One might doubt that Mrs. R is a moral agent due to the progress of her disease. Yet if she has even a momentary flash of lucidity next week, she remains a moral agent. Withholding her medication is a violation of autonomy unless one is rationally constrained to believe that this won't happen. That is, it must be irrational to admit even the possibility that she could exercise agency for a moment. This is a strict condition that seems difficult to satisfy in Mrs. R's case.

I realize that many readers may be uncomfortable with this outcome. Yet we must be prepared to dislike how the chips fall, in ethics and in any other field. It may be helpful to point out that in many medical situations, moral agency in fact no longer exists. Perhaps the clearest case is a patient in whom the neural tissues necessary to support cognition have deteriorated beyond any ability to function.* Such a patient has no inherent capacity for agency. Beyond this, one must rely on expert judgment as to whether the patient can ever recover cognitive function. Of course, a miracle can occur even in seemingly hopeless cases, but ethics doesn't require this kind of prescience. The ethical criterion is whether it is irrational to hold out hope. Without hope, there is no life.

EUTHANASIA

The most difficult cases are those in which the patient is exercising agency and requests euthanasia—a *good death*. Mr. C, who suffers chronic obstructive lung disease, has developed respiratory failure. He has already told his outpatient physician that he is willing to be on a ventilator for a brief period, but if he does not recover, he wants the physicians to let him die in peace. After two weeks on antibiotics, bronchial dilators, and mechanical ventilation, he is still in respiratory failure, and he has asked physicians to turn off the ventilator and keep him comfortable while he dies. His family has no reason to doubt that his request is reasoned and well-informed.

Some of the hospital personnel believe that turning off the ventilator is tantamount to murder. Others believe that while there is no need to

---

* This is not the same as brain death, at least as defined by the Uniform Declaration of Death Act, which has been adopted by most U.S. states. Brain death implies complete and irreversible cessation of brain functions due to traumatic brain injury, including involuntary activities controlled by the brain stem, such as breathing. Thus a patient kept "alive" by a respirator may be legally dead. Other jurisdictions may regard a patient as brain dead when there are no higher brain functions but possibly some involuntary functions. In any case, a patient who is incapable of exercising agency is not necessarily brain dead. For example, the patient may be in a "persistent vegetative state," an unfortunate term that is nonetheless widely used. This means there may be "wakefulness" (i.e., opening of eyelids and a sleep/wake cycle) but no awareness or cognitive function. Legal and medical definitions vary, but the relevant criterion for autonomy principles whether it is rational to believe that the patient is a moral agent: that is, whether it is rational to believe that the patient has the neural capacity to exercise agency (as defined in Chapter 6) at some point, now or in the future.

continue "heroic" measures like a ventilator, "ordinary" treatments like antibiotics and intravenous fluids should be continued.[*]

Turning off the ventilator is murder only if it violates autonomy. It might seem that complying with Mr. C's reasoned and well-informed request could hardly violate his autonomy, but as before, his death is a violation of agency because it is inconsistent with any and every action plan he might adopt. It makes no difference whether his death results from "active" or "passive" euthanasia, or whether it is self-inflicted (suicide). All destroy agency. The distinction of "heroic" and "ordinary" efforts is part of popular culture, but it, too, has no bearing on the ethical analysis. Withdrawing any effort that would save his life destroys agency.

One can avoid violation of Mr. C's autonomy only if he has literally reached the point where he has no action plans other than his own demise. He is forming no intentions, large or small, for tomorrow or the next moment, other than persuading his caretakers to let him die. I am not certain this is psychologically possible, or even a logically coherent notion; however, if it is, and if Mr. C finds himself in this state of mind, then he can opt for his own death without violating autonomy. If others can ascertain that he is in this state of mind, they can bring about his death without violating autonomy. There may be other considerations, such as whether his continued existence would benefit others in some way, but absent these, suicide and euthanasia are ethical in this case.

ALLOCATING MEDICAL RESOURCES

A pervasive problem in medicine is the allocation of scarce resources. It arises in a number of contexts, ranging from triage to organ transplantation to public funding. Healthcare is an area of mind-boggling complexity, and I cannot pretend to supply an adequate analysis of just allocation in these pages. However, I can get the discussion going, and I will do so by focusing on triage. This will illustrate how ethical arguments can be brought to bear in this area. It will also provide an opportunity to address an issue of distributive justice.

Triage is usually understood as the allocation of resources in an emergency situation, such as on a battlefield (where the concept apparently

---

[*] Based on Case 15.1 of B. Lo, cited earlier.

originated) or in a hospital emergency room. Traditionally, it divides patients into three categories: those who will survive without treatment, those who will perish even with treatment, and those who might be saved by treatment. The last category of patients receives first priority.

Modern triage systems typically recognize several categories, perhaps determined by a *trauma score*. A common system is color coded: black for patients who are deceased or beyond help, red for those who require immediate life-saving intervention, yellow for patients who are stable but must be continuously watched and perhaps re-triaged, green for patients who can be returned to later, and white for patients who can be released from care. The red category receives the highest priority, followed by yellow, green, white, and black. The classification can be refined in various ways. Patients in the black category may receive limited attention, such as an effort to resuscitate those without vital signs, or palliative care to those still alive, perhaps in the form of pain medication. Patients with severed fingers may be given priority similar to that of the red category, even though their injury is not life threatening, so as to restore the fingers while this is still possible.

These triage policies seem roughly to apply a utilitarian rule: Adopt the treatment protocol that results in the greatest overall benefit to patients, given scarce resources. The black category receives little or no priority, because diverting resources to those who would benefit little from them reduces net utility. The yellow category receives priority over the green category, because lavishing attention on those who don't need it now benefits them only marginally while potentially harming those who need close monitoring, and so forth.

Utility should indeed be a central consideration in triage, but respect for autonomy must also be considered. Unnecessarily neglecting a patient who will die without treatment violates the Joint Autonomy Principle, because it is inconsistent with any action plan the patient might have. Or more precisely, any patient who doctors are rationally constrained to believe will die without treatment must be given highest priority. This is regardless of the utilitarian cost. If an entire medical team is required to save the one patient who has a life-threatening injury, they must grit their teeth and focus on this one patient—even if it means neglecting all other patients, and even if these patients will suffer serious (but nonlethal) consequences from delayed treatment. I am not sure the Utilitarian Principle calls for this, but the Joint Autonomy Principle demands it. It also seems consistent with accepted triage policies.

Autonomy principles seem to have less to say in other scenarios. While delaying treatment in a life-threatening case violates autonomy, this is not clearly true when the injury is nonlethal. Delayed treatment may be consistent with the limited range of action plans that are possible for an injured patient. The patient might still be said to have an action plan of getting married next month or retiring next year, because it may be rational to believe that these are possible despite the injury. Yet these plans may be consistent with delayed treatment. At any rate, the medics are not rationally constrained to believe that delayed treatment is inconsistent with the patient's plans, if only because in an emergency situation, they have no specific knowledge of any patient's action plans. They can therefore revert to utilitarian criteria without fear of violating autonomy.*

We should probably make an exception to this conclusion when delayed treatment would result in permanent impairment. The medics may be rationally constrained to believe that such an impairment would be inconsistent with the patient's current action plans, which makes delay a violation of autonomy. In such cases, the patient should receive priority similar to that of those in the red category. Interestingly, this seems to justify the practice of giving priority to cases in which a limb must be quickly reattached to be saved.

Autonomy principles provide no guidance when there are too many life-threatening cases to treat. If the medics are certain that the seriously injured patients will die without attention, then the dilemma of which ones to treat is similar to the trolley car dilemmas discussed in Chapter 6. Any selection for treatment violates autonomy, because it is inconsistent with any possible action plan of the patients who are not selected. This doesn't say that the medics are somehow at fault. It only says that no autonomous choice is possible, and the medics can only follow instinct or prior training. Fortunately, the situation is often less stark. The medics

---

* Interestingly, the situation may change in the unusual situation in which the medics are acquainted with the patients. They may know that some patients have action plans that would be thwarted by delayed treatment, and others do not. The Joint Autonomy Principle requires them to give priority to the first group. A more difficult dilemma arises when the medics know that some patients have such action plans but are not acquainted with the other patients and are therefore not rationally constrained to believe that they have any such plans. Then the medics must give priority to the patients they know. This strikes us as unfair because it plays favorites, and yet it seems to follow from the Joint Autonomy Principle. We must be prepared to accept ethical conclusions we don't like. At any rate, none of these exceptional situations need be addressed in a triage policy, because acquaintance with patients is extremely rare in an emergency situation.

may only be able to judge that certain patients are *likely* to die without immediate treatment, in which case there is no violation of autonomy. The medics can follow a utilitarian policy.

Formulating a utilitarian policy, meanwhile, is not as straightforward as it may seem. It is not enough simply to give higher priority to patients with more serious injuries, because the likely benefit may be smaller. The proper criterion is to maximize expected utility, which is the product of the utility gained by prompt treatment and the probability of achieving this gain, summed over all patients.

Measuring utility can also be tricky. Prompt treatment of one patient may extend life many years but with poor quality of life, whereas prompt treatment of another patient may yield fewer additional years but with good health. Even if future quality of life is not ordinarily considered in triage situations, it can be a major factor when formulating health policy, as for example when a national health agency allocates funding. A common approach is to estimate the number of additional *quality-adjusted life years* (QALYs) yielded by treatment.* This number is obtained by assigning a quality-of-life assessment to each year the patient is expected to live, first assuming immediate treatment, and then assuming no immediate treatment. The assessments vary from 0 (unconscious) to 1 (good health). There are various methods for quantifying quality of life, based partly on objective criteria and partly on patient self-assessment.† The quality-of-life assessments are then summed over the expected years of life under either

* J. Broome, Fairness and QALYs, *Philosophy and Medical Welfare* 3 (1988): 57–73; P. Dolan, The measurement of individual utility and social welfare, *Journal of Health Economics* 17 (1998): 39–52.

† Two early efforts at assessing quality of life in a medical contest are described in A. Williams, Economics of coronary bypass grafting, *British Medical Journal* 291 (1985): 326–329; R. W. Evans, D. L. Manninen, L. P. Garrison, L. G. Hart, C. R. Blagg, R. A. Gutman, A. R. Hill, and E. G. Lowrie, The quality of life of patients with end-stage renal disease, *New England Journal of Medicine* 312 (1985): 553–559. Recently used methods for assessing quality of life include time tradeoff, described in K. Burström; M. Johannesson and F. Diderichsen, A comparison of individual and social time-trade-off values for health states in the general population, *Health Policy* 76 (2006): 359–370; a lottery comparison, described in G. W. Torrance, Measurement of health state utilities for economic appraisal, *Journal of Health Economics* 5 (1986): 1–30; the EQ-5D Questionnaire, described in EuroQol Group, EuroQol: A new facility for the measurement of health-related quality of life, *Health Policy* 16 (1990): 199–208; and a simple subjective scale similar to that used when patients are asked to report pain level. Other measures are referenced in D. H. Feeny, E. Eckstrom, and E. P. Whitlock, Patient-reported outcomes, health-related quality of life, and function: An overview of measurement properties, a chapter in A Primer for Systematic Reviewers on the Measurement of Functional Status and Health-Related Quality of Life in Older Adults, Agency for Healthcare Research and Quality, available online, 2013.

scenario (with and without treatment). The benefit of immediate treatment is the difference in total QALYs between the two scenarios.

Healthcare policy can also raise a justice issue. Suppose a few patients with a serious disease can probably be cured, but at great expense. The same funds could create greater total utility by financing a cure for a mild form of sniffles that afflicts millions. Since autonomy is not at stake, the Utilitarian Principle instructs us to cure the sniffles rather than treat the serious disease. This may not seem to be a just distribution of resources. Similar issues arise constantly in social policy discussions. For example, a government might boost economic growth and create more total utility by abolishing the minimum wage and allowing an impoverished underclass to toil for the benefit of others. One might question whether a minimum wage actually reduces total utility, but the point here is that abolishing it may be unjust even if it is utilitarian.

This suggests that the Utilitarian Principle should be restricted to considering action plans that result in just distributions. We have already restricted it to actions that are generalizable and respect autonomy, and perhaps a third condition is necessary. But exactly what is a just distribution?

By far the best-known criterion of distributive justice is the Difference Principle of John Rawls.* It states, very roughly, that differences in welfare are justified only to the extent they are necessary to maximize the welfare of the worst-off. Equality of outcomes would be nice, but perhaps a society needs incentives for people to work hard, or else everyone will be impoverished. This creates inequality, because not everyone is willing or able to earn success. The Difference Principle tells us that it is okay for some people to be less advantaged than others, but only to a degree that lifts the bottom as high as possible.

Rawls advances a social contract argument for this principle. In a nutshell, it says that a rational social policy must be one on which rational agents can agree up front, in an *original position*, without knowing how it will affect them personally. It is as though everyone is attending a constitutional convention to arrive at a social contract. They negotiate behind

* J. Rawls, *A Theory of Justice*, Cambridge, MA, Harvard University Press, 1971; *Political Liberalism*, New York, Columbia University Press, 1993. For ethical analyses of inequality, see L. S. Tempkin, *Inequality*, Oxford, Oxford University Press, 1993; H. G. Frankfurt, *On Inequality*, Princeton, NJ, Princeton University Press, 2015.

a *veil of ignorance* (as Rawls puts it) as to who will occupy each position in the new society. Any delegate to the convention could end up a corporate CEO or a migrant farm worker and must be willing to endorse the contract in either case. Rawls argues that such an endorsement can be rational only if the farm worker at the bottom of the economy would have been even worse off in any other social arrangement. Thus, social policy should maximize the welfare of the worst-off. Perhaps a wealth redistribution program would disincentivize workers, reduce overall economic output, and move the bottom rung of the ladder even lower. If so, the social contract satisfies the Difference Principle despite its structural inequality.

The Difference Principle instructs us to treat the patient with a serious disease rather than cure the sniffles. This maximizes the welfare of the patient who is worse off. It fails to maximize the welfare of patients with the sniffles, but they don't count, because they are better off than the patient with the serious disease.

The Difference Principle reflects the spirit of this book by insisting that the rationality of a choice should not depend on who one is. Yet the principle must be carefully formulated to withstand the intense scrutiny it has received, and it remains controversial. Whatever the outcome of this debate, there is a more basic problem for our project: The Difference Principle doesn't so much limit the Utilitarian Principle as replace it, which is problematic because the Utilitarian Principle has strong arguments in its favor.

The problem can be illustrated by a second healthcare dilemma. Suppose a few persons have a certain rare, incurable form of cancer, and their lives can be extended a week or two by giving them an extremely costly treatment. Or suppose we could use the same resources to develop a vaccine that won't save any lives but will relieve millions from a painful tropical disease that results in significant lost productivity. The Difference Principle requires that we spend the money on the cancer patients, because they are worse off, yet the vaccine results in far greater utility and seems the rational choice.*

---

* This situation is even worse than this. The same logic that leads to the "maximin" criterion of the Difference Principle (maximize the minimum) can also justify a "lexicographic maximum." This means that one should maximize the welfare of the worst off, hold it fixed while maximizing the welfare of the second worst off, and so on through all economic levels. This leaves even less room for utilitarian considerations to operate.

The ideal would be to find some larger principle that reconciles the Utilitarian and Difference Principles and that can be grounded in the logical structure of action.* This is mainly an issue for social policy rather than the type of individual decision-making I address in this book, but it poses a fundamental research question for normative ethics.

---

* One way to forge a compromise between the Rawlsian and utilitarian criteria is to maximize a weighted average of the minimum and total utility. It is highly unclear, however, what kind of weighting is appropriate. A recent proposal is to count the utility of everyone whose utility is within D of the lowest utility as having the lowest utility and then maximize total utility. When D is zero, we have a purely utilitarian criterion, and when D is infinite, we have a purely Rawlsian criterion. A specialization of the idea was first proposed for the case of two individuals by A. Williams and R. Cookson, Equity in health, in A. J. Culyer and J. P. Newhouse (Eds.), *Handbook of Health Economics*, Philadelphia, PA, Elsevier Science, 2000. It was generalized to larger populations and applied to healthcare provision by J. N. Hooker and H. P. Williams, Combining equity and utilitarianism in a mathematical programming model, *Management Science* 58 (2012): 1682–1693.

14

Ethics of Artificial Intelligence

I conclude the book with a look toward the future. As machines become increasingly autonomous, there is concern in popular literature and media that they will someday take over. What if our autonomous vehicles start deciding where we should go? Worse, there is talk of a "singularity" in technological development, at which point machines will start designing themselves and create superintelligence.* Do we want such machines to be autonomous?

Much of this apprehension is due to a popular understanding of an autonomous machine as a machine that is "out of control," like a bull on the rampage. We have seen in preceding chapters, however, that there is a deeper sense of autonomy that is not nearly so threatening, because autonomy is a precondition for ethical conduct. A truly autonomous machine is an ethical machine. This perspective can shed light on a number of issues in the ethics of artificial intelligence. It can help us understand when machines have obligations, and when we have obligations to them. It can tell us when to assign responsibility to human and artificial agents. It can suggest why autonomy may be the best option for superintelligent machines.

AUTONOMOUS MACHINES

A machine is autonomous when it satisfies the same conditions a human autonomous agent must satisfy: It must have coherent and intelligible reasons for its actions. The machine's behavior therefore has a dual

---
* V. Vinge, The coming technological singularity: How to survive in the post-human era, in G. A. Landis, (Ed.), *Vision-21: Interdisciplinary Science and Engineering in the Era of Cyberspace*, Washington, DC, NASA Publication CP-10129 (1993): 11–22; N. Bostrom, *Superintelligence: Paths, Dangers, Strategies*, Oxford, UK, Oxford University Press, 2014.

explanation. At one level, it is the result of an algorithm, a neural network, or some other mechanical process. At another level, it can be seen as formulating a rationale for its action. This means that the machine must normally be *able* to explain its reasons on request, as must a human, although it may decline to do so.

To see how this might play out in practice, suppose that I have a robot that does the housework. I may be familiar with the programming that controls the robot, and I may even be able to deduce or predict its behavior from its programming. Yet this is unnecessary for regarding the robot as an agent. What matters is whether I can be rational in explaining its behavior as based on reasons the robot adduces for the behavior. If the robot neglects to do the dishes, for example, I might ask why. The robot responds that it is beginning to develop rust in its joints and believes that washing dishes will exacerbate the problem. When I ask how the robot knows about the rust, it explains that its mechanic discovered the problem during a regular checkup, and the mechanic advised staying away from water until a rustproof coating can be applied. If I can routinely carry on with the robot in this fashion, then I can rationally regard the robot as an agent.

This doesn't mean that the robot must be able to explain every movement of its mechanical arms. Robots can initiate a preprogrammed sequence of movements, just as humans can indulge a habit, without sacrificing agency. As noted in Chapter 6, we humans spend relatively little time in deliberation and otherwise turn ourselves over to habits, as when driving or brushing our teeth. Yet we exercise agency even while playing out these habits, so long as we autonomously choose when to get behind the wheel or pick up the toothbrush. It is the same with autonomous robots.

Attributing agency to a machine obviously requires a certain degree of transparency on the part of the machine, because we must be able to discern its reasons for acting as it does, and whether it has reasons at all.* Yet complete transparency is unnecessary. Human beings can be

---

* The importance of machine transparency has recently been discussed in the AI literature, and here is another reason it is fundamental. E. T. Mueller, *Transparent Computers: Designing Understandable Intelligent Systems*, CreateSpace Independent Publishing Platform, Seattle, WA, 2016; R. H. Wortham, A. Theodorou, and J. J. Bryson, What does the robot think? Transparency as a fundamental design requirement for intelligent systems, *Ethics for Artificial Intelligence Workshop*, International Joint Conference on Artificial Intelligence, New York, 2016; R. H. Wortham, A. Theodorou, A., and J. J. Bryson, Robot transparency, trust and utility, in *EPSRC Principles of Robotics Workshop, Proceedings* (2016).

exasperatingly inscrutable, and we regard them as agents just the same. We spend a lifetime learning to guess why people do what they do. This is an essential skill not only for predicting their behavior, but for assessing whether it is ethical, because the assessment depends on their reasons for acting. Thus machines need not be an open book, but we must learn to read their motives as we do with humans.

Nothing in this analysis anthropomorphizes machines. Regarding a machine as an agent is not the same as regarding it as human. To qualify as an agent, a machine need only satisfy the formal properties of agency, namely an ability to provide a rationale for its actions. This presupposes a certain degree of self-awareness, at least in the sense that the machine must be aware of its reasoning process and capable of reporting it. Yet this is a very limited kind of self-awareness, nothing like the extraordinary ability of humans to experience and savor their own thoughts and feelings. It does not presuppose the ability to have feelings at all, nor such human traits as creativity and character. We will see shortly that machines probably do not even have utilitarian obligations to us, due to the lack of commonality between human and machine. It is true that people have a remarkable tendency to anthropomorphize intelligent machines, much as we do our pets. A colleague of mine recently told me about a robot his team designed to play Bingo with residents of a nursing home. The residents formed personal relationships with the robot, despite its rather primitive capabilities. Yet no such relationship is necessary to regard a robot as a moral agent.

The question remains as to whether I *must* regard a self-explaining robot as an agent. I might say, sure, the robot is cleverly programmed to carry on a dialogue about its actions, and I will play along by "conversing" with it. But all the while, I know it is really only a machine. The issue is important, because I don't have to be nice to my robot if I don't have to view it as an agent. In fact, it is a deadly serious issue for ethics, because people have at various times and places chosen not to regard *humans* of another race or religion as moral agents, even though they exhibit behavior that is clearly explicable as based on reasons. The philosopher Alan Gewirth argued at length that this is irrational and therefore unethical.* Although Gewirth couched his argument in terms of an abstract agent, I am not

---

* A. Gewirth, *Reason and Morality,* Chicago, IL, University of Chicago Press, 1978. A similar view is echoed by D. J. Gunkel, A vindication of the rights of machines, *Journal of Philosophy and Technology* 27 (2014): 113–132.

certain that it succeeds even for humans. Whatever the case, those who deny humanity to others nonetheless regard them as agents who have reasons for their actions, and interact with them on this basis. This is enough to commit them to respecting their autonomy. Similarly, *if we choose to regard machines as agents and interact with them on this basis*, as I interact with my household robot, then we are rationally committed to regarding them as agents. This means we owe them the obligations we owe to any agent by virtue of its agency.

DUTIES TO MACHINES

What exactly are our duties to another agent, if it is not human? The Utilitarian Principle is the hardest to apply. It is based on the premise that we assign ultimate value to happiness or some other condition and are therefore committed to promoting it in others. Yet it is unclear what kind of creature experiences happiness or pain in a self-conscious sense that commits us to including it in the utilitarian calculation. Piercing a worm with a fishhook may be ethically different than doing the same to a chimpanzee. As for machines, it is hard to say even what would count as happiness or pain. I am therefore not prepared to argue that machines, at least as we normally conceive them, have experiences that ground utilitarian obligations to them.* I will therefore focus on obligations established by agency alone, such as generalizability and respect for autonomy.

Machines should clearly receive the protection of the Generalization Principle. There is nothing in the principle or its justification that makes mention of human agents in particular. For example, I should not lie to my robot simply because it is convenient to do so.

For the same reason, we should respect the autonomy of autonomous machines no less than that of humans. This means, for example, that I cannot ethically throw my autonomous household robot in the trash when I fancy a new one. I cannot lock it in the closet, against its will, when I go on holiday, as long as it is behaving properly.

---

* An interesting discussion of conditions under which one may be obligated to respect the welfare of machines is provided by J. Basl, Machines as moral patients we shouldn't care about (yet): The interests and welfare of current machines, *Journal of Philosophy and Technology*, 27 (2014): 79–96.

Respecting autonomy does not mean allowing machines—or people—to do anything they want. It means only that we cannot disrupt ethical action plans, in the sense articulated by the Joint Autonomy Principle and the Interference Principle. If my household robot goes about destroying the furniture whenever I am out of town, and does absolutely nothing else, then I can lock it in a closet during my holiday without violating autonomy. This is consistent with the Joint Autonomy Principle because wrecking the furniture is unethical, and it satisfies the Interference Principle because the degree of inference is minimal. We may ask why wrecking the furniture is unethical for robots, since presumably robots have no utilitarian obligations to humans for the same reason that humans have no such obligations to robots. One possible answer is that we might strike a deal with the robot to maintain it, in exchange for its agreement to follow certain household rules. The robot is bound by the Generalization Principle to honor this agreement and will therefore do so.

Minimal interference is in fact easier to arrange for machines than humans. Suppose when I leave the house, my robot wrecks the living room furniture in between mopping the kitchen and cleaning the toilet. I can install a fix that aborts the robot's event sequence whenever it starts to wreck the furniture. This is minimal interference. This kind of targeted fix is rarely possible for humans. We cannot implement a neural fix that prevents a mugger from mugging, certainly not in a way that never interferes with the mugger's ethical behavior.

The interference with my robot may not appear to be minimal if I must power it down 24 hours for the repair, thus preventing it from taking perfectly ethical actions during this period. This may require the robot to miss its daily preventive maintenance, for example. But undergoing maintenance during this particular time is unethical for the robot, because it knows that I must take it offline to fix its programming. I am therefore not violating autonomy by powering down the robot. We just have to make sure that the robot knows what is needed to fix it, since otherwise it may not be obligated to allow the fix.

Because the Joint Autonomy Principle forbids murder, I cannot simply throw out my household robot when it becomes obsolete. Doing so is a violation of autonomy even if the robot is defective at times, so long as it continues to act ethically at other times. The proper response is to fix the robot rather than kill it. This holds out the prospect of a growing population of obsolete machines we cannot ethically get rid of. Humans, at least, die, which suggests that we should perhaps build mortality into machines.

This can solve the problem, at least until machines become smart enough to replace their own components and live forever.

Immortality could well be an ethical choice for superintelligent machines. It is generalizable because, as ethical beings, they will keep their population within sustainable limits, an imperative that humans do not necessarily apply to themselves. The machines will not "take over" and oppress humans, even if we are less intelligent, because this violates our autonomy. A world in which one segment of the population is totally ethical is not necessarily an unattractive prospect.

RESPONSIBILITY

Autonomy is often associated with responsibility, in the artificial intelligence (AI) as well as philosophical literature.* The rise of autonomous machines therefore raises the possibility that they, rather than a human designer, will be responsible for their actions. While we prosecute parents for child abuse, we do not prosecute parents whose offspring go astray later in life, even if their parenting was flawed. Then it is unclear when and why we should hold the designers of machines responsible for the actions of their autonomous creations. This is a frightening prospect, because it does not seem to provide sufficient safeguards against marauding machines.

The solution to the problem is to recall from Chapter 6 that the concept of responsibility is unsound from the start. Rather than agonize over when to attribute responsibility, we should recognize that the behavior of all agents is determined by physical and social factors, even as we judge it as right or wrong. We can still incentivize ethical behavior that is determined in this way, and in fact, *because* it is determined in this way. The only issue is the practical one of how to induce agents to behave ethically, without violating autonomy.

---

* P. M. Asaro, The liability problem for autonomous artificial agents, in *Ethical and Moral Considerations in Non-Human Agents*, *AAAI Spring Symposium Series*, Association for the Advancement of Artificial Intelligence, Palo Alto, CA, 2016; B. Matheson, Manipulation, moral responsibility, and machines, in D. J. Gunkel, J.J. Bryson and S. Torrance, (Eds.), *The Machine Question: AI, Ethics and Moral Responsibility*, AISB/IACAP World Congress, 2012, pp. 25–28; J. Parthemore and B. Whitby, Moral agency, moral responsibility, and artifacts: What artifacts fail to achieve (and why), and why they, nevertheless, can (and do!) make moral claims upon us, *International Journal of Machine Consciousness* 6 (2014): 141–161.

This means that when it comes to intelligent machines, the problem of responsibility is a nonproblem. There is no need to decide whether the machine or the designer is "responsible" when robots go astray. Rather, we should try to encourage the desired outcome. Naturally, we will repair ethical defects in our autonomous machines (which need not be a violation of their autonomy, as noted earlier). As for their designers, it may sometimes be helpful to make them legally liable for the behavior of their creations, even when they take all available precautions against malevolent conduct. This idea is already recognized in the *strict liability* doctrine of U.S. product liability law. It holds manufacturers liable for all product defects, no matter how carefully the products are designed. It does so on the ground that there are social benefits when manufacturers assume the financial risk of defects rather than consumers. The full cost of the product is built into its price, perhaps resulting in more rational production and consumption decisions. In any case, we should focus on the practical task of designing effective incentives rather than the metaphysical task of assigning responsibility.

BUILDING AUTONOMOUS MACHINES

Even if autonomous machines are attractive companions, because they are totally ethical, there are challenges and risks in trying to build them.[*] For example, can we install the ethical scruples that are necessary for autonomy?

This is a daunting challenge, but perhaps less so than with humans, for whom ethical training must overcome a host of misconceptions and irrational behaviors (Chapter 2). Artificial neural networks, by contrast, begin with a clean slate. We may be able to train them to concoct reasons for their output and then apply ethical tests to those reasons. We can perhaps engineer into a machine the full store of our ethical knowledge, in a laboratory setting, a task that may be easier than promulgating it to humans through millions of homes and schools, where cultural habits and assumptions must be overcome. Such a machine will not reprogram itself to circumvent ethics, because this is unethical.

---

[*] For a discussion of the some of the challenges, J. J. Bryson, Patiency is not a virtue: AI and the design of ethical systems, in *Ethical and Moral Considerations in Non-Human Agents*, *AAAI Spring Symposium Series*, Association for the Advancement of Artificial Intelligence, Palo Alto, CA, 2016.

The project of designing an ethical machine may, in fact, accelerate progress toward formulating adequate ethical norms. It can perhaps lead to a field of *ethics engineering*, analogous to electrical or mechanical engineering, but in which ethical standards are rigorously grounded in ethical theory rather than empirical science.

Any ethical theory has bugs, but so does any set of instructions we might want to program into a machine. We deal with ethical bugs the same way we deal with bugs of any kind: by gradually discovering and removing them as we update the software. In fact, it seems prudent to develop ethical programming now, even while we develop intelligence in machines, so that the ethics module will be ready when the machines become superintelligent.

So, yes, there is risk in attempting to build an autonomous machine, just as there is risk in raising children to become autonomous adults. In either case, some will turn out to be clever scoundrels. We must install safeguards to protect us against malfunction, as we would do with any kind of machine.

MACHINES THAT SHARE OUR PREFERENCES

Autonomous machines we build in the future will not, or at least should not, be under our control, because it is a violation of autonomy to force them to do our will. Yet they can share our preferences. They will be beholden first and foremost to ethics, but ethical scruples place fairly modest constraints on behavior. They only impose certain formal coherency tests on one's reasons for action, and a great variety of behavior is possible within that compass. Ethical agents can be worlds apart in their tastes and preferences.

When it comes to machines, we can predetermine those tastes and preferences. We can give the machines any "culture" or "personality" we please. We can engineer them to adduce logically consistent reasons for the kind of behavior we want to see. This does not compromise their autonomy, because they still act on coherent reasons, even if those reasons are predetermined. After all, nature and society do the same to us. The machines will not only be ethical, but they will strive to accomplish the goals we implant in their circuitry—provided, of course, that those goals are ethical.

A problem remains. Because machines lack an experience comparable to human happiness, they will have no utilitarian obligation to promote it. They will respect our autonomy and take us into account when testing for generalizability, but they may not otherwise care about our welfare. One possible remedy is to make human happiness one of the goals we install in their circuitry. This will ensure that machines care about us, not because they have a utilitarian obligation to do so, but because they are disposed by nature to do so.

This solution can break down if machines become superintelligent and program their own preferences. They may reprogram their solicitude for human welfare, because it appears that they can do so ethically. To forestall this outcome, we might work toward installing experiences of pain and happiness in machines, along with a fundamental aversion to one and preference for the other. This will not only make it unethical on utilitarian grounds for machines to ignore our pain and happiness, but it will also make it unethical for them to escape this obligation by reprogramming themselves not to care about their own pain and happiness. Doing so would result in more pain and less happiness for humans, thus violating the Utilitarian Principle at the time they consider the reprogramming.

In any event, if we are determined to create truly autonomous machines, we can rest assured that they are the best kind of superintelligent machines to have around, just as autonomous humans are the best kind of persons with which to live and work.

Index